Kisses Sweeter than Wine

Boyd Clack is an actor, writer, singer and musician. He lives in Cardiff with his partner Kirsten Jones.

Kisses Sweeter

than Wine

Boyd Clack

Parthian
The Old Surgery
Napier Street
Cardigan
SA43 1ED

www.parthianbooks.co.uk

First published in 2010
Reprinted 2011
© Boyd Clack 2010
All Rights Reserved

ISBN HBK 978-1-906998-30-1
ISBN PBK 978-1-906998-96-7

Editor: Penny Thomas

Cover design by www.theundercard.co.uk
Cover photo © Kirsten Jones
Typeset by books@lloydrobson.com
Printed by Dinefwr Press, Llandybie

The publisher acknowledges the financial support of the
Welsh Books Council.

British Library Cataloguing in Publication Data

A cataloguing record for this book is available from the
British Library

For my darling Kirsten

THE CLACKS

My father, George Windsor Clack, was born in Barry in South Wales on 31 October 1909. He died of leukaemia in Vancouver, Canada in 1954 when I was three years old. I've met very few relatives from his side of the family. There was Auntie Muriel, who lived in a prefab on the prefab site opposite the grammar school in Tonyrefail in the Valleys where I grew up. I don't remember her well; in fact I can't remember what she looked like at all. I have no physical image of her whatsoever but I do remember an aura of warmth and generosity. Her husband Uncle... I can't even remember his name (sounds like I'm making it up doesn't it?)... was one of those people you never see. He was always in bed or out walking or in the shed. Sometimes you'd go into a room and there would be traces of his pipe smoke still hanging in the air or a half-eaten meal on the table. He was ill. It was probably silicosis or

1

cancer or maybe the result of some war injury. He was very ill for a long time, then he died. I've no doubt he was a nice bloke. I used to visit them quite often at one time but it stopped for some reason. They didn't take me any more. My mother probably fell out with them. My mother fell out with everyone eventually. The prefab was like a toy house. It was an exciting place to visit. They had a dog I think.

I have a cousin, Barry Whitehead, from the same side of the family. He was a policeman in the Tonyrefail area when I was a teenager in the late sixties. I was a bohemian dreamer and he was a copper. I saw him at my mother's funeral service. I have never communicated with him beyond idle chat but he has always seemed a decent enough fellow to me. There was another cousin called Royston James, and his family. Royston was known as Squack. We worked together in the Treffano shoe factory in 1971, the year I emigrated to Australia. Squack was a trendy young man. He dressed fashionably and had an eye for the ladies. I remember he combed his hair a lot. 'Ride a White Swan' was high in the charts. He was a young guy bopping about seeking happiness. I liked him. Haven't seen him in years but I liked him.

I was driving through Trebanog with my brother Blaine and we turned off the main road and stopped outside a terraced house. The people there were Clacks. They had a gorgeous, sexy daughter about my age, a bit younger maybe. I'd've been eighteen. We had a cup of tea then left and I never saw or heard from any of them ever again. I only remember the incident because of the daughter. She was a Doll. There was another Royston too. I think he was

2

from Auntie Mu's husband's side of the family. The family name Whitehead must be from them. There was Barry whom I've already mentioned and there was a teacher when I was in the grammar school named Miss Whitehead, who was related in some way. She taught economics. She was posh by my standards and dressed very smartly. It was rumoured amongst us students that she was having a secret love affair with the physics teacher, Ambrose Hunt, a handsome man with a strong, sad, aquiline face and short lank grey hair. He looked like an SS officer. He looked like Reinhardt Heydrich, the deputy head of the SS, in fact. Anyway, however he looked it did the trick with Miss Whitehead. It was said that she and Ambrose used to drive up to a well-known lovers' meeting point in a forest on a nearby mountainside to be alone and on one such outing they were involved in a serious accident. Ambrose got out of it unscathed; Miss Whitehead suffered some scarring but it didn't stop her being beautiful. I liked her a lot but I don't think she ever thought about me.

There was someone else, another Clack. He lived in a strange old battered house just off the Tonyrefail to Talbot Green road. He was a rag-and-bone man, virtually a gypsy if my memory serves me right. The front yard of his house was piled with rubbish, metal objects, old vehicles and so forth. I think he actually lived in an old caravan outside the house. I was taken to see him two or three times. He seemed eccentric to me to say the least. I think he had a daughter living there too but I don't remember her at all.

There are other people who I think are related to me in some way but I'm not sure how. Maybe they were from my father's side of the family. I don't know. The name

Uncle Eddie rings a bell. Maybe he was Auntie Mu's husband. The fact is that I have had next to nothing to do with the Clack side of my family. This was not by choice, but my father's early death resulted in an unintentional alienation. I'm sorry about this. I would like us to have been closer.

The Clacks had come to Wales from Crewe in the nineteenth century. They'd been railway workers. My grandfather's name was David and my grandmother's was Mabel. I met neither of them. My father emigrated to Canada through a Salvation Army scheme in 1928. He sailed from Southampton on the *Empress of Australia*. He worked in an apple orchard for the first few years and was thought well of by his employers. I have a photograph from this time and I am pleased to say I see something of myself in him. I believe he went on to work as both a gold miner and a lumberjack. I don't really know anything else about his life in Canada until he joined the Canadian Army at the outbreak of the Second World War and after initial training in Iceland ended up on leave in Tonyrefail sometime in 1942. My Auntie Mary, Naine as she was known, my mother's sister who brought me up, spoke of him with fondness. He was a lovely man, very good looking, quiet but humorous. This was high praise from Naine who, like my mother, never had a good word to say about anyone. Uncle Will, Ool as I called him, Naine's husband and my surrogate father, talked to me about him once or twice, not often, but when he did he spoke in an affectionate way too. My father smoked a pipe and was a very good darts player. I've always had the idea that he just bummed around Canada doing an assortment of romantic jobs like a prototype beat poet. I have an image of him being a quiet, intense man, a sort of *Shane* figure. I think he may have been religious. I seem to remember hearing that he'd become a lay preacher towards the end of his life. This suggests that he may never have been the romantic adventurer I imagined him to be. Maybe he was a philosophical man. Maybe, just as fathers are said to want their sons to be like they wish they had been, I have imposed my romanticised image of myself onto him, my dead father whom I never knew. The thing I can say for definite is that it's possible to love someone you never really knew and I loved my father.

THE GRIFFITHSES

My mother, Ellen Elizabeth Griffiths, was born in Tonyrefail sometime towards the end of the First World War. The Griffiths family lived in 64 Pretoria Road, a terraced street that was back to back with The Avenue where I was brought up. The house was on the far side of Pretoria Road, the 'Red Cow' side, the Glyn Mountain side. The Griffithses were a rum bunch indeed. I believe they were quite well off at one time, owning a large amount of land around Gwaun Cae Gurwen in West Wales. The men in the family were a bunch of no-good, drunken, gambling wasters and lost all the family's fortune playing cards. There was an alleged curse laid on the family at that time over some civil dispute. It said that from that moment on the male offspring were damned to ill health, madness and misfortune. It seems to have worked because, with few exceptions, all the Griffiths men that I met seemed to be broken, clownish losers. Anyway, in those days the family was called the Caemelyns. How it changed from that to Griffiths I don't know, but the curse was not 'The Curse of the Griffiths' but 'The Curse of the Caemelyns', which sounds much more mysterious and satisfying to me.

The patriarch of the family at the time my tale begins was my grandfather, Daniel Griffiths, or Dan the Yank, as he was universally known. I've seen an old sepia-tinted photograph of him. He was a thin-faced man with a well-developed moustache. There was no trace of a smile on his lips. His wife, whose name I do not know, stands behind him rigidly in the photograph. They were first cousins. She died of cancer after a long illness. My mother once told me that she had worked herself to death looking after their eleven children. Either way she died young. Cancer has played a big part in the Griffiths' family history. Indeed, cancer had an almost religious role in Welsh Valleys life in those days. It was the Angel of Death itself, judgmental and merciless. Naine was obsessed with it. She'd tell me about a relative she'd nursed with cancer of the throat. She said he'd push his hand into his mouth and try to tear the growths out with his fingernails. Her face would light up when she talked about it.

Dan was called the Yank because on several occasions he'd gone to live in America. He'd just leave his wife and children to fend for themselves and go. He'd desert them. It is said that he lived with the Shawnee Indians for a while on their reservation. He toured with Buffalo Bill's Wild West Show. I believe he even toured the UK with them at one time. My stepbrother Brian (actually my

6

cousin) remembers him well from when he was a boy and liked him very much. He told Brian that when on the road with the Show he would often share a room and a bed with Buffalo Bill himself. He said that Bill would take a six gun from its holster on the bed post and threaten to shoot Dan's big toe off. Dan, I forgot to mention, was a drunk, and I've no doubt Bill was too. After finishing with the Wild West Show, Dan moved to New York, where he opened a restaurant in partnership with Jack Sharkey, the ex-world heavyweight boxing champion. I am unaware of how this venture turned out. There are quite a few Griffithses still about over the pond. Indeed, Uncle Jake became Mayor of Chicago on more than one occasion. At some time it appears that Dan was the owner of The Globe Cinema in Gilfach Goch, a mile or so from Tonyrefail. He also owned a pony and trap, which was the very one used in the sixties BBC serialisation of *How Green Was my Valley*, which was filmed in the area.

As far as I can tell Dan the Yank was a right bastard. Naine told me that he used to beat her and the other children on the back with a pickaxe handle, which he kept specifically for the purpose. The other Griffithses I knew were Naine, my mother, Uncle Ike, Uncle John, Uncle Danny and Uncle Glyn. That's six. There were twins too, I think. In fact I seem to remember hearing that my mother was a twin and that the sister died in childhood. I believe her name was Maude. Maybe I've got this wrong. Maybe there were no twins. Uncle Ike was a chronic alcoholic. It is said he was dishonourably discharged from the army after less than a day, when conscripted in the Second World War. He arrived at the training camp drunk and they couldn't wake him up so they threw him back. I have even heard it said that he was the first man to be dishonourably discharged from the British Army during the entire conflict. I knew Uncle Ike as I was growing up and the story rings true.

Ike lived in digs at 77 Meyler Street in Tonyrefail for years. He was the only lodger and the owner, a kind woman, took care of him. This was no easy task as he was a genuine staggering, trouser-soiling, vomiting type alcoholic; not a romantic literate drunk. She had to wash him and put him to bed on numerous occasions. She was a Christian. Ike was a good gardener. He used to make a few extra bob at it. He did the doctor's garden for years, Doctor Monroe.

Ike dressed quite well. He was given second-hand clothes, good clothes, by the middle-class people he gardened for, and his landlady made sure he wore them clean and laundered. He had some lovely overcoats and ties and scarves and cravats. At first he could control his drinking to the degree that he could attend some social functions relatively sober, and this was admired in him, it being no easy thing for an alcoholic to do. His life fell apart when his landlady died and he started sleeping in the public toilets and gutters. He shared a battered old caravan parked on a patch of wasteground near the Non Pol club with another notorious alcoholic named Tommy Bright for a year or so. Tommy was barely alive. He couldn't even stand up straight. He had the alci's nose too, broken repeatedly in fights with drunken, violent youths. Tommy couldn't fight but he could be hit and there was little mercy about in those days where I come from.

Some twenty odd years ago Uncle Ike was put in an old folks' home in the Tonypandy area. I visited him there once or twice. He got old there and he got stone deaf there too. He was still an alcoholic but he managed not to be thrown out of the home somehow and became a fixture. When I was a boy he used to come to the house quite regularly. He behaved in front of Naine, his big sister, and would often pass for virtually normal on these visits... at first. He was no intellectual. I don't think I ever heard him say a lucid word. Indeed, much of what he said was virtually unintelligible. This was because, despite never having been further than Oswestry in his life, he had somehow developed a flamboyant American accent. My brother Brian claims that Ike was once saved from a severe beating at the hands of some English Red Caps by the intervention of a couple of American soldiers, and that was enough for him. He took to screaming out insults about Wales and the Welsh people in the streets at the top of his voice when drunk and this led to regular visits to the casualty department of Porth Hospital. A bus driver beat him almost to death with his ticket machine once when he refused to get off a late-night bus after soiling it. He was a no-hoper.

One of Uncle Ike's regular appointments was Christmas dinner at our house. We'd be at the table-laying stage and he'd arrive, passing the window looking immaculate in a suit, normally double breasted, an overcoat and a hat. We'd dine together at the table and Ike would limit himself to a single glass of beer with the meal. This would be his first drink of the day and he'd sit by the fire for an hour or so afterwards before going off to do his round of the pubs. He'd get plastered. No, the pubs wouldn't have been open, not on Christmas day in the 1950s. Where did he go then? Yes, he had his rounds to make! Other people he visited. I wonder who the hell they were.

Anyway, as the years passed his control disintegrated and he began turning up plastered on Christmas day. His arrival became predictable and we would fear it. He'd stand outside the window shadow-boxing and pulling grotesque faces like Popeye the Sailor Man. He had an entire repertoire of them, the old alcoholic shuffle. He'd normally wait for Naine to be looking the other way and when she'd finally turn and catch him she'd look really disappointed and say 'My God. Look at the clown!' then rush out and drag him indoors. Once inside he'd sit on the armchair by the fire when Naine was in the kitchen cooking and he'd sing unintelligible songs in an American accent and pull faces and make signs at me as if we were in secret cahoots about something. He was as crazy as a coot, it has to be said. When I was old enough to get pocket money he used to take it off me while making signals not to tell anyone. What did I get out of this secret alliance? Sweet FA...!

When the Griffiths boys were young men in the thirties, they, like Dan the Yank himself, used to fight other blokes for money up on the Glyn Mountain. Crowds would gather and bets would be laid. My Uncle John was a particularly hard man even into old age. He was crackers too but that's another story. I'll tell you about him later. Anyway, drunk from a morning on the beer one Sunday afternoon Dan and Ike, father and son, were stripped to the waist sparring in the back garden of Pretoria Road. They were screaming and shouting, swearing no doubt, and finally the woman who lived next door stuck her head out of an upstairs window and asked them if they wouldn't mind keeping the noise down because her husband was on night shift and couldn't get to sleep. Apparently Dan the Yank shouted back 'Send him down here. Ike will put him to sleep!' Then there was an Alsatian dog in a house a few doors down the street, which used to bark at Dan as he passed by. Dan told the owners to sort the dog out or he'd do it for them. They didn't, so he went into their garden with a shotgun one afternoon and blew the unfortunate creature's head off.

Ike would be taken over by a nightmarish mutated version of his father when drunk. He'd jump up from where he'd be sitting, strike up a fighting pose and then say something ridiculous in his American accent. Something like 'Whooah there Buddy. I'm from New York. I'm the Yank. The Yankee boy. Whooah!' Then he'd tip his hat over one eye and shadow box till he fell over. Like I say, he was crazy, but my mother and Naine loved him. I got the impression that he had been a man of integrity at one time and that some people still held him in regard. They still saw the ghost of that integrity within him, they saw a good soul buried there and maybe they were right. I never saw it myself. I was afraid of him when I was small. Then when I got older he was too far gone for me to relate to him. Indeed he was too far gone for anyone to relate to him by then except for Tommy Bright. Their caravan was burned out by some local thugs. It was torched for a laugh. Maybe Tommy was still in there at the time. If he was then he escaped. I don't know what became of him. Uncle Ike died in the old folks' home when I was living away.

When I was a child our dog Mickey was kicked almost

to death by a passing motorcyclist and Uncle Ike took him to the vet in Porth to be put down. I remember watching the bus going up the hill with Ike holding Mickey, waving goodbye from a window. I asked Naine where they were going and she told me that Uncle Ike was taking Mickey to Heaven. I still relate that image to going to Heaven; that you go there with Uncle Ike on a bus up Collenna hill. I can't think too clearly about Uncle Ike now, to be honest. I never heard of a woman in his life ever. There was no history of love. No broken heart to cling to, not that I knew of anyway.

Uncle John looked as though he had some Negro blood in him. It was unmissable but I never heard anything, no hint of scandal that might explain it. He was hyperactive. He spent his entire adult life working in a watch factory in London. He lived in Kilburn with his wife Edna, a lovely, kind woman. I stayed with them once. I must've been five or six years old. I remember lying in a cot in their room, at the foot of their bed, late one night trying to sleep but too frightened to do so. As I lay there in the darkness I heard the sound of a single drum being beaten slowly and rhythmically somewhere outside, somewhere in the hollow, deserted streets of Kilburn. I remember thinking that this lone drummer was at the head of a silent mob marching towards the house I was staying in. I imagined them assembling outside in the darkness, gathered in the street outside the curtained bedroom window. I was paralysed with fear. It was the beating of my heart.

Auntie Edna died not long after. She'd been ill for a long time. They came to stay with us in Tonyrefail a few months before. Auntie Edna had to stop off at the ladies' toilet on their way to catch the bus back to Cardiff to go back home because she was feeling unwell. We waited outside for a quarter of an hour. I don't know what was wrong with her but I was told that her insides had filled up with pearls and that is what killed her.

They had a daughter Janet, who was a few years older than me. She used to come to stay with us sometimes during the school holidays. She'd stay for weeks, months even. Janet was a tall, gangly, severe-looking girl with short black hair and horn-rimmed glasses. She was as mad as her father. We used to play pretending to kiss in my bedroom. She attacked me with a carving knife, chased me from room to room. She ended up driving the knife into the kitchen door trying to get at me.

Uncle John came into my room one night hysterical and stinking of booze, and gave me a good whacking across the arse with his leather belt. Apparently Janet had told him I'd done something or other. It hurt like Jesus. Uncle John was genuinely nuts. He was a grade-A banana. He could barely get words out such was his constant level of hysteria. He'd dribble and gasp till he'd have to sit down exhausted and mop his brow with a handkerchief. I don't know whether I liked him or not because I never really had any idea what he was like. He was, if you recall, a very hard man. He'd been the outstanding hill fighter amongst the Griffiths boys and his reputation lived on. I was in Hayward's fish and chip shop with him one evening and a group of local thugs entered, drunk and looking for trouble. The ringleader, a huge violent creature devoid of all human feeling or intellect, began pushing people around and Uncle John went for him. It ended up with the bully legging it like a man possessed, with a screaming, dribbling Uncle John hot on his heels. He chased the lad for over a mile.

My brother Brian's then wife, Frances, used to take Janet and me to her place of work as a treat sometimes. She was the secretary to the manager at the Royal Sovereign Porcelain factory. We'd sit typing on machines or playing word games. Janet was very competitive. I never figured out why she hated me so much. She once gave me a coded message, 'LILY' it said. I had no idea what it meant so she told me to drop the first letter and that the other three were the initials of her message. 'I L Y' – I Love You! Well she had a funny bloody way of showing it. I last saw Janet when I was about ten years old. When she got married some ten years later she refused to have me at the wedding. Uncle John died soon after and I never heard from Janet again.

Uncle Danny went to Germany with the Civil Service after the war in some minor clerical capacity to help re-establish a civilian government, and when there became chummy with the upper-class types who were in charge of the operation. It seemed to have given him a home-counties accent and an air of superiority. He reinvented himself as posh in fact. When he returned to England he got work as some sort of apparatchik in Whitehall and became a personal friend of Jim Callaghan's. He was white haired at a young age and had the most peculiar sneeze you ever heard. When you first heard him sneezing you thought he was kidding. It sounded like an expensive firework taking off. Anyway, along the way he'd married Auntie Rene. She was a good-looking woman with pronounced lips. I liked her.

The last time I saw her and Uncle Danny was at

Naine's funeral. Uncle Danny seemed a silly man to me, a pathetic figure. Auntie Rene wasn't silly though. She had an air about her. They had two children, my cousins: a daughter named Eurwen and a son, Tony. I never actually met Eurwen but she was always spoken of with affection by everyone I met who knew her and I have a soft spot for her on the basis of that and her lovely name, Eurwen Griffiths. The son Tony was a globetrotter. He was an adventurer. He was a high-ranking police officer in Kenya at the time of the Mau Mau uprisings: a brutally suppressed rebellion against colonial rule. At another time he was the editor of Kenya's national daily newspaper and a top-class cricketer to boot. He was in fact the scorer of the quickest double century ever scored in Kenyan first class cricket. I remember seeing a newspaper article about it with a photograph of him executing a classic off-drive on his way to the record. He lived on a huge farm in Kenya with herds of wild animals and tribes of black servants. He, along with my cousin Trevor and my schoolmate Geoffrey Holtham, was the shining example that I was constantly urged to emulate when growing up. They'd say 'Your cousin Tony wouldn't be covered in shit' or some such thing at every opportunity in order to belittle me.

I met him once. He came to Tonyrefail, to 10 The Avenue. He arrived in a huge Jeep, which he parked out the front of the house. This would've been about 1960. His wife was with him. I don't remember her at all but he was an impressive figure, tall and athletic, very handsome in a rugged, English-officer way. He wore shorts, the first time I'd ever seen an adult in shorts, and talked to me, albeit briefly, in an adult fashion. He was what everyone had always said he was – a real gentleman. I was very taken with him. I recall him saying 'I have never thought myself better than any man Uncle Will… but I have never thought any man better than me.' Where he, his family and Eurwen are now I have no idea. Eaten by lions maybe.

Uncle Glyn lived in Mountain Ash and we visited him occasionally when I was a child. He died after a long illness. He wasn't like the others as far as I could tell. He was a quiet man; I think there was a bit of angel in him. Then there is Naine, my mother's sister Mary, who brought me up, and Ellen Griffiths, my mother herself. I know little of their upbringing other than that it took place in an atmosphere of lovelessness and drunken brutality. Naine was the eldest sister and became like a mother to the others when their real mother was bedridden prior to her death. Naine would've been about twelve at the time. She worked like a slave for years to bring the others up, while my mother, according to contemporary reports, was a self-centered, lazy little bitch. Both grew up with disfigured characters. Neither could express affection. They hated everyone and everything. They hated each other. I don't blame either of them now but I was a very unhappy child.

When Naine got old she lost most of her bitterness in a sort of second childhood. It was as if the flame had died. I loved her lots then. She'd tell me stories from when she was growing up. She'd act them out. Many was the time we'd end up waltzing around the living room imagining an orchestra playing 'The Blue Danube' behind us. We'd be back in the 1930s. We'd be in the Muni dancehall in Pontypridd. Naine used to go there once a week with her boyfriend Gethin, Friday nights. Gethin was a great

16

dancer. His arms and legs were like dandelion stalks blowing in the wind. He was good looking too, well not 'good' looking, 'nice' looking, and he was always the perfect gentleman. One particular Friday night Dan the Yank forced Naine to take my mother to the dance with her and Gethin so that he and his friends could use the house to get drunk in. Naine had no choice. While waiting at the Ponty bus stop Gethin popped into a nearby shop and bought, amongst other things, a great big half-pound bar of Cadbury's chocolate. It could have been a one-pound bar, a huge bar of chocolate either way. It was a present for Naine. When they got to the Muni and found a table to sit at Naine took the bar of chocolate out of her handbag and broke all three of them off two squares each. They wolfed them down with relish. This wasn't long after the great depression and people were poor. Chocolate was a treat. Gethin whisked Naine away to the dance floor moments later, where they danced wildly until exhausted. When they arrived back at the table the chocolate had gone, the empty wrapper was all that remained. When challenged my mother's mouth was so full of chocolate that she could hardly be heard denying it was she who'd eaten it. She said it was someone else, a stranger. Lumps of chocolate dribbled from her mouth as she spoke. Caught red handed she still lied. It was a pattern she repeated for the rest of her life. Anyway, sometime in 1942 my mother, who was in the WRAF, found herself somewhere in Tonyrefail at the very same time and on the very same spot where my father George Wyndsor Clack, on leave from the Canadian Army and wearing a greatcoat with little polar bears sewn onto the sleeves to show he'd trained in Iceland, found himself. And they met.

THE HAPPY COUPLE

I don't know anything about the circumstances of my mother and father's meeting or from that point to the wedding. They got married in St David's Church in Tonyrefail. There is a photograph. My father is in his uniform and my mother is in white. They are cutting the cake. This was at the reception back at the house, Dan the Yank's house, I presume. My father and mother are holding the knife between them. They are smiling, the knife is held delicately, lovingly. The moment is captured perfectly. I haven't seen the photograph in years. I believe my mother was with child, my sister Audrey. When I was young I was aware of the circumstances of my father's death and I always assumed that my parents' marriage was a love match, another romantic drama thrown up out of the turmoil of war. I imagined the 'loving wife staying at home to care for her beloved husband as he slowly died' scenario. I don't know if this is true. My brother Blaine, who is older than me and remembers some of it first hand, has told me different, but I don't know.

My father was in The Royal Regiment of Canada. He was one of those blokes you see running out of landing craft on foreign beaches being mown down by machine-gun fire. Shortly after he got married his regiment was sent on what has now become known as The Dieppe Raid. I've read about it in military history books. The raid was a deliberate sacrifice of men for the purpose of assessing the German coastal defence capabilities in the area with an eye to the eventual D-Day invasion. German intelligence was aware that the raid was going to take place and British intelligence was aware that the Germans were expecting them. The landing beaches were heavily guarded. It was a slaughter, of course, but contrary to what one might expect it was not the ruthless British High Command who insisted on Canadian troops being in the vanguard of this suicidal attack but the Canadian military themselves who wanted to 'blood' their inexperienced forces in the realities of the European theatre of war. There were incredibly heavy casualties. My father survived the initial landing but was captured by German soldiers a mile or so inland after being given away by a French farmer. There was little sympathy for those captured and my father and a few thousand other prisoners were marched in chains right across France and Germany. There was a German directive to treat allied prisoners badly at the time in retaliation for the bad treatment of some German prisoners. My father was interned in one of the Stalag prison camps, Stalag Three I believe it was, and spent the remainder of the war there, about three years. These camps were not like the camps you see in war films. This was not the sanitised world of *The Great Escape*. Starvation and brutality were the order of the day. My father was in a hell of a mess when he was released, when he came home. I've got no idea how he dealt with it. Maybe his religious beliefs gave him strength. I saw a piece of newsreel film from that time on a television documentary once, Canadian soldiers undergoing a medical, and I was sure that one of them was my father.

As far as I am aware my mother gave birth to my sister Audrey in 1943 and then just hung about in Tonyrefail waiting for my father to return. Naine looked after Audrey no doubt, while my mother continued to gallivant. Naine never missed out on an opportunity to disparage my mother and vice versa. The truth is hard to gauge in such circumstances. My father was repatriated in 1945 and returned to Pretoria Road in Tonyrefail, where my mother should have been waiting for him. There was a mix up, however. She went to Cardiff on the bus to meet him off the train as a surprise, but my father, not knowing this, had arrived in Cardiff early and caught the bus to Ton by himself, so they unwittingly passed each other halfway. Naine was in the living room in Pretoria Road on her own. She was poking the fire when the front door creaked open slowly; this was when you could leave your doors unlocked. At first it seemed there was nobody there but then after a few moments a soldier's cap was thrown in onto the carpet, a Canadian soldier's cap. Then my father came in. Naine said she nearly fainted when she saw him. His face was like a bare skull with a thin layer of skin stretched over it. All his teeth had fallen out due to malnutrition. He weighed less than seven stone. He'd thrown his hat into the room before entering so as not to frighten anyone by his sudden appearance, to warn them. Naine kissed him and sat him down, she really liked him you must remember, and as they talked she boiled him two eggs in a saucepan on the open fire. Eggs were rare then due to rationing and they'd been kept specially. She told me that she was crying her eyes out but she was facing away and kept the tears out of her voice so as not to upset him, that it was heartbreaking to see such a fine man reduced to this. She said that her tears poured down her face and fell into the water with the boiling eggs. I feel really sorry for my father. He had a rough deal. My mother arrived back home eventually and they were reunited.

The next thing I am aware of is that my father, my mother and Audrey went back to Canada to live. Why or how I don't know, though Canada must've seemed an attractive option in the post-war period when Britain was and would remain in a prolonged state of austerity. I imagine that the Canadian Veterans' Association would have seen to many of the practicalities. So in 1946 the Clack family went to live in Vancouver, British Columbia. My knowledge of what happened after that is very sketchy. What I know is that my father was in and out of hospitals regularly from then till his death from leukaemia in 1954. My father's death was long and drawn out. It was caused by the privations and ill treatment he suffered at the hands of his German captors. A close friend of mine died of leukaemia and there was a spiritual tranquillity to him. Maybe it was the same for my father. I like to think so. In 1947 they had another child, my brother Blaine. He was named after the geographical boundary between Canada and America, the Blaine Line. I don't know anything about his early life in Canada except that on the seventh of March 1951 he got a baby brother – me!

THE LAND OF MY FATHER

I was an easy birth. I arrived in the middle of the night. Blaine and Audrey had been difficult births. My mother was worried about me but luckily I was a piece of cake. This is hearsay you understand. I don't remember a thing about it. I was christened Boyd Daniel Clack, Boyd after a local doctor, and Daniel after the Yank of that name.

There is a story that my father called into a local bar on his way to register my name and got plastered on whisky and this resulted in him getting my first two names mixed up. Apparently I was meant to be named Daniel Boyd Clack. Someone once commented that I am fortunate my name isn't Johnnie Walker Clack.

We lived in a town called Courtenay on Vancouver Island. Our house was made of wood and painted white. I really don't remember anything specific about my early days in Canada. I used to think I remembered sitting on a wooden chair outside a garden shed and my father being inside. There is a photograph somewhere of me sitting there and I think I made the bit about my father up. There are some isolated images, an unsteady footbridge high above a river, a party outside near some sort of barn-like building, a commotion in the back garden late at night. I think there was a cougar in a tree and people threw buckets of water up at it to make it go away. I remember banging my face and crying; I fell out of my high chair, I've still got scars on my chin as a result. They tell me I climbed into the back seat of a visiting doctor's car and fell asleep and he drove hundreds of miles before I was discovered. The predominant feeling I have from this time was being aware that my father was dying. He spent long periods in hospital. My brother Blaine tells me that my mother used to doll herself up and go out a lot. I really don't know what happened in those years before my father's death. I have no positive memories of them. He died in 1954 and, feeling isolated and lost no doubt, my mother decided to return us all to Wales.

We travelled across the Rocky Mountains by train. I had a bunk bed. I couldn't sleep one night so I got out of bed and went for a walk along the rattling corridors in my pyjamas. It was dark and I got frightened. A guard found me and gave me a glass of warm milk and a sandwich in his little office before taking me back to the sleeping car. There was a wonderful taste to the sandwich, a taste that lingered in my mind for years, invoking intense memories of the time, like Proust's Madeleine. I didn't discover what it was until a long time later. The sea journey across the Atlantic was a blur. I remember being bought a little sailor rag doll in the shop and throwing it over the side of the ship into the sea. We arrived in Liverpool and I had a ride on a red rocket ship. It was lit with multicoloured fairy lights. We travelled down from Liverpool to Cardiff by train. Naine was with us. She must've met us in Liverpool. We got to Cardiff in wintry blackness. Ool, my Uncle Will, was there to meet us. I remember him walking around a corner by a sweet stall, wearing a thick overcoat. It was very cold. We were taken back to Ool and Naine's house, 10 The Avenue, Tonyrefail, which backed on to Pretoria Road, and we all fell asleep.

I have already told you about Naine, how she and my mother, though sisters, hated one another. I learned later that there had been some incident in which my mother had tried to sow disharmony in Naine and Ool's marriage years before. Naine was eaten up with bitterness. Why the hell my mother chose to run to Naine in her hour of need I'll never know. Neither did my mother apparently, since she spent the rest of her entire life cursing her decision to leave Canada, though since she cursed everything else it

23

may have been just habit. I suppose it's a case of blood being thicker than water. There was an initial period when things were all right between them when we first returned. My father's recent death must've kept the lid on the box of fireworks for a time, but it didn't last long.

Another important player in my tale is Ool, William John Ball. I called him Ool because that's how Will came out in my little-boy Canadian accent, same with Naine. The names stuck. Ool was one of thirteen children. He'd been born in Ynysybwl in about 1910. His family was desperately poor and when he was a little boy he went to live with another family nearby, the Shepherds. He had little education and went to work with the horses on nearby Mynachdy farm when he was ten. He had a younger brother who drowned swimming in a local pond at about the same time. He went on from there to work in the pits when he was fourteen. I don't know anything that happened after that until, one day years later, he was cycling along Pretoria Road and a maiden scrubbing her front doorstep caught his eye. The story goes that he began passing that way regularly after that until one day, suffering a convenient puncture, he stopped and asked her for a bowl of water so he could fix it. They got married some time later. When they got home after the wedding ceremony they had fish and chips from the fish shop as a wedding dinner and were left with six shillings. That was their total wealth. I found out years later that Ool had been married before; he'd had a childhood sweetheart who'd died of cancer and he'd married her on her deathbed.

It seems that from the beginning there was a perceived mismatch here. The Griffithses for some inconceivable reason considered themselves to be a cut above other working-class families. Why this should be is anyone's guess. It may be because of the land they had owned and lost in West Wales years before or because they had relatives in America, who knows? Ool's family on the other hand had no such pretensions. A relative told me that they were of gypsy stock and it makes sense. Ool was a short, dark man with a distinct Romany nose and his brothers were similar. Whatever the reason, Naine always treated him as an inferior.

I have met quite a few of the Ball family because they lived near us. There was Uncle Rhys, a morose man who was very close to Ool. He lived in The Avenue too with his wife Auntie Rene, a big smiling woman worn down by hard work as most housewives were in those days. They had a son Elvert who also lived in The Avenue. He had his toes removed after getting gangrene from a minor operation. I don't remember much about him. There was Uncle Arthur, who had a nasty scar on his lower lip; he died of cancer. I liked him a lot. Then there was Auntie Cassie who lived in Llanharry. We visited her there a couple of times. Going that far was quite an adventure. Uncle Les was a nice bloke. He lived on the housing estate behind the primary school. He had two sons, Clifford and David, and a daughter, Peggy. We didn't hang about together much but they were good lads both of them and Peggy was, and is, simply an angel. All of Ool's brothers and sisters are gone now, as indeed is he, except for Uncle Rhys, who still ambles up and down to the Red Cow most afternoons. Last time I saw him he was still sad. I believe he was on medication for depression and anxiety.

When I was a boy Uncle Ivor was my favourite uncle. He lived in the prefabs near to my Auntie Mu. He had a wife Mavis and a daughter Barbara. Barbara was five years older than me and used to take me to the pictures on Monday evenings. She'd wait for me after school and we'd go back to the prefab and have tea and talk and play before hitting the Savoy on Ton Square. In later life, after Uncle Ivor died, Barbara and her mother both developed schizophrenia and spent long periods in mental hospitals. I never saw Barbara again but Auntie Mavis would turn up at the house once in a while. She'd ring the front door bell, and come in for a cup of tea and a cigarette. She was a short, plump woman and wore a mask of badly applied, cheap, gaudily coloured make-up. Her lips were as red as an electric fire. She dressed in the clumsy, unattractive way that mentally ill people often do. She drenched herself in cheap-smelling perfume and wore a profusion of childishly cheap costume jewellery, the kind you get in lucky bags. Nothing seemed quite right. She was a dear soul. Both she and Barbara are dead now.

Ool's mother, Granny Ball, also lived in The Avenue. She was an old woman even then and in retrospect distinctly Romany in appearance. Her husband, Ool's father, was dead. He was a dapper man by all accounts and used to go for regular long walks every Sunday. He'd take a cloth with bread and cheese wrapped in it, tied in a bundle on the end of a stick, which he rested over his shoulder in the traditional image of a tramp. My brother Brian told me once that when he was a teenager in grammar school he used to sit with the by-then-aged and bedridden Dan the Yank in his bedroom doing his homework and chatting.

On one such evening the doctor arrived and told Brian to go downstairs, which he did. Ten minutes later the doctor came down to the living room and announced to the family that everything was all right and that Dan would be dead by morning, which he was. The family thanked the doctor profusely and they shared a cup of tea before he left. The very same thing occurred less than a year later in the case of Granddad Ball. I contemplated this on-the-face-of-it shocking revelation but came to realise that this made sense at that time. Families were desperately poor, there were no social services as there are now, and an inactive, non-productive mouth to feed was a great burden. Seventy was a very advanced age then and palliative medicine wasn't so readily available. Indeed the National Health Service had only recently come into being and people's memories of the hardship of nursing a person through long-term fatal illness were raw. It struck me that this mutually agreeable euthanasia was obviously common practice. In this post-Harold Shipman age such thoughts are a little frightening but I've no doubt that doctors in working-class communities in those days put an end to probably thousands of such lives in their careers. I'm not equating these doctors with Shipman here, I must point out. These doctors were acting in a vastly different context; Shipman was simply a murderer, these doctors acted with at least the tacit approval of the families involved and, I wouldn't be surprised, with the approval of the invalids themselves in many if not most cases. It is nonetheless fascinating. Anyway, Granny Ball lived on in the marital home on her own for many years after her husband's death. The house smelled of old age, a musty smell that was so strong it left a taste in your mouth, old food and unflushed toilets. The curtains were never opened. Granny Ball was totally blind. I don't know how she became blind or how long she'd been blind but blind she was. She wore long black dresses and shawls. Her face was covered in a network of fine lines. She rarely spoke, not to me anyway, but one of my regular duties when I was a little boy was to go to her house at a certain time every day and lead her by the arm up to the Red Cow, the pub at the end of the street. It would take a quarter of an hour or so because she didn't walk too well either. She'd dig her fingernails into my arm until it bled. I'd leave her there where she'd have five or six bottles of stout every evening and then someone else, one of her sons usually, would lead her home. Her small group of fellow drinkers was an interesting bunch. The woman who ran the pub was named Effie, I can't remember what she looked like, and among the others there were two men who lived together in an old abandoned hut at the entrance to a long-abandoned mine shaft in a copse of trees on the hillside nearby. One had one leg and was known as Ianto Clown, the other was Billy Oof, pronounced like the reaction to a punch in the stomach. I know nothing of their circumstances but I quite like the idea of them living together. Apparently in the winter when it got dark early Billy would lead Ianto down the hillside along the path to the Red Cow by the light of a storm lantern and the people in the bar would chart their progress through the window by the moving light. What a strange clientele they must've been. I wonder what they talked about.

There was a man who lived in the billiard hall in Mill Street who was known to give local children, young boys, packets of crisps and bars of chocolate in exchange for looking at their penises. It was a well-known thing and parents would often warn their children not to partake of this arrangement. He was known to all as Dai the Bummer. There was a young woman named Dolly who lived with her mother opposite the Cow. Dolly was no looker and a little bit twp, as were all the family. Anyway, it came about somehow that she and Dai the Bummer met and struck up a relationship. Marriage ensued and Dolly went back to the billiard hall with Dai after the ceremony to live as man and wife. She turned up back home the following morning however, with her suitcase still packed, sobbing that Dai had forced her to indulge in 'unnatural practices' and that she would never go back to him. What amuses me about this story is that a woman, any woman, no matter how thick or unsophisticated, could marry a man universally known as Dai the Bummer and then react with total surprise and disbelief when he lives up to his epithet. What did she expect – Ronald Colman? It is of course also very interesting in retrospect that Dai the Bummer could have remained at large to carry out his paedophile activities unhampered as he did. In those days it was regarded by many as just another crime. People would talk about someone who'd been put away for 'interfering with children', as they called it then, with no more condemnation in their voice than if he'd been caught stealing lead off roofs. It was a different world then, in some ways better but in many ways much, much worse.

Granny Ball died when I was about eight. I remember Naine standing at the front gate waiting for Ool to come home from work so she could tell him the news. He was about fifty yards away waving to me when Naine shouted out 'Your mother's dead!' I could see his face collapse in horror clearly even at that distance. Naine was not one to stand on ceremony.

After they were married Ool and Naine went to live in London. It was the 1930s and times were hard. They needed to work and some of Naine's brothers were already there, working on building sites in the East End. Ool got a job with them and Naine went into domestic service, as many young Welsh girls did at that time. Her employer was a wealthy doctor. I don't know much about it but Naine said that the work was backbreaking. They returned to Wales sometime before the outbreak of war in 1939. Ool told me that he was picking blackberries on Capel Hill with one of his brothers when someone brought him the telegram telling him he'd been called up. He and Naine must've been back in Pretoria Road, my mother living with them. There used to be a photograph of her in her WRAF uniform. She and a few others girls in uniform were horsing around in the country somewhere, my mother was straddling a kissing gate. She was a large, ungainly woman even then and though people say she was a looker I'm damned if I can see it.

Ool was sent to Africa. He spent the last three years of the war in Kenya and Madagascar teaching black soldiers to crew anti-aircraft guns. He'd been a gunner himself on the south coast in the earlier years of the war when invasion was threatened. He told me that they'd just bang shot after shot away in the general direction of the sky. In the entire war his crew only ever had one suspected hit. He found it difficult in the army at first. In training it became apparent that the Welsh weren't particularly popular and Ool had to use his fists on more than one occasion to illustrate particular points. He was a tough bloke. He'd been brought up hard. After he'd settled in he found army life a dawdle. A lot of men, particularly those from more refined backgrounds, found the practical conditions intolerable but to Ool it was The Ritz. The food was regular and, by Ool's standards, good. He had a comfortable bed and he didn't have to spend ten hours a day carrying bricks up and down ladders. He was fine. He told me that at breakfast in the army the cook would just slam all the food onto one tin plate, porridge with milk and sugar with two sausages sticking out of it and a fried egg on top. Some men found this revolting and couldn't eat it so Ool used to go around their discarded plates getting seconds. He was put on a charge for dragging some joker over the table in the NAAFI and blacking his eye after he'd made an ill-judged comment about Ool's race and eating habits.

Ool always said that the years he spent in Africa were the best in his life. Being white immediately gave him status. Kenya was a colony at the time, of course, ruled by a wealthy white elite, and British soldiers were made very welcome. Imagine it, a rough, uneducated man like Ool, who had never known any luxury in his life, being invited to tea by delicate, well-spoken ladies on the verandas of their colonial farmhouses, served by black servants. No wonder Ool loved it. There was one family called the Roberts whom Ool had very fond memories of. He had a photograph of Mrs Roberts sitting on her lawn with two beautiful tame cheetahs. The Roberts' farm was just outside Nairobi and Ool often had a tear in his eye recalling it. He actually lived among the Kikuyu, one of the two dominant tribes of Kenya at the time, the other being the Masai. He'd lay awake in his tent at night listening to the shuffling dancing and the singing, seeing the flickering of the fire through the open flap. Ool used to call his group of trainees his 'Boys'. One was called Nicodema; I forget the others' names. Nicodema would approach Ool's tent in the early hours and hail him softly from the darkness: 'Gunner Ball. Gunner Ball. Tombacco Gunner Ball!' Ool would give him cigarettes and he'd disappear back off into the night. Ool told me that most of the white soldiers treated the blacks like dirt, punching them, beating the hell out of them for no reason. Ool was no bully and in fact felt a lot more kinship with the blacks than with most of his fellow whites. He liked and respected them and they reciprocated. He shared their food and drink. His affection for the black Kenyans stayed with him all his life and I am grateful for it. It meant that the insidious racism that I was brought up with, ubiquitous in the Valleys, didn't work on me. Well, it didn't engulf me anyway.

Ool found a lifelong friend in Africa too. It was one of those army friendships, a deep trust built up through the experience of common adversity. Ool's mate was an Englishman named Bill Moody or just 'Moody' as Ool always referred to him. Moody was a great bloke according to Ool, and they kept in touch for the rest of their lives, if only by a Christmas card each year. We went to visit him once when I was a little boy. He lived in West Drayton outside Reading. I don't remember him but I do remember that he took me for a ride in the sidecar of his motorbike. He and Ool met in training in England and spent all of the Africa years together. They got into many a scrape. The soldiers drank in a gin house called The Dew Drop Inn, which was well off the beaten track on the edge of a jungle. Ool told me that there was an ongoing feud between the British Tommies and their Canadian counterparts. It was quite a violent situation and a few serious beatings had taken place. One night while walking back from The Dew Drop in their cups, he and Moody came across half-a-dozen Canadians in a similar condition at the far end of a clearing. They'd already spotted Ool and Moody, so legging it was not an option. Ool took off his belt and wrapped it around his fist 'buckle facing out', expecting the worst, but as they approached each other Ool had a brainwave. He walked up to them sharply and said 'What the hell are you doing here? We're on night exercises. There's live ammo being used. You'd better bugger off!' It worked!

I can only imagine what it must've been like for Ool, plucked from the poverty of the Valleys and transported to Africa, with its heat and beauty. It must have seemed another world to him, like being transported to another planet. They say a mile of travel is worth a hundred books and in my experience it's true. I'm not talking about going on holiday. I'm talking about going to live in another country, growing to realise that what unites us is far greater than that which keeps us apart. It is a lesson well learned and it enriches the soul. It was easy in those days for poor people to live and die in ignorance of such truths, believing only what they were told, never knowing anything first hand. Ool knew something for definite. He knew that Africa was really there and that it was a beautiful land inhabited by majestic and noble people. 1945 and demobilisation must have been like waking from a dream.

When Ool got back to Tonyrefail he found two children he barely knew and a wife who'd got used to getting along without him. My mother and Audrey were still living in Pretoria Road at the time, waiting for my father to come home from the prison camp. His return was to take them off to Canada. Sometime in the next five years Ool and Naine moved to 10 The Avenue. I know little about what happened while we were in Canada. Margaret and Brian both went to grammar school and Ool became qualified as a bricklayer. He got into a famous fistfight with Gwynne Evans' father in the courtyard of The Red Gate when his workmanship was disparaged. The blood flowed like spilt beer so I'm told. Gwynne's father was a huge tough man with a bald head but he made a mistake there.

That's about it. No, not quite. There was something else. Ool and Naine took to sleeping apart. There were three bedrooms in 10 The Avenue, Brian had one, Naine and Margaret shared another and Ool had the third; so the decision to sleep apart must have been a conscious one. The war had many knock-on effects socially and in terms of relationships. There were affairs, illegitimate births, agonising deceptions, and terrible guilt. Many marriages fell apart. When the men got back, even if none of these things had happened at home, they themselves had often changed as a result of their experiences.

War makes ordinary men important. It gives significance to lives that had never had any, indeed never

34

expected any. A British uniform in a friendly foreign country acted as a magnet to many temptations. Naine was short and quite pretty in a way but domestic drudgery and resentment had dulled her face. She worked ceaselessly. This was before Hoovers and washing machines. She never really stopped doing housework. The pervading smell of my childhood was laundry and polish. Like nearly all Valleys people at that time, Naine was profoundly racist. It was doubly ridiculous then, of course, because there were no black people in the Valleys, not one but Naine hated them nonetheless. I remember watching a late-night amateur-boxing tournament on the TV with Ool. I must have been thirteen or fourteen. Naine glanced at the screen and noticed a black boxer adjusting his protector on top of his shorts. She stood up, walked into the kitchen and vomited into the sink at the thought of what lay underneath. She shuddered in horror when explaining it to us.

What I think might have happened when Ool got home from Africa was that Naine asked him whether he'd had anything to do with black women when he was away. I don't know whether he had or not but I think Naine believed that he might have and that was it in the romance department from then on. When you consider that they were both still relatively young people you can imagine what sort of effect that had both on them as individuals and also on the family life in general. It was a strained and unhealthy environment for a child to be brought up in and I found myself right in the middle of it.

GROWING UP

My mother and Blaine and Audrey were given their marching orders from 10 The Avenue a few months after we arrived back. I can see why. It must've been impossible for so many people to live together like that, crammed into such a small house. I assume my mother told Ool and Naine it would only be for a few weeks and then just hung on in there. Taking advantage of other people's generosity was a way of life with my mother. She referred to them as Suckers. In order to make things a little easier for her, Ool and Naine said that I could stay till she found a suitable home for us all. In fact I'd moved in permanently. Ool and Naine became my adopted parents, Brian and Margaret my new brother and sister. My blood family Mam, Audrey and Blaine went on their way and I saw little of them for most of my early life. At first they hung around Tonyrefail. They were virtually destitute and spent more than one night covered in cardboard boxes and old blankets, sleeping in the doorway of The Savoy Picture House on Collenna hill. I don't understand how they could have been that poor because as far as I know they were in receipt of a substantial war widow's pension from the Canadian Government. I guess it hadn't come through then. My mother got a certain amount for herself and a smaller amount for each of us kids. When it was sorted out she rented a house in Mill Street and I used to go there to stay some nights. One such occasion was shortly after I'd come out of hospital after having my appendix removed. My mother nonetheless let me go up the snow-covered hill behind the house to play sleighs with Blaine and Audrey and I ended up with double pneumonia.

I was in hospital for more than a month. There was a nurse there named Nurse Allan and I thought she was beautiful. She used to sing a song called 'Bimbo', which was a hit at the time. 'Bimbo, Bimbo, where you gonna goio? Bimbo Bimbo, what you gonna doio? Bimbo Bimbo, does your mother know, you're going down the road to see a little girlio?' She had a lovely face.

I was in an oxygen tent for ages. Everything looked milky and distorted through it. Ool and Naine came to visit me and I remember jumping out of bed and running after them when they were going. There was a little girl a few beds away who'd been badly scalded with boiling water. They used to take her off for treatment on a shiny steel trolley. She'd scream pitiably when she was touched and there were always traces of thin watery blood on the trolley when they brought her back. I'd listen to her crying at night, sobbing her little heart out, the poor, dear thing.

I got better eventually and Ool and Naine decided, since I'd probably die if I went back to live with my mother, me being delicate and her being such an uncaring, thoughtless woman, that they would keep me with them. This arrangement suited my mother fine. She signed over my portion of the Canadian pension to Ool and Naine and that was that. Ool loved me. Apparently he loved me from the moment he saw me. It is said that he loved me more than he loved his own children but that is not true. He did love me, however, and I sensed it and loved him back. It was at his urging that I was accepted as part of his family – I'm sure of that. Why Naine agreed I don't know. Maybe it was out of kindness. I think it was some kind of act of love for Ool maybe, an act of love that was still acceptable. I don't, and can't ever, know the truth here other than the simple fact that it happened. My mother moved home regularly after this, every year at least. They lodged in a flat above the billiard hall in Ton for a short while, I don't know if Dai the Bummer was still the proprietor then but it's not unlikely. They moved and from then on mostly lived in an area bordered by Porthcawl, Bridgend and Penarth.

My mother was a terrible mother. She beat Audrey and Blaine mercilessly. She'd punch them repeatedly in the face, kick them to the floor, batter them with anything that came to hand. She didn't need a reason. I remember her hitting Audrey on the head with a stiletto-heeled shoe and it sticking there in her skull. It was horrific. My mother should have been imprisoned but no one cared. No one did a thing. She starved them too. Audrey and Blaine turned out like they turned out because of the loveless hell of their childhoods, as I have turned out like I am because of the thoughtless hell of mine, though at the time we were jealous of each other's lot. I thought they had freedom, they thought I had stability and comfort. We were all wrong of course. None of us Clack children had it easy. We'd all been through the trauma of our father's death and the subsequent upheaval and now we were frightened. If a parent dies when you're young it feels like they've abandoned you. You can't understand. Everything is personal. On top of this my remaining parent had given me away. I'd been abandoned twice and I wasn't yet five years old. No one thought to explain things to me.

Because of space I ended up having to sleep in with Ool in the small front bedroom, Stalag 1 as we called it. The window looked out onto the street. There was an attic door in the ceiling and for the first few years there was no electricity. There were several rooms in the house that didn't have electricity. The walls were papered and the paintwork was a dull cream colour. I ended up sleeping with Ool till I was eleven years old. We'd talk a lot, lying there in the darkness. We'd sing old-fashioned songs and Ool would tell me stories of his adventures in Africa. I don't think I actually contributed much to these conversations but I enjoyed them and they made me feel safe. Brian's room was cool. It had Boy Scout pennants and posters all over the walls. He had a single bed with a down mattress that was incredibly snuggly. I used to sneak in there some mornings when he hadn't gone to work and cwtch down behind him. Brian didn't bother with me much but I liked him. He was in his late teens then and he was thin and handsome. I liked him then and I love him now. He was a good bloke, a real brother. Margaret was very kind to me when I was young but went off me as I got older. She seemed to regard me as some sort of social inadequate, and then when I got to be about thirty-five she suddenly started talking to me as if I was a normal person. It was a pleasant surprise. I can't second-guess her reasoning but I love her and have always loved her, whatever.

My mother was addicted to gambling. Horse racing and bingo were her loves and that is where the money went. She'd dress up and go out every day and every night. There was no male company though. Well there was one once for a short period of time, a defeated, broken-looking widower whose name escapes me. He came to the house once or twice but he didn't last long. How any man could've been physically attracted to my mother is beyond me, or attracted in any other way either, come to that. I believe the deluded jerk actually proposed marriage to her but that was never going to happen. If my mother had remarried her pension would've been stopped. I suppose Casanova moved on to more fertile pastures. He will never know how lucky he was. In truth my mother's disastrous take on parenting isn't that hard to understand given her own upbringing. Audrey became Blaine's de facto mother, as Naine had been hers. My mother didn't bother with housekeeping so they lived in a state of permanent squalor. She'd go out early in the morning and leave them alone all day, day after day, with nothing but a huge tin of baked beans and a tin opener. Mam didn't care what they did as long as they didn't bother her. They never went to school. They just hung around the house and got into mischief. As a result both Audrey and Blaine grew up wild and delinquent. To me this feral existence that my brother and sister had was Heaven. When I went there to stay it was like being set free. We'd go where we wanted to go and do what we wanted to do. We were like little gypsies. All three of us used to sleep in the same bed; me and Audrey up the top and Blaine down the bottom. There was no timekeeping. We'd go to bed when we felt like, usually very late, and then lay awake for hours frightening each other with horror stories. Audrey was best at this. She'd recount X-rated films she'd seen in graphic and minute detail. We'd work ourselves into states of hysteria, almost paralysis we'd get so frightened. Every breath of wind was a whispered warning, every noise a monster stirring in the shadows. Audrey sculpted nightmares. She'd invoke grey smoky figures to appear in the room, werewolves, vampires and ghosts. Supernatural terror was what replaced toys in our childhoods. We were Enid Blyton's blackest dream.

I used to stay with my mother in the summer holidays. I'd stay for the entire six weeks sometimes. Blaine told me that he and Audrey would look forward to those visits all year. They loved me, you see, and I loved them. We missed each other, we pined for each other, they were my brother and sister; we were a unit. My mother treated them a bit better when I was there too. She fed them and me better and didn't beat them so often. I must have seemed like the Spirit of Good Fortune to them. They seemed free to me. I loved the cats too. One of my fondest childhood memories was when Mam lived in Hill View in Pontycymmer and Dinky, their cat, a female, black and white and a renowned slaughterer of both birds and vermin, gave birth to four kittens. I recall that there was a shallow-lipped bowl full of milk set out on the floor for them and how they galloped in, as only kittens can, when the door was opened, and fell upon it. They were such tiny little things that none of them could reach over the lip of the bowl so all four of them put their front feet into the milk itself and lapped it up from there. Their little paws and faces were white with it. They looked so beautiful. I wasn't allowed to have a cat back home but it didn't stop me loving them and I still do. In fact to this day I have never met a cat I haven't loved.

When the school holidays came my mother would come to Ton and take me back to wherever she was living at the time on the bus. She'd take me to a clothes shop when we got there and buy me some clobber, Ladybird shorts and tops. It was to show willing to Ool and Naine I think, a gesture. It's terrible really how children are used as pawns in grown-ups' games, isn't it? I was one of these pawns throughout my childhood. I was a weapon. It was clear that Naine regarded it as my personal fault that her life was as it was. She had had the enormous difficulty of bringing up her children on her own when Ool was in Africa and now when things should be easier, when Brian and Margaret had grown and could take care of themselves more, she'd been lumbered with me. I lived under the constant threat of being 'sent back' to my mother. I remember Ool and Naine arguing about it. I was standing there between them, each holding me by one arm, pulling me back and fore as I cried and screamed. My father didn't want me, my mother didn't want me and now my new mother and father didn't want me. It was as if I wasn't there at all, as if I wasn't real. Ool was shown less love than I was. He had no emotional succour at all till I came along. I fulfilled that role and this made me the perfect weapon to hurt him with. This constant threat to get rid of me, to return me to my mother, caused him terrible pain, and Naine knew it. I'd lie on my own in bed night after night listening to them screaming at each other downstairs. 'He's ruining my life. I can't stand it anymore. I'm sending him back. Let her take care of him. I've brought up my own family and now I'm lumbered with him!' It seemed to me as though they were talking about someone else. Surely it couldn't be me who was responsible for all those tears and rows. Those diatribes scarred me, the fear and guilt has never gone away.

Naine left home once. She packed her suitcase and went to London. There had been a row at the breakfast table and it ended with Ool smashing all the crockery against the wall. She was gone when I got home from school. She stayed with Uncle John in Kilburn for a few weeks before returning home. Ool was tortured by his love for Naine and his fear that she would separate him from me. The pressure never ceased.

I carried on with my little life. I played up in the fields with my two great friends, Mel and Gwynne. I visited Vaughan Rodgers across the road and played with him in the sandpit in their garden. I read pop-up books about cowboys and Indians, I fought little wars with my toy soldiers and I ate as much as I could. The house was always cold. There was always washing being done, the mangle out the back, the smell of bleach. The district nurse came to the house every day for years to give Naine an injection. She'd boil the needle in a saucepan on the fire to sterilise it. I don't know what the injections were for, anaemia maybe. I had to leave the room. I rarely saw Brian and Margaret. They were growing up, teenagers; they had their own lives. Brian has told me since that he and Margaret knew what was happening to me and didn't like it but felt there was nothing they could do. They had their own problems too, of course, and I don't blame either of them. It wasn't their responsibility. I have acted as a coward when seeing others bullied even as an adult. I am not one to throw stones. I remember coming downstairs late one night, very late when everyone else was asleep, and finding Brian wearing one of his lovely Teddy Boy suits lying in the open fireplace blind drunk and covered in vomit. He was a very stylish guy. He annoyed me another time and I called him a bastard. He was delighted and immediately reported me to Ool. Ool told me that 'bastard' was 'the worst word in the world' and I believed that for years. I even lost bets on it. He also told me later, when I heard the word 'homosexual' on the TV and asked him what it meant, that they were 'the most evil men in the world'. Everything was global to Ool.

I read recently about a condition in young children called 'Night Terrors'. It comes from REM sleep being interrupted and is particularly common amongst children who have suffered early loss. My father's death and my mother giving me away as she did were both obviously traumatic events for a little person like me. I didn't understand the details, the intricacies, but I was in the grip of Night Terrors for many long years. It is essentially a condition where nightmares and reality become confused. I was terrified of the dark until my early teens as a result of it. In practical terms it meant that when I went to bed and it got dark I would be subject to assault by monstrous beings from my psyche. All the monsters from myth and literature, ghosts, demons, evil semi-humans, you name it. Stalag 1 was the anteroom to Hell itself to me. I'd lie there night after night staring fixedly at the attic door, waiting for the sun to set, waiting for it to move, waiting for 'them' to start pouring in. I'd hold my breath and scream inside my head. It was a parade of monsters. As I got older it acquired a lot of religious symbolism. I'd be lifted up out of bed by invisible hands and walked to the door like a puppet. Once out on the landing I'd try to head for the top of the stairs. I believed that if I could touch the top of the banisters I'd be safe, but I never could. It was as though I was dancing with an invisible partner and she'd sweep me away as I got near. Once I saw a woman in a green shawl reading from a book out there. I thought she was the Virgin Mary and I tried to reach her but I couldn't, my invisible dancing partner swept me away into Brian's room instead, only it wasn't Brian's room any more. It was a black endless void, and as I moved helplessly through it disembodied arms and hands reached out from every side to grab me and pull me away, back into the darkness from where they had come. Most modern parents would have realised something was wrong, my hysteria as bedtime approached was well beyond a child's natural reticence. I'd often have to be dragged to bed screaming, in fact. They never tried to find out what was wrong. I'd close my eyes and ask my father to come down from Heaven to protect me. I confused my father and Jesus in my mind. Both were in Heaven, both were kind men, both loved little children. I'd sit on the top of the stairs and cry in the darkness hoping that Ool would hear my tears falling on the carpet and come and get me and take me downstairs, but this rarely happened. I'd see the black and white light from the TV flickering under the door. I'd hear laughter from studio audiences. I wanted to be dead like my father. I was a very messed-up little boy and there was no help, no respite, and no pity. I felt safe sleeping with Blaine and Audrey because if monsters came we could fight them off together. I think they saw monsters too. In fact I'm sure they did.

I started in the infants' school when I was five. I remember little about it other than that it smelled of clay, for model making, and there were stacks of comics. The teachers were all female and very nice. Naine used to take me. I'd have porridge for breakfast, real porridge cooked in a saucepan on the open fire. It was lovely. It rained all the time. I never remember going to the infants when it wasn't hammering down. It would be hammering down when I went home too. Naine would drag me along with one hand, her umbrella in the other, down the bottom of The Avenue, up the lane to High Street coming out by the Gwalias shop, turning left down the hill then along the lane behind the church to School Street. That journey measured out my little life. The headmistress was Miss Evans, one of the two Miss Evanses who lived together in a house at the bottom of The Avenue. They were spinsters. They had a tall thick front hedge instead of railings like everyone else. They valued their privacy.

The Avenue was about two hundred yards long; two rows of more or less identical houses facing each other. The houses were terraced except for Mr Herapath's house which stood, twice as large as the others, on its own at the top end, on the opposite side to us. It was a lovely old house with a large garden to the side. Mr and Mrs Hera-path were posh. He was a bank manager and she was refined. I don't remember actually seeing either of them in my life but their aura was benign. Brian told me that Ool was called over there once when Mr Herapath was away by their daughter, who I never even knew existed. She asked him to help carry her mother, who had collapsed blind drunk while on the toilet, to bed. Ool did so and never told anyone else about it. That was the sort of bloke he was. Other people knew it. He was trusted.

The end house on our side was larger than the other

houses too and had a large garden surrounded by a high wall. It was owned by Mrs Davies Top House. Her husband was blinded in an accident at work; he was electrocuted and his nerves had gone. You'd see him in his dressing gown and pyjamas, standing shaking in the garden sometimes. Leslie Jasper, a contemporary of mine, lived next door to us. His mother and father were stern unsmiling types and he had a sister, Margaret, who pronounced her Rs funny. Leslie and me were friends, we played together a lot, until one day we had an argument and I hit him on the knee with the butt of Brian's old air rifle. He ran crying to his father who came out of the house and gave me a clip. I started crying then and ran in to tell Naine. As it happens my mother was visiting. She went out into the garden, called Mr Jasper over, grabbed him by the front of his shirt, pulled him over the wall and punched him in the face. The chief repercussion of this incident was that the families never spoke again. We saw each other every day in the back gardens, going in and out of the houses, in the street, but never another word was exchanged. Leslie was a strange boy; he had an eerie quality. I think he may have been a vampire. Lyndon Sharpe lived behind us and was Leslie's big mate. When a bit older Lyndon used to entertain us other boys by masturbating his family's pet Corgi, a fat and unattractive specimen of the breed, though obviously not that unattractive to Lyndon. One day he got burned quite badly, Lyndon that is. He hid inside the communal bonfire on the tump for a lark and it got lit.

There was a woman with a huge wiry Afro-type head of shocking red hair who lived a few doors up from us. Her name was Katie Coates. She had big deformed toenails, like snail shells. I remember her taking off her wellingtons – she always wore wellingtons – and thick socks to show me. I was repulsed but said nothing. She was lovely. I've found out since that she wanted to legally adopt me. There were some really nice people living in The Avenue in those days. It was a safe place for a child to be brought up. There was a sense of community. I remember our neighbours with love, especially Mrs Keech who lived opposite with her daughter Frances. There was no Mr Keech. He may have died in the war. Mrs Keech was an ardent Christian, some strange but benign sect, I think. She and Naine were friends. She was the cook in the school canteen and her apple crumble was legendary. She was a lovely woman. Frances ended up marrying a bus driver named Clem.

My mother had a green metal box, which she kept locked on the top of her wardrobe wherever she lived. It was where she kept her 'important papers'. My father's war medals were in there too, campaign medals, a line of them. She was proud of them and so was I. I wore them to church for the Remembrance Day service. They were heavy; I remember the weight pulling my shirt down. Another memento of my father's war was a German infantry bayonet which, it was said, he took off the body of a dead German soldier. There was an inference that he himself had killed the man. It's possible I suppose but if he did it I'm sure he had no choice in the matter. The bayonet itself, about twelve inches long with a groove down the length of the blade, was kept in its scabbard, wrapped in an old cloth on a top shelf in a succession of kitchens and outside sheds. I was allowed to look at it occasionally but not to touch. It was dangerous. When I got older and discovered where it was hidden I got to study it up close. It was a strangely beautiful object. The most remarkable thing about it to me was that the owner's name was printed on the top of the blade, engraved near the base of the handle. The man my father might have killed was named Karl Eikhorn. It doesn't sound real, does it? It sounds made up, but it's not. That was his name. I used to wonder about him, who he was, where he was from, what city. The one thing that became crystal clear to me was that Karl was a man of flesh and blood just like my father. He could've even had a little boy, a little German boy just like me.

I started in big boys' school when I was six. Since it was right next to the infants, the practicalities were unchanged, except I started going on my own. Ool used to cycle to work on his pushbike. He'd do it in the dead of winter, seven or eight miles through the snow to start at six thirty in the morning. He was a fit man. He used to leave me threepence on the mantelpiece every morning to buy sweets from the tuck shop, a threepenny bit or three penny pieces. I'd look for them as soon as I got up. He'd write my name in pencil on the tile under which he'd put it – 'BOYD. 3 PENCE'. I spent it on Blackjacks, Fruit Salads and glasses of pop. I got *The Beano* and *The Dandy* regularly too. I identified with Lord Snooty and his mates. Actually I think I believed that I was a character in a comic myself.

Big boys' school was a bit scary. The boys were – well, big. The headmaster was Mr Locke, a distinguished-looking man with white hair. Then there was Mr Love, a balding English bloke who stayed for two years. He read us poetry: 'I wandered lonely as a cloud.' I identified him with Wordsworth himself for ages; in fact I still find the two images inseparable. There was Mr Owen who had lank, jet-black hair and wore an ill-fitting, shabby suit. He used to take us for football up the playing field behind the school. He'd insist on playing too and he'd throw himself into the game with gusto. I can see him now, jacket off, holding his tie in place with one hand, dashing back and forth after the ball as if his life depended on it. The rest of us were only seven or eight years old. He looked like a deranged cockerel. I really liked him.

I think the weather took a turn for the better after I started at big boys' school. There were long hot summer days to while away. I normally did this in the company of my great mate Gwynne Evans, yes the very same Gwynne Evans whose father had taken the famous hammering off Ool in the Red Gate. This never bothered us and to be fair it never bothered Gwynne's father either. Gwynne and me were inseparable. We worshipped at the secret altar of the Snake God with Emerald Eyes, a cheap ring we found and buried up the mountain. We sat for hours in the cage that Gwynne's father had made us to house Jacky the jackdaw. Gwynne was constantly finding slow worms and lizards and so forth for our collection. He was nature boy. Gwynne's father had his own business and the back of their house was a workyard littered with materials and machinery. It was a great place to play and Gwynne even had a little brother for us to torment as a kind of bonus. We stayed out and played all day, every day. We pretended to be Jap snipers up in the woods. We tickled for crachen in the shallow streams. Life was okay, in many ways it was idyllic. Gwynne was fit and strong. He was the fastest runner anyone knew and could throw a stone with the distance and accuracy of an Exocet missile. He was a great lad. We drifted apart as we got older and went to different schools, Gwynne to Gelli Dawel, the secondary modern which was at the bottom of Pant y Brad near where we lived, and me to the grammar. I still saw him about. He started wearing tight jeans and a denim jacket with black boots and developed an outrageous quiff. Gwynne never left Tonyrefail. He died a few years ago and I was very sad. Friends from childhood remain in your heart forever. My other great friend was Melville Payne. We were and still are the best of friends...

I was in big boys' school until I was eleven. I was a clever little bugger then and did well in all the tests and exams. I had already begun to be frightened of everyone and the humour I used to cover this up made me into a jester figure. The seeds of my future career as an actor were already being sewn. The main reason I was frightened all the time was physical cowardice. I have never been able to understand why but Ool, who as I have said was a hard man himself, quite deliberately set out to make me into a coward. He always told me to run away if there was any trouble. If I'd been bullied and I told him he'd tell me to keep out of the bullies' way. He himself would have broken a few noses and jaws in my position but he told me to run away. Like I say I have no idea why, I can't even hazard a guess, but it has stayed with me. I am easy to frighten, to bully. It has been a burden. It has damaged me.

When I was about eight there was an extension put on the house, a downstairs bit and an extra bedroom upstairs. Ool and me moved into the new Stalag – Stalag 2. Margaret, now a teenager with all that implied, got Naine's old room to herself, and Naine moved into Stalag 1. Stalag 2 was still terrifying but not quite as terrifying as Stalag 1. It was bigger for one thing, and the window looked over the back garden instead of the road. The stairs were closer too. It was actually here that my night-time hallucinations started to be of the religious kind. I had gone to church, St David's, for as long as I could remember. I went three times every Sunday, I sang in the choir at the morning and evening services and in the afternoon it was Sunday school. I liked church. We used to have Bible quizzes in Sunday school and I was good at them. When you won they'd give you prizes of sticky-backed religious paintings, like big postage stamps, which you could put in an album. I had a small library of them. I was told to love Jesus and I did. He was the Good Shepherd; he suffered little children to go unto him. He cared for me no matter what I did.

Robin Hood was on the telly from five thirty to six on Sunday evenings but since Evening Service started at six I had to leave the house at five forty-five to get to church on time, so consequently I never got to see the second half of *Robin Hood* or *William Tell*, which took over from it. This meant that I was constantly exposed to the evil machinations of the Sheriff of Nottingham and the Landburgher Gezzler without ever being there to see good triumph in the end. I think that this may well have something to do with my inherent pessimism. There was a photograph of me in my choirboy regalia hung on our living room wall for years. It was one of those early colour photos that look as if someone had touched them up. My cheeks and my lips were too rosy red. I looked like a little angel. In my teenage years this image embarrassed me excruciatingly but it remained there in pride of place despite that.

Audrey and Blaine didn't go to church. They ran wild. I met some of Audrey's boyfriends. This was the late fifties, the blokes she knocked about with were Rockers or Teddy Boys, violent, good-looking young guys with slashed-back, Brylcreemed hair, jeans and leather jackets. Audrey went through them like Polo mints. She became a biker herself as soon as she was old enough to get a licence. She came to visit me in The Avenue once in full leathers. She was tall and striking looking. There was a silver flick-knife hanging on a silver chain from her belt. No one messed around with Audrey. She was Barbarella. One boyfriend I remember was called Brian, a delicate-looking James Dean type. He took me to Cardiff once to buy toy soldiers. I loved toy soldiers. These were red coats, old fashioned. A few months later I discovered that he'd killed himself when Audrey dumped him. He'd blown his head off with a shotgun in his garage. One day a few weeks later Audrey took me for a ride on her bike and we stopped by a small church out in the country. We got off the bike and walked through a gate, down a narrow winding pathway, beneath overhanging trees to a small graveyard. She showed me Brian's grave. There were fresh flowers on it. It was a breezy autumn day and a sudden sun shower burst over us as we stood there. Audrey never seemed to harbour any guilt about Brian's death and indeed she was right not to. Someone you love not loving you back is something all human beings have to confront and deal with at some time in life. I don't believe that anyone would kill themselves for that reason alone. There must've been a whole universe of problems in Brian's poor little life for him to do what he did.

There was a church hall on a hill just around the corner from Hill View, where we lived in Pontycymer. They held dances there on the weekends and the front of the place was illuminated with multicoloured fairy lights. Some of the Teds and their girls would hang about outside drinking and flirting. Me and Blaine used to stand across the road and watch what was going on. We could hear the bands playing rock and roll inside. We'd catch a glimpse inside when someone opened the doors to go in or come out: we'd see people dancing wildly. Audrey went there regularly. She'd kiss anybody with a quiff. She was attacked once in the changing rooms of the outdoor swimming pool in Bridgend. A man tried to rape her but she laid into him big time and hospitalised him. Then she visited him in hospital and when he got out she started dating him. Audrey was a one-off, a working-class Medusa. She could bend reality the way she wanted it and then take you with her into that world. She had a breakdown when she was about seventeen. She began to believe that she was being stalked by an Egyptian mummy. It used to stand in a shop doorway across the road from the house watching her. She'd point to it from her bedroom window and say 'Look. Can you see him?' I never could. She barricaded herself into the room in the end. She pushed her wardrobe and dressing table against the door and

54

wouldn't let anyone in. She stayed in there for several months. Audrey had mystical powers.

The family lived in Trecco Bay Caravan Park for a few years, in Happy Valley near Porthcawl. I loved going there to stay. I love caravans. I love the little fragile furniture, the folding beds and, particularly, the sound of the rain hammering down onto the roofs when you're cuddled up all safe and warm inside. Ool and Naine used to rent a caravan in Porthcawl for two weeks every year during the miners' holidays. There would be a mass exodus from the Valleys. It would rain from the moment we set out till the moment we got home. The miners' holidays were synonymous with rain. It was a national joke. It was as if God had decided that nice weather would only spoil the miners for when they went back down the pits. We made do as best we could. I remember us sitting on deck chairs on Coney Beach fully clothed, with overcoats, hats and wellington boots on, in fully fledged raging storms. Ool and the other men would collect a pile of discarded deckchairs and build a wall to shelter us a little from the rain, which would be sweeping across the sand like machine gun fire. The deckchairs would blow away in the end and we'd retire to the pubs and cafés by the fairground. I adored Porthcawl fair. It was a fantasyland. I loved the hot dogs, real hot dogs with proper sausages and burnt onions. When I used to stay in the caravan with my mother, me and Blaine used to spend all day every day just hanging around the fair. Audrey was working on the Dive-Bombers. She used to sit in one of the whirling, spinning capsules to eat her lunch. Grown men would be screaming and begging to be let off. Audrey should have been an astronaut. The ladies in the fair got to know that we were Audrey's brothers and they'd give us free faggots and peas. I love faggots and peas. Two faggots, gravy, pepper and vinegar and two pieces of white bread and butter. Heavenly! Blaine and me took to sniffing the empty Calor Gas canisters that were left by the caravanners in a big pile for collection when they'd run out. There'd always be a bit left and we would inhale what we could. I don't remember it having any effect but it was fun because it felt naughty. Blaine was a great brother. My mother chased him outside one night when he was having a bath and wouldn't let him back in. He had to hide himself behind the caravan shivering and naked as the women passed, coming home from bingo. He was as thin as a pipe cleaner.

My joking brother Brian was in his early twenties. I hardly ever saw him. He was always out drinking, tomming and fighting with his mates. This was the time of early Elvis, Lonnie Donnegan, Billy Fury and Gene Vincent. *The Wild One* had just been in the pictures, Bill Haley and the Comets were touring Britain. His best mate was Sion Evans, who lived a few doors up from the Red Cow. Sion was a tall, bony guy who looked a bit of a handful. They both had pigeon coops, white flamboyantly feathered tumblers. They had good jobs too: Brian was a trainee ventilation officer in Coedely colliery and Sion was a welder. They spent their money on booze, Brylcreem and clothes. They had identical white suits made and looked quite a sight getting on the Porth bus together. They'd buy a half bottle of whisky each and drink it in the back row of Porth pictures. Brian had a bit of a reputation as a fighter but as he explained to me later it was a myth. What

Boyd's maternal grandfather (Dan 'the Yank' Griffiths), grandmother, Uncle Danny and Uncle John

Boyd's father, George Clack

Ernest Clack, Grandfather David Clack, and George Clack

George and Ellen at their wedding, Tonyrefail, 1942

 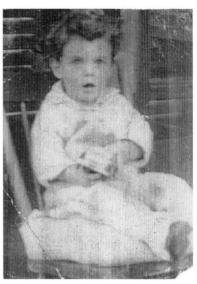

Ool in army clobber   Little bemused Boyd

Santa's grotto, David Morgan's,
Cardiff, 1957

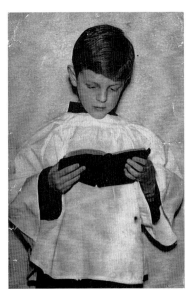

Choirboy Boyd

Boyd and his cousin Janet,
daughter of Uncle John, 1958

Boyd and Ool, High Street,
Tonyrefail, 1961

Boyd as Charles Atlas,
Porthcawl Beach

Boyd in the garden, High Street,
Tonyrefail, circa 1961

Boyd as a teenager on the
rooftop at Pencoed

Boyd in the garden, Ford Street, Sydney

Kate and Boyd, courting couple,
Sydney, 1972

Boyd and Kate, the happy couple,
Speers Point, New South Wales,
Australia, 1972

Petah, Kate, Boyd, Hugo, Wedding Day 1972

The Ball family, Wales, 1973

Boyd, Blaine, Audrey, Sig, Wales, 1974

Boyd and Mam, Wales, 1973

Boyd, Naine and Ool,
133, High Street, Tonyrefail

133 High Street, Tonyrefail

Boyd, Blaine, Audrey, Sig,
Wales, 1974

Naine, Boyd, and Mam
High Street, Tonyrefail

Boyd and Ool,
High Street, Tonyrefail

Hugo, Boyd, Athens, 1974

Lindsay, Foxy the dog, and the cats, in the kitchen, National Street, Sydney, 1976

John Strangeways, Kate, Ian Bruce, KT the cat, Boyd, and dogs Marion and Foxy, playing volleyball in the back garden, Victoria Road, Drummoyne, Australia, early 1975

had happened was that he had once punched some well-known hard knock in the mouth and downed him outside the fish and chip shop, but he'd only done it because he was drunk. It was a lucky punch. Indeed, the hard knock in question sought revenge but Brian managed to keep out of his way by hiding whenever he saw him. Brian was a lover not a fighter.

We had a record player in the parlour. The first music I remember was Al Jolson. Naine loved him. He always sounded hysterical to me. I preferred Nat King Cole. 'Around the World', 'Mona Lisa', 'Autumn Leaves' – he had a warm, all-encompassing voice and was such a cool guy. We had Slim Whitman singing 'Rose Marie' too. 'Oh Rose Marie I love you, I'm always dreaming of you', in that far off, wistful voice. Beautiful! There was an EP of gospel songs by Elvis as well – 'Peace in the Valley'. It was Brian's and I remember Ool and Naine quite liking it and saying that maybe the demonic Elvis wasn't as bad as was made out since he was so obviously genuine in his religious beliefs. There were other records too. 'Sailor' and 'Lay down your Arms' by Anne Shelton and a couple of singles by Michael Holliday, the British Perry Como as he was billed. There was 'The Story of my Life' and 'Kisses Sweeter than Wine'. Holliday was a big star at the time but his star waned and he committed suicide some years later. I believe he shot himself in a caravan. Strange how music stays with you, isn't it?

Auntie Gwen, not a real auntie but Naine's best friend, used to visit us quite regularly in The Avenue. They'd sit in the parlour together listening to the wireless in the firelight. I'd sit on the floor and play with my soldiers at their feet. I'd've been five or six years old. There was a play on once about a woman whose husband had died in the war. She'd remarried but then one day her first husband just turns up. He'd been in a POW camp and lost his memory. This chimed with my father and mother's situation and I got fantasy and reality mixed up in my little boy head. I thought that my father wasn't really dead, that he'd come back. I ran out of the room to the back door and waited for him to appear. It was snowing.

Brian and some of the other lads bought motorbikes and he used to take me on the back for rides up the mountain roads sometimes. There were no helmets in those days, he'd just jump on in his shirtsleeves and we'd be off. The shirt used to billow in the wind like the sail of a sailing ship. I'd cling on behind. One of his close friends, Lyndon Dix, was killed coming off his bike outside the Co-op in High Street near where we lived, and Brian and most of the other boys sold their bikes. He was never a biker by nature. Brian was the sensitive type. He was very political, a Marxist in fact. This was not unusual in the Valleys at that time. It was a fortress of socialism. I remember Ool taking me up to Gelli Dawel School to vote in a general election. He didn't even go into a booth. None of them did. They just ticked the Labour box on the voting slip in front of everyone, and put it in the box. I asked him what the difference between Labour and the Tories was and he told me that the Tories were for posh people and Labour was for us. I believed that until just recently. Ool would turn in his grave today, he really would.

When I was nine years old Brian met a girl on holiday and she became his first proper girlfriend. She lived in London and Brian went up regularly to visit her and stay with her parents. We saw photographs. Her name was Frances Mary Osbourne. She was a few years younger than Brian and very pretty. Her family was poor, working-class Cockneys. She had two sisters, one of whom was called Nancy, and a brother Billy. Her father was an on-course racing tipster but he obviously didn't make a fortune at it. Frances had seen a man killed by lightning on a racecourse and it left her with a lifelong fear of thunderstorms. The day arrived when Frances came to pay a reciprocal visit to 10 The Avenue. Brian went to meet her off the train in Cardiff. It was winter, a Friday evening, they didn't get back till latish and I was in bed but couldn't sleep. I heard them arriving, a strange new voice; a different accent. I strained my ears to hear what was being said. Not five minutes later I heard unfamiliar footsteps on the stairs. I was sat up cross-legged in bed in my pyjamas. The door, which was slightly ajar, swung open and Frances stood there in silhouette. She came in, sat on the bed and gave me a kiss. She told me that she'd heard all about me from Brian and how she'd been so looking forward to meeting me. I was overwhelmed. She was so pretty and she smelled of fresh night air. She had beautiful long black hair that fell in cascades over her shoulders. She was like an angel to me. That night Frances came into my room to say hello was the first time I ever remember anyone talking to me as if I was a human being. Talking to me as if what I thought or felt had some significance. She visited regularly after that and became the first person to latch on to the possibility that my fear of going to bed might be more than just an annoying affectation. She'd sit with me in the dark and tell me how it was no different to the light. She'd switch the light on and off to show me that the world was still the same place whether you could see it or not. It worked slowly and my Night Terrors began to fade away.

Brian and Frances got married in London but I didn't go. I stayed with Auntie Maggie in Collenna Road instead. My cousin Trevor lived nearby and we played bows and arrows in Auntie Maggie's back garden. It was a beautiful summer. We'd tie pieces of rag dipped in petrol on the points of the arrows and set them alight, then shoot them over the back wall towards the railway line at the bottom of the field. Nice, good fun! Auntie Maggie was very old. She had white hair and a lovely delicate face. I don't know why she was my auntie, what part of the family she was from, but I stayed with her several times when people went away. She lived in a large house on her own. Trevor would sleep over when I was there. We'd go to bed quite early but Auntie Maggie would let us get back up again later to watch *Seventy-Seven Sunset Strip* on the TV, Gene Barry, Efrem Zimbalist Junior and Eddie 'Kookie' Byrnes. 'Park my car Kookie.' Cool! Auntie Maggie used to eat what was known as sop. It was a bowl of tea, with milk and sugar just as you'd drink it, with broken-up pieces of buttered toast thrown in. It was inedible to most people but quite common among the very old and Auntie Maggie was very old, she was in her eighties. Sometimes pieces of sodden toast would slip from the spoon and hang down her chin as she put it to her mouth. She'd slurp them back up. I can hear it now. Auntie Maggie was a strange, ethereal woman. She was quite lovely.

Brian and Frances came to live with us in The Avenue after they were married. They had the parlour and their own bedroom. I used to play in the street with the Avenue Boys, Raymond Tucker, Royston Coles, Roger 'Slasher' Webb, Graham 'Hawkeye' Hawkins. We'd play 'kick the can' and 'outings', sort of gang versions of hide and seek, in the long winter evenings. We'd search for each other by street-light. There was the occasional skirmish with the Pretoria Road Boys, but nothing too serious. I started getting into comic books about then too, the small square British Second World War ones, the ones where the Germans all said 'Achtung Englander' and 'Himmel!' From there I moved on to American comics. I had a particular liking for stories about huge machines: giant earthdiggers and cranes and so forth somehow coming to life and terror-ising people in cut-off communities. These comics were popular for a time. The machines would be personified: *Mechanisto!* or *Metallica* or some such thing they'd be called. Then came comics about mutants, I liked those too. I think a lot of people who couldn't identify with superheroes found it a lot easier when the superhero was a mutant. I know I did. My favourite of all though was Green Lantern. 'Through brightest day and blackest night, no evil shall escape my sight!' I lost myself in a fantasy world. I felt at home there. We boys used to have a barter system with our comics but I was never any good at it. Raymond Tucker used to inveigle me into his front room and beguile me with his sales pitches. I was a sucker and often ended up handing over precious gems in exchange for some rubbish with a spectacular but misleading cover that Raymond would palm me off with. I was always easy to fool, still am. It's a byproduct of being a coward, I think.

From the age of seven or eight I started going to the pictures on my own. I went to the Savoy on Ton Square. I'd go four or five nights a week, often seeing the same film three nights in a row. I've no idea why Ool and Naine let me do this, but they did. When I was very young I used to go to the children's matinee every Saturday morning, a cartoon, a cowboy film, *Flash Gordon* and *The Three Stooges*. It was great fun but then I graduated to the real thing. Now the thing about the Savoy was that it showed virtually nothing but black and white American horror movies: *The Blob*, *I Married a Monster from Outer Space*, *I was a Teenage Werewolf*, that genre. Despite this the audience was made up entirely of children under ten, the old matinee mob in fact. These films may look tame now but they frightened the hell out of us. There would be rows of us with our heads hidden under the seats screaming hysterically most every night. The bloke who ran it would walk up and down the aisles with a torch yelling at us to stop screaming or he'd throw us out, which he did regularly with sadistic pleasure. I think he was a nutter. After the pictures I'd walk home in the dark through the old lane behind the church. I'd walk fast with my eyes shut, trembling with fear. A house in School Street just across the road from the Savoy was quarantined when the man living there died of smallpox during the epidemic of 1960. There was a red cross painted on the wall out the front. I stood and looked at it for hours on end.

I loved television from the moment I first saw one. It started with Children's Hour. I was a big *Wooden Tops* fan, and *Bill and Ben*, *Rag, Tag and Bobtail*, *Prudence Puss*, even *Picture Book*. I loved the lot of them. Later I started watching *Billy Bunter*, *The Range Rider* with Dick West and *Whacko* with Jimmy Edwards, who later went to live in Australia with a male ballet dancer. Ool and Naine used to watch *What's My Line?*, *The Four Just Men* with Vittorio De Sica and *The Invisible Man*. Later on there were shows like *The Human Jungle* with Herbert Lom. I really liked that. Herbert played psychiatrist Doctor Korda, and there'd be a different case for him to cure every week. Joan Collins was the guest star in one episode. She played a neurotic society woman who'd started getting her kit off in public and Herbert had to find out why. It began with a long running shot of her going into a tube station and stripping as she walked along. She looked blankly ahead as if in a trance. It was nearly all reaction shots but it was still very sexy. I wonder how old I was then. Old enough to fancy Joan obviously! I remember us getting our first telly that showed ITV clearly. I remember the man plugging it in and tuning it for us. The first program I ever saw on ITV was *Junior Criss Cross Quiz*.

In 1961 Naine and Ool sold 10 The Avenue to Brian and Frances, who were expecting their first child, and we moved to 133 High Street, not far away. It was a beautiful big house that had belonged to Mr Madge, a school-teacher, and his wife. She had died and he had lived on a few years before hanging himself in the front room. It was very posh by our standards but Naine set her mind on it. She went to London several times to see various solicitors but there was a problem contacting the owners, their children presumably, so we ended up, on legal advice, cracking the house and moving in as squatters. The deal was done eventually and Y Bryn Golau, 'The House of the Light on the Hill', was ours. It cost £1350, a phenomenal amount in those days. This was a delineating point in my memory. Before this, things seem far away. Like they happened to someone else and I'd been told about it. They exist in images and flashes and even then the story retold gets changed in the telling. What I've told you up till now is a representation of what happened. Essentially, my childhood was spent in a Welsh Valleys town in the 1950s. Let's draw a line under it. 1960 was an exciting year in Britain's history. We were at the start of a decade of great change. I was a thin bespectacled little boy with a strange, sparkling little mind. The future was there especially for me and people like me. I was an embryonic hippie!

ELEVEN PLUS

133 High Street had been empty for two years when we moved in and both the front and back gardens were overgrown to the point of impenetrability. The house itself was in need of decoration and some structural work but Ool could do most of it himself and he started on it straight away. Naine took control of clearing the gardens, assisted by Uncle Ike, who got stuck in like a trooper. The house itself was very beautiful. There was a stone on the front showing the name and date it was built: 'Y Bryn Golau 1861'. It was semi-detached and had a wooden garage to the side with double wooden gates and a short driveway. The front door and entrance porch were also on the side and there was a large stonework coal shed up the

back, in which Ool used to keep his tools and building materials. Karl Eikhorn's bayonet was deposited in a cavity on the wall too high up for me to get at. There was a conviction that if I got my hands on it, blood would be spilt. Nowadays kids would take it to school in their satchel. There was another, smaller shed and outside toilet behind the garage, hidden by a lovely holly tree. Inside the house itself the two front rooms had been knocked into one, which created the biggest room I'd ever seen in my life. There were built-in bookshelves with glass fronts on either side of the fireplace and an upright piano against the opposite wall. Being two rooms knocked into one there were also two windows. Two windows in one room! The living room was smaller, but still a fair size, and beyond that there was a pantry and kitchen leading out to the back garden. Upstairs there were three bedrooms and a large bathroom. This was the first time we'd ever had a bathroom. In The Avenue we'd still used a tin bath in front of the fire. There were two bedrooms at the front and one facing the rear. The stairs were wide and had a hand banister along the side. It was a fantastic step up in terms of living space and a statement of the family's upward social mobility. Ool had got a job at the coke ovens in Coedely colliery a few years previously and the regularity and security of the income had allowed us the move. I loved it. Not long after we moved in Margaret surprised everyone by getting engaged to Brian's mate Sion. They had been courting for a while but the actual engagement had not been expected. Margaret had been working in the Civil Service in Cardiff since leaving school and had been mixing with sophisticates. It was assumed she'd find a bloke amongst them and indeed she gave quite a few test runs, but it turned out that the love of her life was just around the corner. Sion was a quiet, moody man. His family were well respected and doing quite well in business. They lived only a hundred yards away from us in our new house and I think the match was seen as a good one. They got married and moved in with us until they found a place of their own. Marrying Sion appeared to be something of a compromise for Margaret. He had a good job but he wasn't 'impressive'. He was too working class. It was the same pattern as with Ool and Naine, the old Griffiths sense of superiority. Still, at first they seemed happy enough. The problem for me was that they took over the big front room and I wasn't allowed to go in there. They also got the main bedroom, which meant I had to carry on sleeping in with Ool, though by now I wanted a room of my own. Margaret soon fell pregnant and Sian Evans was born not long after Brian's first son Stuart.

I was gearing up for the all-important eleven plus exam that year and even at that age we were all aware of how important it was to pass. If you didn't pass you went to Gelli Dawel, which ironically means 'Grove of Peace'. It was renowned as a dumping ground for the thick and the violent. Not to get into grammar school was unimaginable. I was very clever as a lad. I never did any work but still shone. I was always first in exams. My exercise books positively sparkled with gold and silver stars. People used to comment on how bright I was. Naine would always reply that I might be intelligent but I didn't have any common sense. On the day the eleven plus results were read out my name was first on the list and I ran all the way home to tell the family. I was feted and we went on a week's holiday to London as a reward. We stayed at a bed and breakfast in Paddington and spent the time doing normal tourist things like going to the Tower of London and the Zoo. There is a photograph somewhere of me in my grammar school uniform eating an ice cream cone in Trafalgar Square. It was a great holiday. We'd been to Mevagissey in Cornwall the previous year, where Frances' grandmother lived. I remember us going for a walk along the harbour where Ool and Naine fell into conversation with two middle-aged English women and their brother, who were also on holiday. It was a foul day. The sky was dark and the sea very rough. Despite this I wanted to walk out along the semicircular harbour wall to the little lighthouse on the end, and the brother volunteered to take me, which he did. I started to regret it quite quickly. The waves were crashing onto the wall and sweeping over the top beneath our feet. I was frightened but the brother insisted we were safe and we carried on to the end. He was a tall bony man with receding hair. When we were at the end of the harbour wall far away from the others he took out some seaside postcards and showed me one, which had two women looking at a lighthouse with two large rocks at the base. One woman was saying 'That reminds me of my boyfriend'. He asked me if I knew what it meant. I felt very strange, very vulnerable out there with the huge waves smashing and the grey swirling sky. He told me that he had a big cock, and would I like to touch it? I don't know what I said. It began to rain then and he took me back. I didn't say anything. I didn't understand what had happened. If I had told Ool he would have literally killed the bloke, and I mean 'literally'. How significant that, despite the fact I was only nine or ten years old and that nothing actually happened, this memory should have remained so clear to me.

I started in Tonyrefail Grammar School in 1962. It was what was known at the time as a 'good' school. Its record of academic achievement was high and it had produced some notable sportsmen, specifically the Welsh rugby legend Cliff Morgan. The building itself was red brick and strangely impressive. It had been built in the early part of the century with the idea that it could double as a hospital for soldiers in time of war, the First World War. The basic vibe of the place was smugness. This was the place to be if you were a teacher, a 'good' grammar school. The students, at least when I was there, were taught in a dead, almost threatening way. It was the prevailing culture. The total emphasis on examination results and getting to university created a battery-hen system of education. It's a shame. My Night Terrors had all but stopped and my life entered a soporific stage. I didn't feel happy exactly but time passed in a summery sort of way. I played cricket in the field opposite the school in the evenings or soccer up the old school field. I hung about with boys from the housing estate. They were a nice bunch of lads in the main and just as daft as I was. I watched television fanatically, whenever I could. It was an empty, unreal time, the early sixties. The Beatles hadn't appeared and it was as though everyone was waiting for them. I hated school. The truth is that I was a dreamer. I wasn't prepared to waste my time studying. I did try, in fact, but I couldn't do it. I didn't want to know what they wanted me to learn. I had other interests. My reports were good in year one, where my natural intelligence pulled me through, but when it came to having to revise and do homework in year two and beyond I fell dramatically by the wayside. I was tall and thin and unworldly. Life is not easy for a boy when he's tall, thin and unworldly. People seemed to think I was unusual. Even my friends scorned my company. I was gauche, I think, I didn't reflect well on them. Ool used to tell me you can always judge a man by his friends and he was right. The teachers couldn't deal with me at all. I was regarded as an empty-headed chatterbox. I was always being chastised no matter what I did. When I tried not to do anything at all I was still chastised. In the end I gave up trying. I wasn't like them; it was as simple as that. They had no idea what went on in my life. I was a sort of lesser form of Holy Fool. That said, I had some friends, Mel Payne was there and Gary Newman, Mugso Morgan, Des Bevan and others. There was a wonderful boy named Raymond Kember who was very tall and very strange. He too was scorned by the Normals but he was no pussy and often got into fistfights defending himself. Good on him. Another thing he did was to pick his nose and put the boogies into holes in the wooden desktops till they were filled right up and then flatten them out. Sometimes people would sit at one of his desks and be sickened. Girls would squeal in horror. We used to play football with a tennis ball in the schoolyard every lunchtime and Raymond was a keen and committed participant. One day he came out from dinner a bit late and rushed to join in the match, which was already in full swing. As it happened some boys were playing cricket down on the field at the same time and one of them hit a towering six which was coming down on the yard near to where we were playing. Raymond, obviously thinking that it was the tennis ball being used to play the football with, leapt majestically into the air and headed it towards goal. He was knocked out cold. There was a lump on his forehead the size of a pomegranate. That was just the sort of stupid thing I'd do. Good old Kember! There were other loser types too of course, a whole subculture of us, but we had no sense of solidarity. The main boys, the alpha males, were Geoffrey Holtham, David Bonner, Mudge Jones, Anthony Scarrett and Dennis Ward; they were young, smart, personable and good looking. Being an emotional cripple I desperately wanted to be one of them and took to being a de facto jester as a means of entry into their circle. I was tolerated but never accepted. They'd plan to go places and not tell me. Don't get me wrong, they were good lads, I regard most of them as friends to this day. They were just young and full of themselves. Anyway, they'd sussed me out correctly; I wasn't an impressive chap.

All of these normal boys were tough, of course. There was no respect for anyone who wasn't able to look after himself and I failed miserably on that count. There were a few straightforward bullies among the perfects. Anthony Scarrett was a nasty guy. He was a sadist, a Flashman type. He liked belittling people. There was a lad named John Carter or Jeanne Louis as we called him. He'd been brought up in Belgium and could speak French. He moved to the school in year three with his sister Louise. They were delicate, gothic types, all air and nerve. Jean played the violin badly and had a pronounced stutter. Scarrett made the poor fellow's life hell. He used to punch him practically whenever he saw him. He'd make him cry and then laugh at him because he was crying. He'd spit in his face. Jeanne Louis couldn't defend himself. He was helpless. Bullying was accepted in those days, some teachers actively encouraged it. It was part of becoming a man. The first non-white person I ever met joined the school in year four. His name was Navinder Sachdev and his father was the new doctor. He too was a gentle, quiet person. Scarrett used to beat him mercilessly. Punch him repeatedly in the face. Call him a nigger. Tell him to fuck off back to Wogland. Scarrett wasn't the only one. Navinder was a punch bag. I tried to communicate with him but I was too stupid to know what to say. What I wanted to say was I'm very sorry, I don't hate you. I like you but I'm too frightened to help you. If I helped you they'd beat me up as well. One of the many terrible things that a bully does is to reduce witnesses in their own eyes for not having the courage to intervene on behalf of their victims. Anthony was a damaged person. I met his parents once. I was going to see the Rolling Stones with him in Cardiff and we stayed in his house overnight. They were very nice people, young and modern. He acted like an angel in front of them. Navinder's father had taken over Dr Monroe's practice after Monroe had retired. Monroe was a legend. Patients sat in his waiting room in total silence. They were terrified of him. Just the sound of his footsteps on the stairs coming down from his living quarters to the surgery in the basement made people gag with fear. You never knew what mood he was going to be in. Grown men fixed their eyes on the ground at their feet as he approached. He was, however, universally acclaimed as a doctor.

Sion and Margaret were having a difficult time living with Naine. She didn't have much time for Sion and didn't hide the fact. Sion had some psychological problems with it all and I remember him sitting on the stairs one night crying his eyes out for hours. Doctor Monroe came to the house in the middle of the night to see him and sat there on the stairs with him, talking him through it in his gentle Scottish brogue. He was a fine doctor. Everyone respected him. Navinder's father had big boots to fill. He didn't get the chance, however, because his surgery was firebombed by local racists and the family were driven out. Tonyrefail was a violent place in those days, make no mistake about that. All the Valley towns were.

Margaret and Sion eventually moved to 147 High Street, just a few doors away from us, and so I finally got my own bedroom. At first I'd have to check in the wardrobe and under the bed every night for vampires etcetera before I could go to sleep, but I gradually became satisfied that there were none about and dropped the routine. I read a lot. I'd got six classics in red leather binding as a Christmas present and despite being bitterly disappointed I read them all many times. *Tom Brown's Schooldays* and *Kidnapped* were my favourites. I love those books to this day. I reckon every young boy should read them.

Auntie Gwen now lived just around the corner and became a regular, almost compulsive, visitor. She'd appear at the back door like a ghost and Naine would let her in. They'd sit there for hours in the fading sunlight talking, drinking tea and, in Auntie Gwen's case, smoking Woodbines. She smoked so much that she appeared to be permanently shrouded in a low-lying mist. Ool and she were avowed enemies. She was Naine's friend, not his. Ool used to tell them that they ought to move in together into a little cottage up the hills where they could spend 24 hours a day gossiping and running people down. Auntie Gwen thought Ool was a pig. Gwen lived with her mother, who was ancient. She had Alzheimer's disease or she was in her second childhood, as they called it then. I remember chasing after her down the road one winter's evening when she'd seen an advert on TV imploring people to rush down to their local shop to get a big discount on washing machines before the offer ended. She was in her nightdress and it was snowing. She was lovely. I have always really loved very old people. Auntie Gwen and me always got on fine too. I liked her chutzpah. Brian and Frances were well settled in at The Avenue and I used to go there often. We'd play quizzes. I was very good for my age but Frances was better.

Audrey was living with a bloke named Terry Smithers in Llangeinor, a small village on the other side of Blackmill. He was a nice guy with two kids from a broken marriage. Blaine had been spotted running wild by Social Services and sent to a boys' home near Abergavenny. This really upset me but Smithers drove me and Audrey up to see him and take him out for the day a few times and that was wonderful. The boys' home was a heavy place but Blaine had learned how to keep his nose out of trouble and seemed okay, so I could rest easier...

The first world event I remember was the Cuban missile crisis. It was on the news every day. People felt frightened. Then one night when I was getting a quarter of Merry Maids for Naine from Sydney's sweet shop, the man on the wireless behind the counter said that John F. Kennedy had been shot and killed. There was an unreal air to it all.

It seemed that something fundamental was being undermined. The world trembled. Come to think of it I remember the Mau Mau uprising in Kenya too, and that was probably before this. There was a report saying that the Mau Maus had murdered some Belgian nuns and eaten their raw livers while they were still alive. Who knows if it was true? I wouldn't put it past them. My cousin Tony would have put paid to a good number of them, I've no doubt. Just thinking about all this makes me sad. The first things I remember about the outside world and they are all bad, heavy duty bad. I got to see newsreels from America. I watched Jack Ruby murder Lee Harvey Oswald on the news. The popping sound the gun made was eerie; it didn't sound real. We started seeing film of the early civil rights movement soon after. There were marches being broken up by baton-wielding police with snarling Alsatians and black people being punched in the face by short-sleeved white men in schoolyards; they were getting beaten to the ground and swept away by powerful jets of water from water cannons. It was like a war. In Cowboy and Indian films I was always on the side of the Indians. I thought the black protesters were very brave. It was inspiring to see such courage and dignity under pressure. The white police seemed barely identifiable as human. London and the rest of Britain meant nothing to me. Cardiff meant nothing. These places didn't exist. America is what existed. I was obsessed with the idea of going there, living there. Oh God, I just thought, maybe this love of America and all things American is hereditary. I might have got the DNA shoveled down to me from Dan the Yank. It had happened to Uncle Ike, why not me? I didn't talk about it or tell anyone at the time but, genetic or not, I began to walk with a lazy stride. The odd thing is of course that my brother Brian regarded America as the antichrist. He was an ardent communist. He had a pile of books on politics. One of them was called *Inside Russia Today*. It was a thick volume with a red leather cover and the title embossed in gold print on the front. I must have read it half–a-dozen times from cover to cover. It had tables of statistics, population distribution, exports of various minerals, racial geography: all incomprehensible. I studied them nonetheless. Some chapters were on social problems. There was an underground nihilistic, beatnik movement among young Russian intellectuals and artists, which was called Nibonicho. It meant 'nothing' or 'nobody'. These people were a minor subculture. They held poetry and literature meetings in secret, where they would greet each other by saying 'I am Nibonicho'. A dead giveaway if you ask me. The KGB men would be home early for tea that evening. There were some examples of their poetry in the book. It was rubbish. If I had been a young Russian in those days I'm sure I too would have been Nibonicho.

Brian would talk to me for hours, he'd tell me about the exploitation of the proletariat and Marxist ideology, about dialectics and trades unions and the struggle of the working classes. I listened to stories about Trotsky and Lenin and Stalin, how the Russian people had raised themselves up from poverty and servitude by blood and courage and revolution. I loved Russia, the great Soviet Union: our noble ally in the war. Women soldiers fighting like men. I loved the Russian people. You might have noticed that I loved both Russia and America. Weird, huh? Then there was Sputnik. When was that? The late fifties or early sixties? Yuri Gugarin, Valentina Tereshkova, little dogs wearing spaceman helmets, it was fascinating. Russia was to the front of the public consciousness at that time too. It was round three or four of the Cold War, there was a tangible fear that there could be a nuclear flare-up at any time. We were conditioned to expect an unexpected attack. No wonder everyone was numb. Me, I don't know what I was doing from day to day. Time just seemed to pass. The ages nine to twelve are transitional years in a human life. They disappear in a flash. Then at thirteen or fourteen individual thought begins to blossom. I started to realise how crazy the world was and how awkward I felt in it.

One afternoon I went up Brian's house and he played me a new LP he'd bought. It was *With the Beatles*, the band's second album, the one with the lovable moptops' faces staring out of a black background. I listened to it and liked it. This would have been 1963 or 1964; I was thirteen. I had also begun getting preoccupied with the female form at this time. I thought of the girls in my class with uninterrupted lust. I could have masturbated for Wales, though I'm sure I would have had some stiff competition. I didn't know anything at all about sex, absolutely nothing. It was a subject that was never broached in our family. I believed that girl's private parts were on the front, a sort of moneybox slit, and that the sex act consisted of the bending down of the erect penis to a ninety-degree angle and then pushing it forward into the vertical slit in front of the girl's crotch. It was inaccurate of course but it was good enough for me. It was mastur-bation that hammered the final nail into my fear of vampires, in fact. You cannot masturbate successfully if you are frightened that a vampire might attack you at any moment. One of them had to go.

Audrey found a serious boyfriend named Malcolm Sargent, the same as the famous conductor. He was a boyish, tassel-haired chap with a kind face and I really liked him. His great love in life was motorbikes. He had two, a BSA Rocket and a Norton Commando. He'd spend day after day in the blistering summer heat taking them apart piece by piece and then putting them back together again in the front yard. He'd clean the individual pieces, nuts, bolts, washers, strange bits of metal with tubes coming out of them, all of them by hand one at a time. He'd polish a single washer till it shone and then put it back where it came from. I suppose in retrospect that there must've been some purpose to this but at the time I thought it was just what blokes with motorbikes did. It seemed to make him so happy. Audrey seemed calmer than she had been. I think she might have been happy too. I remember us riding down to Porthcawl one night. It was late, a crisp and clear sky, black and dripping with stars. Audrey was on the back of the bike, the Norton I think, Blaine was in the middle in front of her and Malcolm was driving. I was on the petrol tank in front of him. We were belting along a long curving coastal road. The sea was huge and dark and silent to one side. I remember Malcolm shouting out for me to look at the speedometer, which was lit up in front of me. It was pointing over the ton. Audrey and Blaine were screaming with delight. It was thrilling. I felt alive. The four of us there on that beautiful bike zooming through the sparkling darkness. It was contact with the infinite.

Audrey and Malcolm got married and moved into a small stone cottage outside Bridgend. There was a row of three cottages together but the other two were uninhabited. They were very old. They didn't have proper sanitation; there was a septic tank in the back garden. There were no other houses in the area, it was common land. The cottage was just a few hundred yards from the Parc Gwyllt psychiatric hospital. The Parc, as it was known, was a huge forbidding Victorian asylum. Auntie Daisy was locked up there for fifteen years. We'd see patients wandering about the common quite often. Thin men with blank expressions and misshapen heads or middle-aged women dressed like little girls. The Beatles' influence was tangible at this time. They were in the newspapers, on television; people were talking about them, singing their songs. Fashion was changing overnight as young men rushed to imitate them. There was a boy named Paul Crocker in school and he was a dead ringer for Paul McCartney. Within weeks he'd become a virtual doppel-ganger. The fringe, the suit, the cute smile, the Cuban heels, he had the lot down to a T. It worked too: girls started flocking after him.

School was getting increasingly weird. There were all these incredible things happening all over the world and they expected us to sit in rows in big rooms and listen to rubbish about convectional rainfall or what some strip of paper would do if you stuck it in a chemical of some kind. It was crazy. It was a waste of time. I could barely stand it. It wasn't that I was a rebel: it was that I couldn't breathe. The only positive thing about it was that I could be near girls. I thought about them all the time. I tried to get Naine to buy me cooler clothes and it worked to a limited degree. She got me a waistcoat-type thing with black synthetic leather stripes down the front from the Grattan's catalogue. I loved it. I took to walking into assembly with my thumbs tucked into the front pockets. I thought it made me look sexy and interesting. It was a bohemian affectation. Someone commented on it after a few months and I stopped immediately.

I started going to the roller-skating rink regularly too. There was a girl from school there named Pauline Morris. She was a few years older than me and had raven-black pageboy hair. She was as sexy as hell. Her father owned the rink and Pauline was a highly accomplished skater, a serious one. She entered competitions. I could barely stand up on roller skates; in fact I was frightened of them. I used to go round and round the wooden-floored rink three or four times hanging on to other people, and when it got too fast I'd stop myself by going straight into the wooden counter where they sold bottles of pop. How I didn't seriously injure myself I'll never know but the risk was worth it to see Pauline practising. She filled my thoughts day and night but I never actually got to speak to her. I would probably have fainted if I'd got the opportunity but I never did.

The other place where I got to be near girls close up was The Urdd. The Urdd is an organisation to promote the Welsh language and culture amongst young people and there was a branch at the school. It was run by Johnny Williams, the Welsh teacher and deputy headmaster. There was a meeting every Tuesday night after school. We could go home first so it became something of a fashion display. After reading some Welsh poems out loud together or some such thing we'd clear the chairs and have a social get together, a dance in fact. I used to stand to one side watching. I'd go near girls sometimes and maybe exchange a nervous smile or a few inane words. I noticed that girls didn't only look nice but they smelled nice too. I was sure that they'd taste nice as well if I ever got the chance to taste one. I was in serious danger of doing irreparable damage to my left arm at that time. Naine who, like my mother, was repulsed by any hint of sex, started making unpleasant comments about my bed sheets. She used to sniff them and pull a disgusted face. 'What is this stink on your bed sheets?' she'd ask. What could I say? Naine was not one to let nature take its course. At one time she took to bursting into the bathroom under the guise of needing to put things in the airing cupboard when I was on the toilet – the latch on the bathroom door was faulty. She wanted to catch me at it but she never did.

As it happens we could see into the upstairs windows of the newly built council houses on the estate behind us from the bathroom window and there was a girl from school living in one. I don't remember her name but she was really beautiful and one night when I was looking out of the window she walked into her bedroom with a big towel wrapped around her after having a bath. The curtains were open and I could see her clearly. She stood in front of a mirror in her room for a moment and then let the towel drop to the floor. I stood and watched her looking at herself. She turned this way and that; rubbed her hands down her hips and cupped her heavenly breasts in her hands. I could even see the expression on her face. She was a bud bursting into bloom. Someone called to her from inside the house and she stopped and drew the curtains. I tell you, friends, it was a Holy moment. If only she'd have let me cup her breasts. What fun we could have had. I would have filled her up with all the love she wanted. She missed out there but unfortunately so did I.

THE DREAMER

The next few years were painted in broad strokes. There were long hot summers and bitter winters. The routine of school dictated the pace of my life. I started going to stay with Audrey and Malcolm in the holidays instead of with my mother. I don't even know where she was living at the time, but she showed up regularly. Needless to say, she hated Malcolm and he soon learned to reciprocate. Blaine was around too. I don't know what was going on in my mind in those days, what I was thinking. My head was full of bubbles. Audrey had a baby son, Anthony John Sargent. He was a sturdy little fellow. Malcolm used to throw him up into the air and catch him. He'd throw him so high sometimes that he'd scrape the ceiling. It frightened hell out of me but Tony loved it. He'd laugh and laugh and laugh. I started wearing a denim jacket and a Donovan cap. 'Catch the Wind' had been a huge hit. There was always music in the cottage. The radio was left on all the time, day and night. Everyone had gone to the Moon. Dusty Springfield's love lay in the middle of nowhere and John Lennon implored us to help him. He was feeling down. They were happy times.

I'd started supporting Cardiff City. A bunch of us lads from Ton went to almost every game. I didn't miss a home match for four years. City were never a great team but they were entertaining. They took to the field to circus music blaring out over the tannoy system and this was apt because they usually played like a bunch of clowns. Ronnie Bird, a left winger with lightning pace and a hammer of a shot, would hare past the opposition full back and run a good thirty or forty yards down the pitch before realising he no longer had the ball. Sometimes the bemused defender would hare after him. Everyone would roll about laughing. It was a hoot. Don Murray, the Scottish centre half and club captain, was such an uncontrollably violent man that he'd sometimes attack players from the other team before the game had actually started. He had to be sedated on more than one occasion. The other players joined in with the spirit of things by often demonstrating a degree of ineptitude that could only have been deliberately planned. That said, Ivor Allchurch was and still is the finest player I have ever seen anywhere. He was a genius.

I think I have made it clear that I was breaking records for self-abuse in those days but it wasn't just me. We'd all go to my cousin Trevor's house after coming home from the football on a Saturday night, when his parents were out, and masturbate en masse in his front room while watching telly. There'd be a dozen or so of us at it sometimes. Young men are strange creatures controlled by hormones and a pack mentality. To have suggested to any of us that our behaviour could have been construed as deviant would have met with incomprehension. In fact there were no homosexuals in Tonyrefail in those days, none in the entire Rhondda Valley as far as I knew, except Dai the

Bummer, and I'm not even sure he was still alive at that time. A known homosexual would have been beaten to death. It was a totally macho culture and yet it wasn't only the football-playing guys who indulged in this mass masturbation. I also hung about with the Pretoria Road boys and they were a really tough bunch. I hesitate to mention names here because it might embarrass them and they may come looking for me. Suffice it to say they had a tree house up the Glyn Mountain which was rhythmically dislodged over a period of several months and fell to the ground. It was normal adolescent behaviour, of course. We were all as horny as hell and couldn't get any girls – it was as simple as that. It did us no harm except for several strained wrists and a residue of good old-fashioned Christian guilt.

1966 saw the World Cup in England. I watched the final in Mugso's house. His family owned a small shop on Collenna Road and I used to go there a lot so we could revise for exams together. Mugso's parents were charming people. His dad was an avuncular man who always wore an old cardigan and his mother was a genteel, refined woman. They were both lovely to me and I still hold a place in my heart for them. Mugso himself was a clever and open lad. He had a gentility of spirit that must have been nurtured in him by his parents. He didn't look at me funnily or think I was strange at all. We were good mates. The cup final was a buzz. I wanted Germany to win of course, as did all Wales, but you can't legislate for cheating and England won 4–2. I bet you didn't know that!

Later that year we went on a school holiday to Germany. We travelled by coach and then a ferry to

Ostend in Belgium. I was as sick as hell on the ferry. One of the crew members told us that he'd been doing the run for twenty years and that this was the roughest crossing he'd ever remembered. I managed to find a spot on the lower deck at first and was feeling relatively fine until someone vomited all over me from the upper deck and that was it. I thought I was going to die. We stayed in a small hotel on the harbour. There was a famous sailing ship in full sail moored there as a tourist attraction and it was illuminated at night: a spectacular sight. We were four to a room, Mugso, Gary Newman, Des Bevan and me, and we were presented with an unexpected and unusual dilemma at bedtime. There were no sheets or blankets on the beds, just big fat eiderdowns inserted like pillows into great big pillowcases. None of us could figure them out. We finally came to the conclusion that the idea must be to unbutton the top of the cover, get inside it and then button it up again around your neck. Then we couldn't decide whether the eiderdown bit was supposed to be on top to keep you warm or underneath to keep you comfortable. I opted for the latter.

Young though we were, we were obviously right into the booze as the entire week was spent tipping it down us at every opportunity. The boys had told me that they were going to force me to smoke cigarettes on the trip too so I pre-empted them by practising secretly on Ool's Wood-bines for a few weeks beforehand. We went from Belgium through Luxembourg to Germany, stopping off in a host of wondrous cities en route. It was fantastic. This was our first sight of the world beyond. The foreign girls looked the business too. Des Bevan actually got off with one and disappeared for a day. Des was mature for his age. He'd already started shaving and carried a packet of Frenchies in his wallet. It was always one light. One evening in Düsseldorf we found a beer garden that was by the side of a river overlooked by a steep vine-covered hillside. We were told that the grapes were used to make the local wine so we decided to give it a go. None of us had ever drunk wine before. It was served chilled in huge glasses and, knowing no better, we knocked it back like beer. We got plastered and were violently sick later, vomiting copiously into the small sink in our room. Eventually the vomit, beefed up as it was with German sausage and sauerkraut, refused to go down the plughole and we were forced to scoop it up with our hands and sling the solid bits out of the window. A few nights later we got into trouble with the teachers when they coincidentally came into a back street pub we thought we were safe in and collared us. They chastised us at breakfast the following morning and we had to stand up and apologise in front of everyone. How cool was that!

The following year was GCE O-level year and for some reason, despite my obvious laziness and surly indifference, I was still expected to do well. I think they thought that I'd pull myself together, knuckle down and come up trumps, but I didn't. I didn't want to be a teacher or a bank manager, I didn't want a nice house and kids, and I didn't seek society's acceptance. I was a free spirit. I wanted to travel the world living in beautiful places and shagging beautiful women. I was a hippie. I was into peace and love and I wasn't the only one, there were others like me even in Ton. Even in the grammar school there were little signs of rebellion, a flowered shirt here, a pair of moccasins there, the occasional discreet bead necklace, and who could blame us. We were inundated with images from America, thin cool-looking guys in black top hats putting flowers into the barrels of National Guardsmen's rifles. Wide-eyed girls with butterflies tattooed on their faces writhing semi-naked in fields of mud, people blowing bubbles into the air and making love in sleeping bags in open fields. I wanted to be one of them. I wanted to go to San Francisco. There were other images too, new words joining the vocabulary. Words like Napalm and Tet and Vietcong. Martin Luther King addressed huge audiences in Washington while other young black men had started wearing dark glasses and long black leather coats. They wanted the change to come quicker, they wanted it right then, and they were prepared to do something about it. How the hell did they expect me to concern myself with quadratic bloody equations with all this going on? You get my point. I was getting drunk instead of studying. Me and some of the other lads would walk up to the Lamb and Flag along the winding country lanes between Ton and Beddau and drink Whitbread Tankard. It was a tidy stroll, four or five miles there and back, but it was out of the way and they'd serve us, so needs must. We'd stagger and stumble back home in the dark laughing and singing and shouting at the stars. I'd go straight to bed as soon as I got in and sleep it off. Ool and Naine must've known what was going on but I was rarely rebuked. I kept myself pretty much to myself.

There was still no real action on the girl front but I did almost get a date. I was slipped a note in religious instruction class saying that the girls in our form had taken a vote and decided that the most fanciable boys in our year were Geoffrey Holtham, David Bonner and me! I was speechless. I couldn't believe it; in fact I didn't believe it. I thought it was some kind of social experiment. If it was true how come they didn't want to shag me? What I didn't realise at the time of course was that young girls had dreams of love and sex and adventure just like young boys, but that they too felt awkward and unattractive and unlovable. It may seem obvious now but at the time I had never really even talked to a girl about anything other than asking to borrow a pen or some such thing. I knew nothing about them. This note came like a bolt from the blue in more ways than one. I didn't know what to do. I didn't know if there was anything I could do. What I wanted to do was to grab one of them and say 'Okay if this is true, take off all your clothes and let me kiss you and feel you and lick you all over', but I didn't. I just smiled inanely and trembled inside. Somehow, I've got no idea how, but somehow it was arranged that I was supposed to meet the prettiest, sexiest girl in the class at the Gilfach bus stop near the park at half past five one night after school. I don't remember asking, maybe it was she who suggested it, but I had what could loosely be described as a date! Her name was Gillian Archer. She wore a famous red anorak and had lovely lips. Every boy in the class fancied her. Anyway, I waited in the Italian café on the corner about fifty yards from the designated meeting place on the night in question, playing the flipper machines, drinking coke and getting more and more nervous. I popped out between games and peeked around the corner to see if she was there and the last time I popped, she was. I was taken aback, I hadn't expected her to turn up at all. I just stood there looking at her, watching her. She was a vision of beauty, she really was. I felt weak, hypnotised, I couldn't move and I'm afraid I didn't move. She waited for a time, looking at her watch occasionally, and then finally left on the Gilfach bus. I walked home crying. Gillian never mentioned it and was still friendly to me. She wasn't just beautiful; she was sweet and understanding too. Gillian herself may not even remember this incident. I'm sure it meant a lot more to me than it did to her. I bumped into her a few years ago with her husband in a street in Cardiff. She'd become a schoolteacher. She was as pretty as ever.

Audrey had another baby, another boy. They called him Jarrod after a character in a TV western called *The Big Country*. Things were going wrong between her and Malcolm though, the cottage lost its sparkle, the laughter stopped. Then one day she turned up with another bloke. He was a Norwegian named Sigurd Ellingsen. She'd met him when he was working on a geological drilling project on the common near the Parc. He was a diamond driller, which doesn't mean that he drilled for diamonds but that he used diamond-tipped drill heads. I was very confused and unhappy about the situation. Audrey left Malcolm and took the kids. They moved into a house in Pontycymer with Sigurd. I went to stay with Malcolm on his own for a weekend soon after. We drove out to some meadow where there was a gypsy encampment and we fed the horses. We ate fish and chips out of newspaper in the car down by the docks in Barry. We watched a big ship leaving. Malcolm was yesterday's man and he knew it. He went on to start a successful transport business but died young. I have a theory that couples who have ever been in love at any time remain in love forever somewhere in the stars. I believe it.

Sig was tall and thin and had a mess of black curly hair and piercing ice-blue eyes. He was very handsome, strikingly so, sort of moody looking too and as hard as nails. When he'd been a teenager in Norway he used to go down to the docks and fight foreign sailors for fun. Sig wasn't just hard; he was vicious. You wouldn't want to fuck with him. That said he was always friendly and kind to me. Him and Blaine didn't get on but that was as much to do with Blaine being an arsehole as Sig being unreasonable. Blaine joined the army, the Welsh Artillery, and disappeared from view. Audrey had two more sons in quick succession, Gavin and Nikki. My mother moved in with them. The very words portend disaster, don't they? I stayed there whenever I could. My mother hated Sig even more than she had hated Malcolm. The difference was that, knowing Sig to be a short-tempered man of violent disposition, she wasn't so quick to say it. By my mother's standards this was shrewd thinking. Another thing I should mention about Sig was that he was psychotically possessive. If another bloke so much as smiled at Audrey he would get a quite unambiguous warning to stop it. Sig would even get jealous if Audrey sat on my lap. He never said anything but I could detect he wasn't best pleased. I tried to get Audrey not to do it but she knew it annoyed Sig and that was enough for her. Sig was hard but there was a gentleness, a kindness there, hidden away inside. He didn't show it often but I remember a time when a neighbour's dog had a litter of unwanted puppies and Audrey volunteered Sig to get rid of them for her. He did this by hitting them over the head with a lump hammer and then drowning them in a bucket. I was with him in the back garden. It was late evening, almost dark. He didn't enjoy it. I think I detected a sniffle or two at one point and he mumbled 'poor little fuckers' under his breath at another. He dug a hole and we buried them. I liked Sig a lot, there was a kind of Nordic madness there. He was exciting. I've no doubt that's why Audrey ran away with him in the first place. After Audrey's divorce came through they got married in Bridgend registry office. The only guests were my mother, Blaine, the kids and me. After the ceremony we went for a fry up in a café then went home and got blind drunk on home-made vodka.

The O levels finally arrived. I tried to study; I really did try even at this late stage. I sat at the table in the front room and stared at my books for hours on end but nothing ever went in. The exams themselves were stressful, boring and unpleasant. On most papers I simply couldn't find enough questions to answer. They seemed to be full of questions about things I'd never even heard of. I'd have to answer five, say, but there were only three I could answer in any way at all, so I ended up having to write essay-long answers about subjects I had no knowledge of whatsoever, the Canadian fishing industry, for example. I wasn't even aware that there was one. I got three out of twenty for that. Anyway, I ended up getting six poor passes and you know, despite my laziness and existential nausea, I was still conceited enough to feel disappointed. Crazy isn't it? I should have been doing cartwheels but I wasn't. I was the Green Lantern, you see. The normal rules didn't apply to me.

About this time me, two mates named Steve Dudley and Paul Davies, and Paul's girlfriend Sandra, started a charitable organisation called GAS, the Gelli Dawel Action Society. We organised a sponsored walk and collected unwanted toys from better-off families to distribute to poorer ones at Christmas time. We based ourselves in Gelli Dawel School and dedicated ourselves to the task for the entire winter. In the new year we took a cheque to the Julian Hodge Home and presented it to the matron. They didn't seem that impressed. We played with the kids for a while and then were asked to leave. There was a girl known as Dead Sheep who was on the fringes of the group and people tried to pair me off with her, but it was a no-goer from the start. She wasn't my type, and that's saying something! I believe they locked us in a small room together once. At home the prevailing idea was that despite only getting six O levels I'd stay in school for another two years and get two A levels, thus giving me enough qualifications to get into teacher-training college. What a carrot to dangle in front of a boy, eh? Halfway through the first year, however, it became apparent that it wasn't going to happen. Ool and Naine discussed things and said I could finish school and get a job if I wanted to. I didn't need asking twice. I was seventeen. It was 1968 – the year of the student riots in Paris, the Summer of Love. I applied for and got a job as a trainee taxation officer in the Civil Service. My mate Mel Payne had done the same thing and we started working at Cardiff Marine tax office together on the same day.

WORKING MAN

Cardiff Marine dealt with the income-tax affairs of merchant seamen. The nature of their work, irregular contracts, long periods away from home etc, made it more complex than the normal PAYE. They were taxed under a different system. The 'office' itself was a series of small, one-storey, prefabricated buildings set just off the main Tonyrefail to Cardiff road in Llandaff. Our fellow workers were all right, some of them were quite nice, but the work itself was tedious in the extreme. I didn't know then that all work is shit, of course. I was young. We got luncheon vouchers though, and the food was good. There was a games room, too, with a table-tennis table, and me and Mel used to go at it hell for leather for hours. He had the annoying habit of beating me while holding his tie up out of the way with one hand. I don't know why but it bugged hell out of me. We almost came to blows on several occasions. We caught the Cardiff bus to work every morning from outside Dai the Bummer's billiard hall. We'd watch the bikers and other local ne'er do wells lining up outside the chemist shop opposite waiting for it to open so they could buy bottles of 'Dim' – Dimeryl cough mixture – which they drank as a cheap way of getting wasted. There was opium in it apparently. I often wondered what the chemist used to think these guys were doing turning up there every morning like that. None of them ever had coughs anyway, and that was a good thing.

There was a girl named Ellie Cole in the office. She was a dish, dark sleepy eyes, luscious lips and as naughty as hell. She'd come to work straight from her boyfriend's house and she'd sit next to me and tell me what they'd been doing all night. It was to tease me, to embarrass me. She liked it. She'd whisper it up close. I could feel her breath. I could smell her. She smelled like she'd just woken up, musty and sexy. I was overwhelmed in her presence. I would have crawled on my hands and knees to Moscow for ten minutes in the sack with her but she was way out of my league, not that I was actually in any league at the time, but you know what I mean. There was another girl, not such a stunner but possessed of fine white teeth and the largest breasts I'd ever seen. I got to snog her at the office Christmas party. She had a boyfriend with huge sideburns but they'd fallen out over something and she grabbed me. I felt her up. We were hidden away in a corner while others danced. She lifted her top and I sucked her nipple. It was fantastic. I'm sorry I was too drunk to appreciate it properly. She and her boyfriend made up and our moment of passion was forgotten.

The Cardiff Marine office housed the logbooks of all British merchant ships since the 1850s. They were kept on shelves in a special shed and I used to browse through them whenever I got the chance. They were wonderful, filled with tales of murder, thievery, horror and romance, all written in the functional but exquisite prose of the ships' captains. The handwriting itself was often very beautiful too, copperplate in some cases. There was a fantastic entry in one log where they'd found the first mate bleeding to death on the gangplank with his throat cut in the early hours of the morning when they were laid up in New York harbour. There was a trail of blood leading to one of the seamen's cabins and they found the culprit there 'soaked in blood drinking from a cask of brandy'.

In the fight that followed he stabbed one of the ship's officers in the stomach before being subdued. He and the victim had been out on the town drinking together and had fallen out over a woman. The murderer had attacked the first mate in an alleyway on the way back to the ship and left him there for dead. He then returned to the ship on his own, but the victim had managed to stagger and crawl as far as the gangplank of the ship before succumbing to his wounds. The killer was taken away sobbing by the New York police. I'd sit there reading these accounts for hours sometimes. It was like travelling through time. I loved it.

I'd started frequenting The Boars Head on Ton square. It was a pub with a bad reputation but I seemed to fit in okay. I drank, with several other aesthetic types, in the small lounge next to the bar in the company of the bikers, who sat by the window and the Destroyed Middle Aged Men, tieless in ill-fitting suits, who sat next to the juke box. We co-existed in harmony. There were a few very common girls, with names like Nympho and Mot, who hung around too. One night Mot came in screaming, drunk and hysterical, and punched her fist through the glass of the door. She cut her wrist and the blood spurted up like a geyser, hit the ceiling and fell in a lava-lamp-type globule into my half-drunk pint. One of the bikers walked over and said 'Are you going to drink that?' I said I didn't plan to and the biker took the glass and drained it in one. Mot was taken away in an ambulance. Nympho used to suck blokes' cocks in the basement of the secondary school across the road from the pub. She never sucked mine. I'm sure she would have but I was too afraid to ask.

There was a lot of LSD about at the time, Orange Barrel and Strawberry Fields at ten bob a tab. Disneyland stuff, incredibly strong. The Boar boys ate them like they were Smarties. I recall going in for a pint one early summer's evening and finding the Destroyed Men all gathered by the window staring up at the roof of the Co-op furniture shop opposite. They thought that there were 'scientists' up there observing them and making notes. It was causing serious concern. I looked but did not see. They were ducking down behind the chimneys apparently. The Destroyed Men were mostly ex-miners who'd finished work early due to depression. They were all divorced and had children they rarely saw, and they were all alcoholics. Sometimes one of them would cry and they'd all sit there together in silent empathy. I understood their sadness. I could easily see my life turning out that way. If I'd stayed in Ton I think it would have. These guys were rarely violent but you wouldn't want to put it to the test.

Around this time I developed a belief that I was special. I felt special. I felt like the lead actor in a film. Other people were other actors in lesser parts. Most were simply extras. This probably sounds daft but it's the truth. It wasn't drugs either. I was just a piss head in those days. In fact I only took drugs twice before I went to Australia. The first time I swallowed two Black and Whites, which Barry Meyrick pushed into my mouth on Ton square one night when a police van pulled up to arrest him. He said 'Swallow them quick' and I did, then I went home to bed. I had no idea what speed was or what it did. I spent the entire night with my eyes closed tight, zooming through the blackness like I was on a huge roller coaster. My heart pounded like a Gatling gun. It was like someone had thrown me off a bridge and I just kept falling. I must have been crazy. Meyrick was a genuine, twenty-four carat psychopath. Those pills could have been anything; they could have been cyanide. The second time I had a few belts on a spliff sat in Keith Darlington's mother's front room listening to Led Zep Two. I don't remember it having any effect but I was drunk at the time so maybe that's why. Oh yes, I got knocked out. I was walking home from the Red Cow one rainy night when Steve Dudley, one of the boys I was with, banged his fist on the roof of a car that slowed to pass us on a narrow stretch of road. The driver, John Povey, captain of Tonyrefail rugby team and no retiring flower, got out to remonstrate and he and Steve started fighting beneath the light of a street lamp. A moment or so later a minibus screeched up and a gang of drunken thugs poured out. One of them knew Steve from somewhere and seeing him in a fight they were intent on backing him up. Steve told them he didn't need any help, which indeed he didn't, but they were drunk and laid into everyone in sight regardless of affiliation nonetheless. I was wearing my famous white raincoat so I suppose I offered myself as a prime target, and before I realised what was going on some unseen assailant smacked me on the jaw. My glasses flew off up into the darkness and I went down like a sack of spuds. I felt kicks raining into my chest and ribs but no pain. The thug who was kicking me was pulling the kicks at the last second. He didn't really want to hurt me. The savagery was for the benefit of the onlookers. I remember lying there in the mud feeling quite touched by this unexpected and unusual manifestation of human kindness. Anyway, as the melee died down I got to my feet and retrieved my glasses. Then, bleeding from the nose and sobbing, I went over to the minibus and started to regale the occupants, the accompanying females mostly, with my hippie ravings. I told them we should all live in peace with one another, that life was too short, that we shared the same world. I told them there was no need to fight. I told them that there was a universal love just waiting for us all to tune in to. I offered them my friendship. They drove off laughing.

The only lasting thing to come from my time at Cardiff Marine was meeting Hugo – Hugh Thomas Jones – a tall, thin guy about my age who worked in one of the rooms off one of the long corridors. We played for the office football team together and got into the habit of going over to the Half Way Inn, a local pub, after the game for a pint. Hugo was a cool guy. He chain-smoked French cigarettes and drank scotch on the rocks. He too was Nibonicho. He made me laugh. We became firm friends.

Things at home weren't great. Ool and Naine resented my morose posturing and I resented their resentment. There were constant rows. I started going to stay with Mam and Audrey and Sig and Blaine in Pencoed on weekends. The vibe was looser there. I shared a room with Blaine and we painted it all black. He convinced me to go in shares on a car, which was stuck in the garage. It did six miles to the gallon and eventually we had to smash it up for scrap. Blaine was a great one for schemes. He'd been in the army by this time. He didn't last though. He deserted and fled abroad to America. They caught up with him somehow and he'd been sent to military prison in Germany for six months and dishonourably discharged, incidentally keeping up the family tradition started by Uncle Ike decades before. He was home now though living a life of idleness.

KAY

My mother was obsessed with playing cards, pontoon and three-card brag. She claimed to have studied in what she called a 'gambling school' in America. She was crackers, as I've said. Anyway, one night we were all indulging her as we occasionally did, sitting around the dinner table drinking and playing pontoon in the living room. There was me, my brother Blaine, my mother, Audrey and a girl named Rose who was staying with us for a few weeks till her boyfriend got out of prison. Rose was sitting next to me and as the night wore on she started touching my thigh under the table. Her manner didn't change. No one could have been aware of it. I got a hard on and she started to unbutton my flies. Someone called a break in the game and Rose said she'd go and make us all a cup of tea. A minute or so after she left I made my excuses and got up and followed her. She was standing in the passageway in the dark leaning against the wall. I went up to her and we started kissing. She was right up for it. Something interrupted us and she went to make the tea, and when she came back we carried on playing cards into the early hours. When everyone had gone to bed, I got up and went back downstairs. She was waiting for me in the living room. We stripped naked and we had it off on the floor in front of the fireplace. This was how I lost my virginity. I was eighteen. Rose was a plain girl about the same age as I was. Her boyfriend Twiggy was a petty criminal. He was a lot older than her. I think she may have been very alone and frightened. The poor girl didn't have a family. That's why she was staying with us. She had nothing. She was looking for kindness. We carried on having sex regularly for the rest of the few weeks she was there.

The week that Rose left I got set up with a blind date. Her name was Kay Evans. We met at a friend's house and caught a bus into Bridgend. After a few drinks at The Palais de Dance, a large fifties-type dancehall, we went on to the Railway pub opposite the bus station. We sat in the upstairs bar and listened to the jukebox and drank and talked the night away. She'd kicked her shoes off under the table for comfort at some point and a nutter from a group of nutters who'd been getting steadily drunker and nastier all night at a table opposite picked it up and refused to give it back. He'd offer it to her and then snatch it away when she tried to take it. He wouldn't give it back – full stop. Having no choice she finally gave up and we went downstairs to find a taxi home without the shoe. She told me that she was very upset and asked if I'd go up and get it back for her while she waited there. Can you imagine it? I mean, you've got some idea what I'm like, right. These blokes were alcoholic psychos. Think for a moment what they had just done to two innocent strangers. I mean, you can see where they were coming from, right. These were sick people; they were not into peace and love. These were Bridgend Boys. What she, this girl I had just met, had just asked me to do was tanta-mount to committing suicide. Anyway, I stared at her for a few moments standing there looking so pretty in the rain, and then said 'Sure, I'll be right back,' and I went back upstairs, walked straight up to the howling drunken thug who was brandishing the shoe at the time and demanded its return. I said that my girlfriend was upset. At first they were too dumbfounded to react, then they started to push me around and threaten me, setting me up for a hammering, until one of them, a leader of some type, snatched the shoe off the nutter who had it and handed it to me. He escorted me back along the landing with a friendly arm around my shoulder, explaining that it was just a bit of fun got out of hand, and then he threw me down a steep flight of stairs into a packed Chinese restaurant on the ground floor. It was a hell of a fall. It could have killed me but it didn't – as a matter of fact it didn't hurt at all. The manager of the restaurant approached but I didn't want to hang about, so refusing any offers of assistance I got up, dusted myself down and exited the place with as much dignity as I could muster in the circumstances. Kay was standing there waiting for me as she'd promised. It was still raining. I knelt down and put the shoe back onto her lovely little foot and we got a taxi back to Pencoed. We kissed in the back seat. Kay was a fantastic kisser.

When we arrived at her house she invited me in and then excused herself and left me on my own in the living room while she went upstairs. I looked out of the window but it was black – all I could see were the outlines of the backs of other houses. When she came back into the room a few minutes later she was wearing a baby doll nightdress and her hair had changed. It had been raven black with white ribbon woven into it but now it was short, like a boy's, like Joan of Arc's. There was a double bed in the room; she slept downstairs because it was warmer. She got in and took off her nightdress. I got undressed and got in with her. I've never had a deeper sexual relationship with anyone else ever in my life than I had with her. I loved her. I loved her as much as anybody ever loved anybody and she loved me the same way. She was the prettiest, sexiest, kindest, most wonderful person I had ever met. She gave me so much. We were still awake at daybreak, thin lilac light seeping into the room, then I fell asleep, and when I woke she was dressed and had made us some tea and toast. I drank the tea and left. She had to go somewhere. We kissed goodbye at the back door and she told me that she was sorry she'd been drunk the night before and that next time she'd be better in bed. That meant she wanted to see me again. I got back home before my mother had stirred and got in through the bathroom window so as not to let her know I'd been out all night. Kay and me became lovers. I didn't exist when she wasn't there. I really didn't. Hey, I just thought, the reason I went back for the shoe, the reason I did that insane and chivalrous act, was both that the girl I loved had asked me to and that I, like her, must have been drunk! Yes, I must have been, I drank like a fish in those days. I was quite possibly plastered. Yes, this would also explain how I managed to avoid serious injury in the fall. I was a rubber-limbed bouncing drunk. Lucky for me.

We spent all the time we could together. We went to pubs and clubs and stayed in a lot making love and watching TV. Her mother lived nearby with her brother, a curly-haired boy known as Jazz. He had a best mate called Kenny whom he always hung about with. I discovered that Kay was married. Her husband, Gene, was in prison, but from what I could understand she'd given up on him. I don't know the exact story. She had two children, girls, little more than babies. They lived with her mother. All this should have bothered me more than it did but I loved her and nothing mattered except us being together. I believe that her family was concerned about our relationship but that they saw that she was happy, possibly for the first time in a long time, and didn't know what to do for the best. I more or less moved in with her. We moved the bed back upstairs. I remember going to Porthcawl fair together and then getting drunk in the Buccaneer pub on the seafront. Later, when it got dark, we went down to the beach and kissed in the starlight with the waves falling around our feet. I was a lot taller, so she had to reach up to kiss me. Her teeth tasted of rum and blackcurrant. It was like being in Heaven. I thought it at the time. This is what Heaven must be like, I thought. Thank you, God.

One night a few months after we met we were in her house lying in bed, it must've been about twelve midnight, when I heard voices, angry voices, outside the window in the street. Jazz and Kenny were drunk and Jazz was in a very bad mood. Kenny was trying to calm him down, to reason with him, but Jazz was having none of it. He kicked the front door open and tumbled into the hallway. Kenny joined him. I could hear Jazz saying that he was going to kill me. Kay, lying there by my side, didn't stir despite the noise. She must have heard what was going on but I think she decided to just lie there because it was the wisest thing to do. I did the same. I closed my eyes and waited. Jazz stumbled up the stairs and opened the bedroom door. A wedge of electric light from the landing cut into the room. I peeked at him unseen from one eye. He stood in the doorway in silhouette, still, unmoving, looking at us lying in bed. I closed my eye and just lay there. Jazz stayed there looking at us for a long time, a few minutes at least, and then he closed the door quietly, went back downstairs, and he and Kenny left. The way I read it was that Jazz, ashamed that he wasn't looking after his friend Gene's interests when he was away, had decided enough was enough and had come to the house with the intention of dragging me out of bed and beating the living shit out of me. Then when he opened the door he saw us lying there in the dark in each other's arms like children and realised that it wasn't that simple. Gene may have been a good mate but Kay was his sister and he loved her. He was basically a good guy and despite his anger and frustration he acted in her interests. He was a good brother; I admired him. I wasn't frightened. I somehow knew that we were safe. Kay and I never mentioned the incident. I think that we decided it was a dream.

Kay wanted to leave Pencoed so I quit Cardiff Marine and we moved to Southsea on the Solent across from the Isle of Wight. I went down first and got a job and a place to stay, then Kay joined me. I met her at the train station. I'd missed her. We went home and went to bed. She got a job as a silver service waitress at an exclusive restaurant and I was night porter at the Solent Hotel on the seafront. It was summer, very hot. The big hit song of the time was

'Something in the Air' by Thunderclap Newman. I learned later that it had been the theme tune to the IRA's murderous campaign in the late sixties. I can see why. The main road through the town was called Elm Grove, or Elm Groove as we liked to call it. Southsea was a holiday resort. It was full of pubs, there was entertainment everywhere, amusement arcades, live bands, crowds of pretty young girls and packs of tomming young thugs. It was like living in Majorca. We loved it. We'd go out walking amongst the crowds of tourists, then go home and lie in bed and watch the telly. We watched the first man set foot on the moon. We discussed it, what it meant, but we didn't know. We talked a lot, all through the night sometimes. I don't remember what it was we talked about but it didn't matter. I just loved listening to her voice, especially when she was tired and it went a bit husky. Being a night porter wasn't a bad job. I had to change the barrels in the cellar, Hoover around the reception area a bit, polish some brass fittings and ornaments and then just mooch about till the day porter came on duty. I had to serve in the bar too if residents wanted it to stay open late, which was quite often. The Solent was owned and managed by an ex-army officer named Adrian Grant. He lived on the top floor with his mother, a very distinguished old lady. He was well liked in general but not a man to cross. He was an interesting guy in fact. I saw him throw a belligerent drunk out of the bar one night and it was clear that he was not averse to violence when called for. It's an unfortunate fact of life that countries need armies and, that accepted, Mr Adrian, as he was universally known, was just the sort of guy I would like to think of as being an officer in ours. He had a warrior spirit.

I remember sitting outside the hotel having a fag on the front steps one evening and hearing music from the Isle of Wight festival floating over the water. Life was pretty idyllic. Then Kay's mother came down to visit us. The family was concerned. I think it was to do with the children. She wanted us to go back to Wales but Kay didn't want to. I did. I have no idea why, I really don't. It seems crazy now but at the time I think I was afraid but I don't know what of. Things started to go wrong for us after that. We were working different shifts and didn't see as much of each other as we had done. She started going out with the girls she worked with and didn't get home till late. I'd sit up waiting. She used to wear my red checked shirt as a nightdress. She looked so beautiful in it. I'd open it down the front one button at a time. It's almost impossible to explain what was going on in my head at the time because I don't understand it myself. I loved her more than ever. You know how it is when you're in love. Everything was dreamlike and magical and yet even in that divine state I could see our relationship falling apart. I left and went back to Wales on my own. I betrayed her: there's no other way of looking at it. I was her bloke and she expected me to stand by her and support her and I didn't. It was because I was a coward. Kay gave me so much, she loved me, and I repaid her with desertion. To say I regret it is futile, but I do. She is still in my heart. Remember my theory that couples who have ever been in love at any time remain in love forever somewhere in the stars? I pray that she met a decent bloke who brought her the happiness and love that she deserved. I wish it had been me but it wasn't. I never saw her again.

THE AFTERMATH

I moved back home to Ton. It was clear that everyone in the family knew where I'd been and what I'd been up to but there was an uncanny silence on the matter. It was as if they'd all agreed never to mention it and they never did. No one did, not even my mother. I don't think they knew what to say. I mean, what could they say, right? I got a job working on a building site in Cardiff. Ool's nephew, Georgie Shepherd, was the site agent. I had to get up at quarter past five in the mornings to catch the bus to Porth, where the works bus picked us up and took us to the site. We clocked on at seven thirty. It was winter by now. I remember standing there that first morning, shivering with cold, the sky still the pitch black of night. Then a man came out of a hut and handed me a pick and shovel. It was the first time I'd ever touched either. It was surreal, fantastic. I just stood there not knowing what to do. Suffice it to say that swinging a pick and digging holes was not for me. I was put to work labouring for a brickie named Eddie. He was a good-looking Valleys guy in his mid-twenties, married with a child. He showed me photos of them. She was lovely and the baby was too. She owned her own hairdressing salon. They seemed a perfect couple. One Monday he told me about a party he'd been to on the weekend. He'd shagged his mate's grandmother, who was in her seventies, in an outside shed. He said that she had big orange bloomers on and false teeth. I was disappointed in him. Not that I had any right to be, but I thought it wrong for a man with a wife and a little baby to shag another woman. It wasn't the age of the woman involved, it was the adultery I didn't like, the deceit.

The wages as a labourer were good, twenty quid a week. Twenty quid was a lot in those days. It was a magic number. I went out on the razz most nights and bought hip clothes from the Grattan's catalogue, but it couldn't last. It lasted about three months, in fact. They knew I was a waste of space. I was lucky it lasted as long as that.

Audrey and the family had moved from Pencoed back to Pontycymer, Hill View: the very street Mam, Audrey and Blaine had lived in years before. Hugo and me went up to stay most weekends. Day to day life under Audrey's regime was total mayhem. She never stopped screaming. The kids never stopped screaming. My mother never stopped screaming. It was impossible to relax. We laughed though. We laughed a lot. Sig was working in Norway. He sent photos of himself at work in Arctic clothing, his long beard white with snow. Audrey began to resent him being away so much. I think she mistrusted him with women too. When he came home for a few weeks off things would soon descend into bitterness and recrimination. He'd go away and the cycle would start again. I got a job as a stock control clerk at the Dewhurst Butchers warehouse in Penarth Road, Cardiff. I kept a graph of the number of flies I killed using thick rubber bands on the wall of my office. The boss, Mr Mole, was from the North of England. He liked me but my attitude disappointed him. He told me so on several occasions. There was a girl there named Julie Sparks. I started working evenings as a wine waiter in the Angel Hotel at the same time. Hugo worked there already and since we finished so late I took to crashing at his house. The boss at the Angel was a man called Mr Aldo. He was a small, neat, good-looking Italian guy. 'I tell you what to do in work, you jump to attention and say "Yes Mr Aldo; No Mister Aldo". You see me in the street you smile and wave and shout "Hi Aldo!"' There were two Italian waiters, Hectore and Luciano. Both were very good looking and obsessed with getting their leg over. It was quite something for a chap like me to watch them in action. It was so simple for them, a flicker of the eyes, a beautiful smile, a few softly spoken words and women would melt at their feet. They both had wives and families back in Italy and regarded the women they bedded with contempt. I got the bullet after tipping a glass of Nuit St George over the Lord Mayor of Bristol at a banquet and I got sacked from Dewhurst's the following week for absenteeism.

Blaine had started working at the Parc, the old mental hospital outside Bridgend on the common next to where Audrey and Malcolm had lived years before. I went for an interview and started as a student nurse the following week. I lived in. The rooms were side rooms off the wards, poorly furnished but cheap. I started on ward eight. We had about thirty subnormal adults so I spent the majority of my working day elbow-deep in shit. The social life was good, though. There were quite a few pretty girl student nurses all budding into sexuality. We drank in a pub a short walk from the hospital and there were many drunken snowy afternoons and evenings spent in adolescent flirting. I went to a party once and a woman washed my hair for me. It was very erotic. She was grown up, married. We slept in a sleeping bag on the floor together. There were other couples sleeping on the floor and we could hear them shagging all night. It was a sort of middle-classish libertarian vibe.

The Parc was a grey forbidding place. My Auntie Daisy was a patient there at the time. Remember her, Barbara's mother? She was on the female wing so I only saw her occasionally. They had social evenings in the main hall on Fridays and I'd escort the male patients from time to time. Auntie Daisy would be there. She'd dance alone beneath the twirling glitter ball in her white frock with blue spots, lost in the arms of some unseen lover. She'd sing along with the songs. 'Sailor' by Anne Shelton was a favourite. She'd sing as she danced. I'd say hello but I don't think she recognised me out of context. She was in the Parc for some twenty years. She'd tried to murder Barbara; she'd tried to drown her in a mountain stream. When Auntie Daisy was old, after she got out of the Parc, they gave her a council flat in the Valleys. Brian visited her there once with Ool and he told me that she sat on a kitchen chair with no seat and a bucket underneath into which she'd urinate while talking. The world doesn't give a damn about people like my Auntie Daisy, the world is embarrassed, the world is disgusted. There's no point me banging on about it. It was ever thus and thus it will ever be. People fear things that they don't understand. They hate their own imperfect reflections.

Some of the nurses were very unpleasant bits of work. They'd delight in 'subduing' patients who had often done little or nothing wrong. They'd beat hell out of them. One such nurse was a fat psychopath named Thompson. He'd goad and insult patients and staff alike. It sickened me. If I had had more guts I'd've busted his nose for him, but I didn't. There was a night nurse on my ward, named Cliff Bowen, an old guy, South African, and he was bananas.

Some nights I'd get back in the early hours and I'd join him for a cuppa. We'd sit there in the darkened day room and chat for half an hour before I hit the hay. One night he stopped me mid sentence with a sharp 'Shhh!' He stared fixedly across the room for a while and then asked me in a whisper if I could see a lady dressed in grey beckoning to us. I couldn't. I found out later that Cliff had been seeing things for a long time. His favourite expression was 'Well fuck me with a pink-handled tooth-brush.' Later he got cancer and died. There were quite a few gay guys working there. They felt freer to express themselves in that sheltered environment. I recall walking down the long corridor to ward twenty-nine late one night and having a group of them come running, dancing towards me, in loose-fitting garments, clutching roses in their teeth. They swept past me like a herd of Thompson's gazelles. One bloke, a handsome devil with black curly hair, became a drinking mate. We'd get drunk and sleep it off in the pharmacy. I didn't know he was gay; he never tried it on with me, anyway. I liked him. There was also a group of nurses from Mauritius training there. They were all Muslims but it didn't stop them being very funny or swearing like troopers. One of them, named Hassan, used to wake the resident nurses up every morning. 'Come on Clackee. Time to stop wanking!' They had a lot of shit to put up with. Racism of the crudest kind, not just from patients but from other nurses too.

I don't want to give the impression that all the nurses were racist thugs, far from it. There were some excellent people working there. In fact the majority were excellent. It's the old rotten apple syndrome that was the problem, and there was a closing-ranks mentality inherited from the dark ages of psychiatric care, which made it hard to put things right. I found one incident particularly disturbing. There was a young patient named Phillip Redding who was an epileptic. He'd fallen face first into a fire when he'd had a fit as a child and one half of his face was horrifically burned. It was bright red and deeply grooved with scar tissue. He was a young guy, probably the same age as me, and tuned in to the Age of Aquarius. He wrote poetry and he'd read it to me. It was good too, much better than mine. We struck up a friendship. He grew his hair long and trained it so that it covered the burned half of his face. He was a poor, damaged fellow. I was told not to trust him. He was a psychopath. I had a week off for some reason and when I got back I popped in to his ward but he wouldn't see me. I found out later that he'd got into a minor scuffle with one of the nurses when I was away and to teach him a lesson they'd grabbed him, held him down and cut all his hair away, leaving his scars, cherry red, for all to see. I mean, what can you say, right? I tried to talk to him but he never spoke to me again.

Winter turned to spring and the old wanderlust returned. Southsea had been a mere prelude to my next great adventure. Me, Blaine and Hugo decided to go and live abroad. We quit our jobs and got on a bus to Folkestone. When we got there Blaine threw a spanner in the works by informing us that he didn't have a valid passport. He must've known for ages but he was too thick to let us know. This is not untypical of Blaine. I believe that he has some sort of autism. Anyway, there was a poster on the wall of the booking office place advertising the delights of the Channel Islands. We got the ferry and arrived in

St Helier, the capital of Jersey, early the following day. The sun shone on us as we walked down the gangplank. We found a one-room flat above a baker's shop and paid a month's rent in advance. This left us pretty strapped so after a few days on the piss we had to start looking for work. This proved a lot harder than we'd thought it would. All the real jobs were kept for locals. We tried bars and restaurants and farms and shops and amusement arcades and, well you name it, but to no avail. We ran out of money completely by the beginning of the third week. A local priest used to leave half-a-dozen eggs, a pound of bacon and three bottles of beer out for us for breakfast every morning in a small outhouse next to his church. He asked for nothing in return.

We bumped into two girls from Watford we'd met on the ferry over, Lynne and Sue, and we hung about together for a while. They were young hippie types looking for romance and adventure. Lynne was gorgeosity itself, a delicate pre-Raphaelite sex kitten. I snogged her several times but got no further. She had come to Jersey as a friend and confidante of Sue, who'd been raped by a dozen players from the local rugby team after she accepted a lift home in their coach after a match. She was only seventeen, a child. She and Hugo fell out in a pub. She was angered by Hugo's perceived arrogance and uttered the immortal line 'You think you are so clever but back home in Watford I know four people exactly like you.' It was around this time that Hugo, who'd been feeling a growing kinship with insects, tried to change his name by deed poll to Hugh Eight Point Five Fluid Ounces Master Of All Spiders Jones. The girls sought other company. In our desperation we decided to 'roll' a queer. We'd seen it in *Midnight Cowboy* and thought it was worth a shot. I can't remember how we went about it but I ended up in a room behind a kitchen in some sort of restaurant or guesthouse with a sad, oldish bloke in a white suit. It didn't take him long to suss that I was heterosexual, I think it was because I was Welsh. He gave me a quid and I went home. I couldn't hurt anyone on purpose. I feel sorry for everyone, you see. I even felt sorry for him. The other boys accepted that it had been a bad idea in the first place.

We got to the stage where we thought we'd have to bite the bullet and return to Wales but a chance meeting in a pub led me and Blaine to apply for work in St Saviour's Psychiatric Hospital near Gorey on the other side of the Island. The boss was an ex-professional football player named Bollington. I'd heard of him, he'd played for Wolves for years. Our experience working in the Parc gave us the edge and, after a perfunctory interview, involving filling out a form, we both got taken on to start as nursing assistants the following day. We had a sub from our first month's wages and took Hugo out for a slap-up meal. As fate would have it Hugo got a job a few days later, as a barman at Les Arches Hotel, which overlooked the beautiful Arichondel Bay, the Bay of Angels, from the hill above. Blaine and me moved into the staff quarters at St Saviour's and Hugo got a room at the hotel.

JERSEY

St Saviour's Hospital was similar to the Parc but less dilapidated. The building itself was newer and had been modernised at some point. The grounds were better kept. There was a sports field to the front where staff and patients played football and cricket. Our soccer team suffered from having a catatonic schizophrenic in goal. The local village team beat us twenty-nine nil on one occasion. The only way our goalkeeper could stop a shot was if it hit him on the head, which, interestingly enough, it did on a surprising number of occasions. We'd have to stand him back up and reposition him. Our cricket team was little better. The staff quarters were away from the main hospital and consisted of two adjacent one-storey buildings. Blaine and I moved into the smaller of them. There were five bedrooms, two on one side of the dividing corridor, three on the other, a bathroom, a kitchen and a communal lounge. There were only four of us living there at the time: the other two were Dennis Michelle, a short stout man with a small moustache, and Albert Wickham, a beaten-down looking fellow with a defensive stoop. Wickham had had all his toes removed by surgery. He said that it was because his mother forced him to wear shoes that were too small for him when he was growing up. He wore special shoes with wedge-shaped lead weights in the toe area to keep him balanced. Michelle claimed to have seen action in the Canadian Marine Corps and been awarded endless medals for bravery. He was an expert in virtually everything. He could throw a knife like Jim Bowie and shoot the eye out of a jack of spades with a pistol at

114

fifty paces. He was a drunk. He'd drink on his own in his room till the early hours. Sometimes he'd have the radio on quietly and he'd sing along with the old-fashioned songs. Wickham was a poor soul, a social inadequate. He told me once that the most intelligent person he'd ever met was his sister, who worked in a food store and could add up quite long lists of numbers in her head. He and Michelle had been living there in the nurses' home together for years and they despised one another. They couldn't be in the same room for more than a minute without it spilling out. They had created a Sartrean nightmare for themselves, a symbiotic hell. It was like *Who's Afraid of Virginia Woolf.*

I was sitting alone in the lounge late one night when I heard Michelle coming in from the pub. He was with a woman. They stumbled drunkenly along the corridor together, whispering and suppressing laughter, and went in to his room. There was the familiar clink of whisky glasses and the radio started playing love songs. I caught snatches of their conversation. 'Come on love, get that down you!' Girlish giggle. 'You're a pretty little thing aren't you? Oh yes, don't blush, don't go all shy on me. It's the truth!' Girlish reticence. 'What about a little kiss?' Shortly after I decided to go to bed and as I passed Michelle's room I saw that the door was half-open. I peeked in. Michelle was sat on the edge of his bed in his shirtsleeves with a tumbler of whisky in his hand and he was alone. He'd turned his bedside chair towards him for the ghostly girl to sit on. There was an untouched glass of whisky on the dressing table next to it.

St Saviour's was a smaller hospital than the Parc, with a smaller demographic, so they had no speciality wards. The patients were all lumped in together. The nurses were more sophisticated than at the Parc. This was a sign of the times too, of course; R. D. Laing and LSD had challenged conventional ideas about mental illness. What is madness anyway? We are all mad, aren't we? Ideas like these filtered through the system. Working in mental hospitals when I was young had a profound effect on me. I was a hippie. I was a seeker after wisdom and truth. I loved my fellow man and my heart bled for these poor people. There is nothing more terrible that can happen to a person than to suffer a psychotic illness. Schizophrenia is living hell for many. I used to cry about it. In truth I was not cut out for the work. Being objective is not one of my strong points. I get sucked in.

There were several padded cells on the ward. One, in the basement, housed Joe Blake. He'd been a butcher and ended up killing his wife and kids, hacking up their corpses and hanging the pieces on hooks in his butcher-shop window. It was a big case, in all the papers. Joe was 'The Butcher of Jersey'! When I met him, he'd been banged away for seventeen years. He was confined to the padded cell at all times except for half an hour a day when he'd be taken into the enclosed garden and allowed to exercise. He'd walk around in circles. His teeth had been stained almost black by nicotine. They were foul and his breath stank. He was gone. There was a faraway look in his eyes; he was somewhere else. He called me Mr Boyd. There had to be at least two nurses present when Joe's door was opened. He'd attack you out of the blue; snarling and spitting like a mad dog. He was really serious about it; he wanted to rip your eyes out. There was a senior nurse, a Jock whose name escapes me, who had Joe's measure of old, and I always stood behind him.

Joe had to be force-fed for a period of time. He'd gone on a hunger strike over something and this was the hospital's response. We'd pin him down on the floor of his cell then someone would stick a fat rubber tube up his nose – he wouldn't open his mouth – push it down into his stomach and tip a plastic jug full of thin gruel down a funnel directly into it. It was an unpleasant procedure but Joe, despite making a fuss, seemed to enjoy it. He'd have a little smile on his face as the tube went in. It was something different I suppose. I think he found it relaxing. Joe was seriously ill.

There was another patient named Maine. He was tall, six-three maybe, and cadaver thin. He was probably in his forties but it was difficult to tell. He'd had not one but two pre-frontal leucotomies, brain operations meant to help chronic schizophrenics, and they'd left him paralysed down one side. His right arm was tucked up like the wing of a wounded bird and he had a profound limp. He had a long, crescent-shaped face and no teeth. He looked like Mr Punch, in fact. Maine spent his days striding around the corridors and wards shouting out rubbish. He developed the habit of offering me his hand in greeting whenever he saw me. I'd ignore it most of the time because I was working and had to get on with whatever I was doing, but I'd take it from time to time and that would delight him. He'd clasp my hand very firmly, then push his maniacal, smiling face close to mine till we were almost touching and say 'I like you. I love you. I believe

117

in you more than anyone else,' then he'd start shaking my hand in a sort of slow-motion arm wrestle and repeat it. 'I like you. I love you. I believe in you more than anyone else.' Then he'd fling my hand away and stalk off squealing with pleasure. He was lovely. I found him in the storeroom next to the kitchen once, an area that was out of bounds. He'd got in there somehow and he'd found a catering-size jar of pickled onions. When I found him he'd eaten the entire jar and was on to drinking the vinegar. He stopped mid-gulp and stared at me guiltily. I could see that he felt really sick but he didn't have the nous to relate it to the pickled onions. He smiled at me forlornly and belched. Come to think of it, Maine would not have been out of place in one of those George Romero films, *Night of the Living Dead* say. He'd've loved it too. He'd've stalked around with the best of them. He was a great guy. You see what I was saying about how the work affected me. Thinking back now I wish I'd given him a hug every time I saw him. I wish I realised what was going on, that he was a person like me. I just didn't think of it. There were others – The Man with Women's Breasts, The Boy who Behaved Like a Horse, The Posh Lawyer who Felt Nothing, Johnny the Mongol, Cyril Le Sailor. Cyril was fascinating. He'd been as sane as you and me until his forties. He'd been a big-wig legal type working for the Jersey government, an important man, and then Zap! He was gone. He used to eat his own shit. I got him up one morning, he slept in a pad because he disturbed the other patients, and he'd been at it all night. The walls and the floor were smeared in shit, his naked body was daubed in it and his mouth and teeth were covered in it. He saw me and his face lit up with a smile. 'Good morning my love.' Then he held out his hand and offered me the shit he was eating and said 'Here, have some. It's good!' I couldn't help but laugh. He was so refined, his accent was cut glass and he had a beautiful, delicate face. Another time I was bathing him and he became suddenly agitated. He grabbed my arm, pointed to something unseen and said 'Hey! Hey Pierre! Look, it's slipping. Hurry, get a rope to it! Quickly!' I could see it, the boat, the water, the men in their shirt-sleeves, the women in their summer frocks. I could see it in his eyes. A brief but vivid glimpse of the man he once was, the life he'd once had.

It was the summer of 1970. The World Cup was on in Mexico. I bought flowery shirts and red crushed-velvet trousers. I wore them everywhere. My hair was longer than it had ever been. I saw *Easy Rider* in the pictures and became convinced that I was Peter Fonda. I got clip-on sun visors for my glasses and felt very cool. I started trying to talk less. I wanted to come across as a deep interesting guy who didn't feel the need to jabber like a lunatic all the time but I couldn't keep it up. I was too hysterical. I was nineteen. Blaine had started shagging a Scottish nurse who he'd seen through a bedroom window giving a blowjob to a bloke with black curly hair. He started hanging about with her. It seemed to make him happy.

A new nurse came into the lounge one evening. Her name was Pauline and she'd just arrived from Hull or somewhere. She was gorgeous. She had white socks on. I told her that where I came from if a girl wore white socks it meant she was a virgin. She assured me it wasn't the case where she came from. She was twenty-six. It makes me shudder even now to think how damn sexy she was. We became friends. It turned out that she was the estranged wife of another nurse who'd been working at the hospital for some time. He was a short, somewhat tormented looking bloke who'd been in the army. I never figured out the entire story but it seems that they'd separated the previous year and he'd left and come to St Saviour's for some space to sort his head out. Now, even though she didn't want to rekindle their relationship, she'd got a job there herself. Who knows why? Someone once said that all men are pricks and all women are crazy. I started hanging about with her and her husband. They were still 'friends'. We used to walk down Daisy Hill to Gorey in the evenings. Gorey was a small harbour town with a big white fortress on the headland above, over-looking the sea. We drank at The Dolphin Inn on the quay. It was a fun place. There was a guitarist singer named Barnie, an Irish guy who belted out IRA songs to the tourists. They loved it. Pauline, her husband and me would get drunk, then walk back home in the dark together. We stopped by a small cove one night and Pauline and me went skinny dipping while her husband stood on the shore. She stumbled in the waves and I grabbed her as she fell. I held her close. She was so pretty. She felt like Heaven. A few nights later we found ourselves walking up Daisy Hill alone. They'd been at each other all evening and her husband had stalked off in a huff. I stopped for a pee in the bushes by the roadside and after a few moments I felt her standing behind me. She put her hand around and said 'I'll hold that for you' and she did. She wanked me off while standing there, on Daisy Hill in the starlight. I kissed her over my shoulder as I was coming. It was fucking great. She pulled my trousers up, buckled my belt and we walked home. She went to her room and I to mine. The following weeks were disconcerting. Pauline was nice to me, sweet even, but there was a new, unspoken distance. I was upset, unhappy. I wanted her real bad. One evening I was sitting on the wall next to the sports field having a fag when her husband came over to me. He told me that if I ever touched his wife he'd do me a serious injury. He wasn't nasty, he wasn't bullying, none of that, but he meant it and I've no doubt he was capable of delivering it. I got the message. I saw Pauline one last time after that and we kissed. She and her husband left Jersey together a few weeks later. I think they went back to Hull.

Blaine and his girlfriend Morag got married. The ceremony took place at St Helier Registry Office. They'd quit their jobs at the hospital and were off to set up home in Edinburgh. Hugo and me went to the airport with them. Blaine got so drunk that he had to be carried onto the plane. Morag waved out of the window and they were gone. The following week Hugo and me followed suit. We decided to go to France, travel around Europe for a bit till we ran out of money, and then find jobs wherever we ended up. We bought a tent, a small stove, some cooking and eating utensils and two sleeping bags and got a flight on a twelve-seater to Dinard on the French coast. We arrived on a Saturday evening. After we left the tiny airport we walked till we found a roadside pub and stopped for something to eat. It was a beef dish, big chunks of beef in a red wine sauce. It was gorgeous. I'd never eaten anything like it before. We had a few beers and by the time we found a place where we could camp it was dark. We'd never put up a tent before and ended up having to tie the strings to a steel post of some kind to get it to stand upright. It started to rain. We crawled beneath the crumpled canvas and fell asleep.

The next day we decided to get a train to Amsterdam. We had to change trains in Paris and got there late in the evening. The Amsterdam connection wasn't until the following morning so we settled on walking the streets till then. We sat on a wall and ate bread and cheese, then set off to find the Eiffel Tower. It was dark but we could still see it high above. We cwtched down in a shop doorway for a while but it was too uncomfortable so we went for a walk by the side of the river instead. It was the middle of the night and the city seemed deserted. It was very still. The only people I remember seeing were two men, dandies in black capes, walking along together in intimate conversation. One had a cane. Their voices were low and expressive, their talk littered with soft laughter. They saw us and nodded in casual greeting. They looked so cool. We got the Amsterdam train from Le Gare du Nord and arrived there in the early evening. Amsterdam was a magnet to our generation at the time. It was the European San Francisco. There were people from all over gathered there. Arab boys on pushbikes swept past us outside the station. 'Hashish? LSD? You want a girl? Somewhere to stay?' We had no idea what to do but we were aware that there were some nasty bastards about in the world and that we were the sort of naïve dreamers that they fed on, so we kept ourselves to ourselves. We went to the red-light district and gazed in awe at the scantily clad girls displaying themselves in the illuminated windows. They took no notice of us. Most of them affected an air of superior indifference, in fact. The idea of paying for sex didn't enter our minds. I think I expected one of them to fall in love with me at first sight, but it didn't happen. We carried on exploring. There were Americans aplenty. They all seemed to be incredibly good looking. Long hair, rugged features, eyes that had seen things I had only dreamt of. They sat cross-legged on the stone steps of beautiful old buildings and strummed on acoustic guitars. They had women dripping off them. This was the detritus of the Flower Power generation. I was where I wanted to be but I wasn't like them. I sensed a falseness to it. These people were pretending.

A bloke told us that there was a multi-storey car park in a square called the Leidseplein where people could stay in relative safety for a few guilders a night so we headed off there. I thought the place was called Led Zeppelin Plain and told everyone about it when I got home. We laid our sleeping bags on the floor on one of the lower levels and looked around. It was a council-run thing; there was cheap food and a picture house showing Marx Brothers films twenty-four hours a day. When we were getting ready to hit the hay two blokes in suits turned up and laid their sleeping bags next to us. I thought them incongruous. They looked straight. They were Turkish, I believe. They had proper suitcases too. Anyway, we drifted off to sleep. I began to have a very vivid dream. It was hard to pin down but it involved being out in a field with a huge crowd of people chatting happily and laughing all around me. They sounded like birds. I woke up and felt that I was floating. The dream was true. There were people standing around. It was a party. I sat up and saw that the two blokes in suits had lit an opium lamp right next to my head. The hippies had gathered like moths to a flame. Hugo woke up too. We got up and walked up to the highest level of the car park. From there we looked out at the city spread out below us. It was glittering with tiny lights. It looked like a diamond necklace in the window of a jeweller's shop. I felt as if I was Jesus on the mountain top being tempted by Satan. 'All this could be yours.' I couldn't wait!

Hugo and me didn't really have any idea of what we were up to, that's the truth of the matter. Unlike the Americans, we lacked sophistication and experience. We were like two little kids who'd run off to Porthcawl on the bus without telling our parents. We had no plan, no overview. We had no money. For some unknown reason we decided to go to Basle in Switzerland. We paid out what little money we had left for tickets and got the train. Basle was a cold unfriendly place. We got jobs washing up in hotels. Mine was horrific. Washing up in a big commercial kitchen is hellish work, hot, hard and relentless. On top of that the chef was a German who made no secret of his hatred for the British. His father had been killed in the war. I had to work split shifts too and since I was so knackered from the morning half I'd have to sleep all afternoon till the evening half, so I was in effect working all the time. I couldn't handle it. I told Hugo I was going home. Hugo said he'd join me but unfortunately we were flat broke by this time. We went to the British embassy and told them our position. Since we were working illegally they agreed to pay our fares home provided we paid it back. We agreed and got back to Folkestone by train and ferry. We forgot about our sleeping bags and other equipment and left them in a locker in Basle railway station. We hit the Social Security in Folkestone and they gave us money to get home. I left Hugo in Cardiff and got the bus back to Ton.

I got a job selling vacuum cleaners door to door. I saw it advertised in *The Echo*. It said I could earn two hundred pounds a week. We had two days' induction at the firm's offices in Swansea. There was a patter that we had to learn word for word. It was gibberish. It was about all the things that the vacuum cleaner could do as well as vacuum – paint, dry clothes, collect leaves, make tea, varnish floors etcetera – and there was a practical demonstration of each. Then at the end we had to say 'Well Mr and Mrs Jones you will be amazed to hear that you can get all these household devices, all here in the one unit, for the startling price of just eighty-five pounds.' People used to look at me as if I was crazy. This was 1970. It would be the same as saying fifteen hundred pounds today. It was ridiculously expensive and it was crap. No one on earth was going to buy one. By the end of the five weeks that I stuck it I'd knock on people's doors and instead of using the 'We're doing a survey in the area' spiel, I'd just say 'I'm selling vacuum cleaners, eighty-five quid. Do you want one?' We stayed in cheap rooms in cheap boarding houses. None of us earned anything. We went hungry. I was teamed up with a young Cardiff lad named Alex. We had to share a double bed. The second week he informed me that he had crabs. Alex was a cool guy. He'd been hoodwinked into the job the same way I had, i.e. he'd believed the ad. This was a long time ago. Alex taught me to eat a Mars bar in thin slices like they did in approved school. We used to walk along the streets of Swansea together singing Al Jolson songs with all the actions. We'd kneel in front of old women and sing 'Mammy' with the palms of our hands outstretched. 'The sun shines east, The sun shines west, but I know where the sun shines best. Mammy!' The women used to laugh. He took me to a strip club in Cardiff one night called Gino's, his uncle owned it. Alex told me that he was a criminal of some note and he looked the part. His name was Pablo and on the night I met him he was accompanied by a bodyguard, a famous Cardiff nutter called Johnny Gouchi. I say all this because it's what I was told at the time. Alex may have been bullshitting. They seemed nice enough guys to me. The stripper was a blonde Amazon. She had an ethereal quality and the most beautiful tits. I got plastered. It was a memorable night. The following day I jacked the job in, went back to Ton and signed on. It was early spring. Keith Darlington and me would sit on the hillside opposite the dole office and discuss the world and the nature of life. Keith was a lovely, gentle guy. He joined the NCB after leaving secondary modern with no qualifications, went to night school, got the necessary O and A levels to get into university, got a degree in higher mathematics and is now a highly respected professor of maths at some big university.

Me, Mel and Hugo used to go up to Audrey's in Mel's car on the weekends. She'd moved to Blaengarw, which in those days was a horrific inbred town, at the very tip of the Garw valley. She lived in the street right at the top of the highest hill. A terrace overshadowed by an enormous mountain of slag. Something terrible had happened when I was away. I don't know why or how exactly but Audrey and Mam had driven Sig to a state of mental disintegration. He'd been abroad and when he'd come back they'd managed to convince him that MI5 was after him, to imprison him for breaking some vague European law. He thought they were patrolling the streets. They hid him in the attic. He came down when I visited and he was obviously ill. He was thin and pale. His eyes were dead. One day we were all huddled in the kitchen and Audrey brought out a letter she'd received from a bloke she'd met when Sig was away. I think he was an American. I think his name was Randy. She read it out to us, me, Mel, Hugo, Mam and Sig, all sat around drinking tea. The guy wrote in the crudest sexual terms. Audrey read it as though we should be amused. Sig sat there staring at his feet, belittled and broken. When she finished there was an unbelieving silence. It was excruciating. Audrey had something missing inside her. Mam too. They lacked empathy and that lack of empathy allowed them to do unspeakable things. We smuggled Sig down to Cardiff docks in Mel's van. He covered his head in a blanket for the dash from the front door and he dived in the back. We dropped him off in Tiger Bay and he got a ride home on a Norwegian ship. Some time later I heard that he'd gone to some coastal town to recuperate and found a dead body on a beach. He turned it over and it was himself. Sounds a cliché but it's what they said happened. He was hospitalised then and he and Audrey got divorced. He recovered and they remarried! What a crazy world, eh? What a crazy fucking world! I used to believe that my family was the maddest family on the planet but it's not true. We are about seventy-two per cent mad on the scale of zero being oneness with reality and one hundred being belief that you are a one centimeter cube of fat. There are a lot crazier than us about and over the years I've met quite a few of them.

I got a job through the dole. I became a trainee Scientific Leather Measurement Officer at the Clark's shoe factory. The boss was a gently spoken West Country bloke named Roy Fuzzard. My best mate there was Maldwyn Evans. Maldwyn and me used to go to the local pub at lunchtimes to play darts. We'd have two pints and a cheese and onion roll. The factory was a big place full of sewing machines and benches. I don't really know what anyone did there. I knew where they stood or sat and that was about it. Factories were like an extension of school in those days. Hierarchies and bullying were not uncommon, but I knew a couple of the lads on the factory floor so I got on okay with everyone. Ronnie Rasmussen worked there and he was a grand lad, big and bony and friendly, and Glyndwr Bowden or Canon as he was known. I never heard him say anything ever that was not a joke. If you woke him up in the middle of the night to tell him his family had all been killed in a car crash he'd reply with a joke. He had no other means of communication. There were a couple of other people in our office, Joan Jones, a slender pretty girl, another girl, blonde, sexy in a sort of dumb, Marilyn Monroe way, a bloke with a limp, a strange guy, and a bloke who started just after me named George Farrago. George was a waistcoat-wearing dandy in the Jason King mode. He talked posh and had a little moustache, which

128

he was not averse to twirling. How he got the job I'll never know. He was a nice guy but despite his appearance he was as thick as a plank. It was great hearing his posh voice discussing work with people from other departments. They'd listen for a while and then you'd see it dawn on them that George was talking drivel. He sounded so confident, so sure of himself. He was funny too, and I'm pretty sure that he was just a chancer, I believe he knew he didn't know anything. He was a dreamer bouncing through life like a dried pea spilled onto a kitchen floor.

I went on several week-long courses in Scientific Leather Measurement at Clark's HQ in Street, Somerset. I'd saved up and bought an Afghan coat. It was green with leaves and trees woven into the design. I'd seen it in a window in Cardiff and I had to have it. It was the most beautiful thing; it expressed my inner self. I loved it. One Sunday evening I was going to Street for one of these courses and I got on the wrong train at Bristol. It took me to Abergavenny and by the time I got back to Bristol the trains had stopped and the station was virtually deserted. I turned up a flight of stone steps to exit the place and saw that it was lined on either side with skinheads. They just stood there staring at me in my Afghan coat and John Lennon glasses. What to do? I couldn't run; I couldn't falter. I just walked up the steps between the rows of skinheads and tried to avoid eye contact. To my amazement I got to the top. There must have been twenty coppers up there. Someone had just been knifed. I hitched a ride in the direction of Street in a van of hippies. They didn't talk much. The girls looked like they never stopped shagging. They dropped me off somewhere in the middle of the night and I started to follow the signs for Street. I must have walked five or six miles and I got very tired so I hopped over a wall and had a lie down on the side of a hill. I fell asleep and when I woke a cold, misty dawn was breaking. I'd slept in an old graveyard. I got up and continued my walk. I got to Street about an hour before the first lesson started. I put my clothes in my digs and went straight to the factory. I told one of the teachers about the graveyard and he told me that it was where legend had it Jesus had stood to preach when he came to England. I'd sensed something when I was there. It was a beautiful dawn, I'll never forget it.

The courses were ridiculous. The work was so tedious and uninteresting. The people were okay, though. We used to go to a local boozer every night. One of the teachers played guitar and sang folk songs. We'd all join in. When I got home I got a letter from a pretty girl with blonde curls who'd been on the course with me, inviting me to go to Weston-Super-Mare, where she lived, and see Marc Bolan at the Wintergardens. She still lived at home. Her mother and father said I could stay there for the night. She was only seventeen. It was a lovely letter and she must have been so brave to write it. I didn't even reply. If I could go back in time I'd have gone to Weston-Super-Mare that night and I'd've kissed that beautiful and brave girl on the boardwalk outside the Wintergardens. She was lovely and I was a mindless prick.

I was there in Treffano's throughout the summer. I played football with the boys and got drunk. I went to Porthcawl and stumbled through sand dunes in the dark. I sat in our back shed and stared out at the flowers. I felt that everything was passing me by. There was love and adventure for me out there somewhere just waiting for me to come and get it. If I stayed in Wales I'd end up mad. I'd kill myself. I wrote away to the Australian emigration people and filled out one of their application forms. A few weeks later I got an interview in Cardiff and was sent for a chest X-ray the following week. It was September. The bad weather came early. It got dark at six and it was unseasonably cold. God punishing us for the nice summer was the general consensus. I felt as mad as hell. Something had to happen or I'd start howling like a dog and shitting in the streets. I listened to Radio Luxembourg and heard Leonard Cohen singing 'Dress Rehearsal Rag'. 'Once there was a path and a girl with chestnut hair.' He understood. Leonard knew.

AUSTRALIA

I got up to go to work one Thursday morning a few weeks later and there was a telegram. A telegram was a big thing in those days. It said that I'd been accepted as an emigrant to Australia under the assisted passage scheme and that my flight left from Heathrow the following Monday morning. It was fantastic. It was magical. It was the answer to my problems. I'd be somewhere where nobody knew me. Nobody would expect anything of me. I could do what the hell I liked. I could become a debauched, drug-taking hedonist and have my way with as many girls as I could convince to let me have my way with them. I could become bait, human bait. I could offer myself as a sacrifice on the altar of love. I went into work and told everyone the news. I finished the next day. The weekend was spent packing and saying goodbyes. We had a piss-up in the Red Cow on the Saturday night that went on into the early morning. There were lots of people there. I felt that I was in a dream. Ool gave me a watch. He was very upset. Though we'd been through some difficult times he loved me and he was going to miss me. I gave no thought for how he felt. It's hard for me to explain my behaviour. I was just self-centered I suppose. I loved Ool and would not have dreamt of hurting him. He was my father. I don't think Naine was concerned. Maybe she knew that I could take care of myself, she wasn't stupid. Me and Ool went to Heathrow by coach on the Sunday evening. I had one suitcase and sixty quid. The flight was at noon the next day. We stayed in a hotel at the airport and Ool was stunned at the price, seven pounds a night. He refused to pay it for himself and said that he'd get his head down on a bench outside. It was a nasty night and I managed to convince him to get a room or I'd worry. We sat in the bar together drinking and talking. He gave me the benefit of his experience about going to another country. He was Polonius to my Laertes, the dear man. I woke up with a crushing hangover. We checked in and carried on drinking. There was a call for me over the tannoy. A group of the boys had driven up from Ton to see me off. It was a touching gesture. We tipped the pop down us like madmen till I finally had to go. I waved goodbye through the departure lounge gates and boarded the 707. I'd done it!

The plane was surprisingly small and packed solid with young blokes about my own age. Almost all of them were from Northern Ireland. They were getting away from the troubles. There was free booze on the flight and it was like a saloon in the old West. There was leaping about and play fighting for the first six or seven hours until exhaustion kicked in and then endless hours of incredibly uncomfortable attempted sleep. I sat by a window and looked down at the snow-peaked Alps below. It was breathtaking. Later there were huge swathes of purple desert. This was the world, set out before me in all its delicate beauty. We made several refuelling stops where we could get out and stretch our legs. One was in Tehran. There were young soldiers with machine guns in high towers. We waved to them and they waved back, smiling. A bloke in a white cloth thing asked me in broken English if I had any arms. I thought it a very strange question. It seemed obvious to me that I had so I said yes. He told me to wait there and fetched a guy in a suit who frisked me in a small room. He figured out that I was referring to my upper limbs and he let me go into the holding area, where I willingly paid a quid for a glass of chilled orange juice. The Irish lads were sobering up and I got to talk to them. They were all Catholics, every one of them. They'd been wooed by the IRA but weren't interested. It was wise to leave the country after that. One of them limped from where he'd been kneecapped. The journey took thirty-four hours. When we were approaching Sydney we took turns to look down at the city from the tiny windows. There was street after street of red-tiled roofs and gardens with small blue circles in them. They were swimming pools. When we'd taxied to a halt a man in a mask came on board and sprayed everyone with some sort of disinfectant. Then we trouped out to a large hall where immigration people processed us. There was a bus waiting outside to take us to the initial reception centre in Burwood, but I had to stay behind because my baggage was missing. They said it had been put on the wrong flight and they'd get it to me the next day, so I went through customs without it. I had nothing to declare but the bloke asked me where my Afghan coat was made. I assumed it to be Afghanistan and told him so. He said that they didn't allow unprocessed animal skins into Australia and I'd have to have it treated to kill possible bugs. It would cost a hundred quid. As I left customs and stepped out into the waiting area for the bus I had nothing, no bags and no Afghan coat. The air was so humid that my shirt and trousers stuck to me like they'd been glued on. I was shattered.

Burwood reception centre was a sprawling, barracks-like complex in one of Sydney's outer suburbs. It was deliberately Spartan so that people wouldn't want to hang about finding jobs and getting out of there. I had a small room with a bed, a wardrobe and a wash basin. It was too hot to stay indoors in the daytime so we used to assemble outside on the pavement. There were people from all over staying there, white people of course, though some of the Turkish guys were brownish. Sometimes cars full of young Australian thugs would cruise past and they'd shout out racist abuse. We took meals in a canteen. The food was crap but the people in charge were generally very helpful. The second or third day we were there I went into the city with two of the Irish boys to have a look around. It was a Sunday. We walked across the Harbour Bridge and stared at the skyscrapers. It was wonderful just to be there, all that way away. On the way back to the camp the boys, Joe and Barry, hard young men with sparkling eyes and laconic senses of humour, decided to go to church and I went with them. It was an enormous church, the biggest I'd ever seen, and it was packed. I assumed that this was what Australian churches were like. I went up front and knelt with the others when they said to, and the priest gave us a bit of wafer and a sip of wine from a silver goblet. It was odd but quite nice. It was later that I realised that it was a Catholic cathedral. The Irish lads laughed. I really didn't think there was any difference between Catholics and us. They believed in the same God, the God of Peace and Love and Forgiveness, what did it matter how they chose to worship him? I still don't get it. It's the same with all religions. Joe told me that if we'd been back in Belfast I would have been dragged out and beaten unconscious. He told me he was glad to be away from there. I kept in touch with them for a while after we left the centre. We went to the pictures one evening. It was in Bondi. We'd been on the lash and saw a film with Jack Nicholson in it advertised. We knew and liked him from *Easy Rider* and went in. The film was *Five Easy Pieces*, an art-house film about a disillusioned bloke from a posh family of classical musicians who'd left that world behind to work as a labourer on an oil field. It was an intense, brilliant film but we were expecting something different. We were expecting a story with goodies and baddies, we were expecting guns and car chases. None of us had ever seen a film like this before. We watched it in silence. When we got outside we all agreed that though it wasn't what we expected it was good nonetheless. I was surprised. Joe had hired a car, a convertible, and we drove along the Bondi road in the sweltering late evening with the roof down. There were palm trees lining the street and the sky was huge and full of pink rolling clouds. Two weeks before I'd been staring at my reflection in the bus window coming home from work down Capel hill in the bitter Welsh winter and now here I was. It was hallucinogenic.

Sydney is a wonderful city and Australia is a wonderful country. It has a unique beauty. The land is russet red and the seas are wild and sparkling. It has a living heart. I love it, I really do. It had been dominated by extreme right-wing politics since the end of the Second World War. There was a solid core of mostly older people who identified strongly with the country's colonial ties to England. They didn't like Darkies and they feared the Commie threat. They were as right-wing as hell. They were like our Tories. That said they had sustained a strong aftertaste of the fifties in Australian society, which I really liked. The politics was Stone Age. The national government was in Canberra but each state had its own state government to deal with the day-to-day running of business. They were at each other's throats like rabid dogs most of the time. Queensland was a gerrymandered fiefdom for an embittered Bible-bashing psychopath called Jo Peterson and his cronies. It was quite openly referred to as a police state. It was as corrupt as hell, needless to say, and a dangerous place to visit if your hair was below your collar. At the same time the New South Wales state government and the police were actually run by criminals, straightforward gun-toting criminals. They were busted for it when I was there. They used to hold up banks, the lot. The Australians were in

Vietnam too, of course, and it had caused as much division in Australia as it had in America. The establishment loved it. It was credit in the bank of American gratitude. Spurred on by a *Der Sturmer*-like press, a large number of ordinary folk liked it too. An awful lot of folk didn't, though. The divide was what it always is, the Nutters versus the Dreamers. The Dreamers had already lost in America but Australia was a few years behind. The Dreamers were still dreaming. Sydney was a nest of hippies.

I saw the employment people in the camp and they fixed me up with an interview at Gladesville Psychiatric Hospital. I got the job. There was a guy being interviewed at the same time and he got in too. We chatted and decided to follow the hospital's advice and save money by getting a place to live together. His name was Ted Christensen and he was a Canadian. He was a handsome guy in the classic American hippie mode, a thick black beard and moustache and kind eyes. He was a philosopher. He was a few years older than me. He'd been travelling around Asia. He fell in love with a prostitute somewhere but it ended in grief. He'd come to Australia as the final part of the American version of The Grand Tour.

We got a two-room apartment in a single-storey house in Drummoyne, a suburb near Gladesville. It was a dump. Neither Ted nor I were domestic in any way so we came to an agreement that we'd live in squalor. Ted slept in one room, me in the other. Ted had the window. It looked out over the harbour. I got home one day and Ted shouted for me to come and see something. I went into his room and found him standing bollock naked on the mantelpiece in a crucifixion pose. 'Look, I'm Jesus,' he said. Ted was crazy. He got his leg over a lot though. I had to lie there in my bed many nights listening to him servicing a succession of tasty-looking Sheilas through the paper-thin wall. The floors were two-foot deep in garbage too. It was frustrating. Vince and Mavis occupied the rest of the house. Vince was a short, stocky Australian bloke in his mid-twenties and Mavis was a Northern English woman about ten years older than him. Mavis had left her husband, an arsehole she'd come to Australia with, and she and Vince met and fell in love. The husband was a copper and he was still causing them some grief. Vince was nugget hard and not averse to physical confrontation and Mavis was a woman of substance. They were good people. They were very good to me. I spent a lot of time with them. They introduced me to their friends. We ate out and they took me to a Lebanese restaurant. We had hummus and stuffed vine leaves, pitta bread, olives and goat's cheese. I'd never eaten anything like that before. Australia is a great country for food. They have wonderful tasty fish like barramundi and red snapper, there's oysters and prawns and scallops and lobsters and fantastic fresh meat. Steaks the size of a T-shirt cooked over charcoal. There were great shops, delicatessens catering for the different nationalities who lived in the city, Italian, Greek, North African. I ate cabanos, mango and avocado. I tasted cashew nuts. I had steak and eggs for breakfast. Remember I told you about the taste of the sandwich that the guard on the train across the Rockies gave me when I was a little boy, the taste that lingered in my psyche like Proust's Madeleine? It was peanut butter! Crunchy peanut butter in fact. I'd heard it mentioned in American films but didn't know I'd tasted it. I had money too. Everybody in Australia had money. It was incredible. The wages were twice what we earned in Britain and the cost of living was a third less. They were three times as well off as us. I had money to go out, to buy clothes, to get taxis. I designed a jacket and had it made for me. It was white and longer than usual, tapered at the waist. I thought it made me look like a riverboat gambler. I bought cool shirts. I had my red velvet trousers from my Jersey days and I bought an American flag vest, and shoes to match. I bought new glasses. The lenses were made from blue plastic and the frames were octagonal. The lenses were so thick at the edges that they wore grooves in my forehead above my eyes. I tried contact lenses but they nearly blinded me. They were horrific.

I started drinking in a big pub near the hospital. The first night I entered the darts competition and I threw a one eighty with my first darts. I won a dozen bottles of beer. It was a rough place. There were some really nasty dudes hanging about. There was a strong macho culture. I tried to keep myself to myself but got threatened on several occasions nonetheless. Eventually I got talking to a particular group of lads when one of them told me he'd been born in Wales and wanted to know what it was like. His name was Gerry Orr. He had long straight hair and an obsession with Lilith, the mythical wife of Satan. He wrote dark, crazed poetry. He loved Black Sabbath. There was a tattoo just below his navel saying 'HOT ROD' and an arrow pointing straight down. Gerry's big hero was Charles Manson. He wanted to go to Hell. He was a psychopath and he hung around with other psychopaths. There were two in particular, half-caste Aboriginal brothers named Col and Mick Hennessy. Col was married with children and was as handsome as hell. I never met his brother Mick but both Col and Gerry told me that he was seriously violent. They used to go out together attacking homosexuals. They hated them. They'd cut them up. They'd seriously hurt them. They'd hospitalise them. Gerry told me that he took a tab of acid every day. They were frightening but they never picked on me once, not even in fun. I don't know why. They hated Wogs too. A Wog in Australia is any immigrant whose first language isn't English. If they were not totally white either so much the better. Gerry took me out to the pub car park once. It was where he'd take someone if they wanted to fight him. He put his arm down into the hollowed trunk of an old tree and pulled out a sword that he kept hidden there for such occasions. He told me he'd cut a man's arm off in a fight the year before in Queensland. He didn't value human life at all. I drank in a pub in Drummoyne as well. It was a haunt of older blokes, Jocks and Paddies. Quite a few of them were firemen stationed nearby. We played darts for two bucks a game. These guys were nasty alcoholics. They were middle-aged destroyed men who'd emigrated. I was drunk most of the time myself, otherwise I don't think I could have stood it. It was horrific.

The hospital consisted of a spread-out group of buildings over about ten acres of verdant tree-filled land. It was ultra-modern by British standards and the staff were involved and caring. The hierarchy was old school but the majority of the nurses had a compassionate ethos. This was in no small part due to the fact that most of the younger ones were hippies. They enjoyed looking after the patients. They worked hard with smiles on their faces. I was put on ward eight. It was for the severely mentally and physically disabled. All the patients were wheelchair bound, I had eight of the worst affected and my job was to do everything for them. I got them up in the morning, washed them, dressed them and fed them. They were all doubly incontinent and a lot of my day was spent showering them and changing their clothing. They were a sweet bunch. Frankie Geldard used to swallow his own hand down to the wrist. He'd push it right down into his stomach. The fingers were white and thin having been slowly eaten away over the years by his gastric juices. He was restrained most of the time but seized any opportunity to get it down him. Another bloke used to punch himself repeatedly in the face. There was a hard lump the size of a duck egg on his cheek. He was tied up to his bed at night but often managed to pull free and succeeded in beating himself to death one night. A guy called Maldwyn spent all his time masturbating. He'd learned to do it with no hands. He pushed his cock between his thighs and just rocked back and fore. There was a blind guy too, who just sat on his haunches and screamed. They were of varying ages but were all referred to as children. There was a swimming pool on the ward and we'd go in with them. The weather was glorious. At meal times I'd sit them in a row and feed them like on a production line. Franky Geldard could eat his dinner and desert in twelve seconds. He'd regurgitate it though, and spend the next hour rolling his eyes and churning the food around in his mouth like a cement mixer. It was hard work but the vibe was good. The charge nurse was a great bloke. He treated the patients with affection and dignity and made sure everyone else did too. He was liked and respected by everyone. The other nurses were young and hip. It was a good place. There was a social side too. They'd organise rugby matches and barbecues. I played against another hospital one Sunday afternoon. Vince was on the other side. Both he and Mavis were nurses too. I got battered to a pulp. I think they were intent on giving the Pom a kicking but I acquitted myself well. Vince was sent off for fighting. I began writing poems for the hospital newspaper under the name Squire Morlock, an old name for the Devil.

There was a social in a club one night and I dolled up in my finery to go. The main attraction was a band called Chain which had the number one song in the charts at the time. I got talking to a girl. I discovered that she too was a regular contributor to the poetry section in the paper and she told me that she liked my work. I ended up going home with her. She lived not too far from me. When we got there we talked for a while and then hit the sack. She was very fat, obese and when we got down to it I found it off-putting. I have since learned that women of all shapes and sizes are sexy but at the time I guess I was offensively unenthusiastic. After we'd finished we had a fag and there was an awkward silence. The door opened and her flatmate, another nurse, walked in. She'd just come off duty and was still in her uniform. She sat on the bed and started to kiss me. She was no Audrey Hepburn but then again I was no Cary Grant. She got stripped and got in bed with us. The first girl just laid there. The second girl wanted it Russian style, something that had never crossed my mind before, but I reckon a man has got to do whatever a woman wants him to, so I plunged in and I must say I thoroughly enjoyed it. It was my first sex in Australia. I left before dawn and went home.

We worked on a rotating shifts system, a week of seven am to three pm, a week of three pm to eleven pm and one of eleven pm to seven am. When I wasn't in work I was drinking. I finished a night shift one morning, the last of my week, and having four days off decided to go to an early opener – some Australian pubs opened from six am to six pm – with two other nurses who'd knocked off the same time. We were drunk by half eight and the other guys suggested we went back to their place to chill out. They lived quite a way out so we got a taxi. It was a nice, hippie-type house and we smoked fags, listened to music and drank some cans in the kitchen. One of the guys said that it would be an idea to drop some acid. I was drunk and said fine. I'd barely smoked dope before. I had no real idea of what acid was like other than my observations of the boys in The Boar. We had half a tab each. It took half an hour to kick in. I started to feel like I was in a strange and delicate fairy world. There was a mood of benevolence. I felt good. We decided to go into the city, to Kings Cross. I don't remember how we actually got there but there we were. It was a brilliant hot morning. The place was teeming with people in their summer clothes. They were shopping and talking and laughing. I saw a guy I recognised from the camp. He was a Turk, bald-headed, about twenty stone. I smiled at him and said Hi. He stopped, turned and looked at me and asked, 'Do I know you?' 'The Camp. Burwood!' I said. 'Oh, yes,' he answered and walked on. We came to a beautiful fountain, a silver orb shooting streams of sparkling water into the air. Droplets of ice cold water fell on us. Everyone looked happy, they all looked like they were enjoying a day out, they looked like they were enjoying the best day out they'd ever had. This was how the world should be. I passed a shop that sold hippie gear and went in. I bought a green suede jacket. It had long fringes like the one Billy wore in *Easy Rider*. I bought a wide-brimmed black hat too. I put them both on. I passed another shop. It sold toys. There was a teddy bear in the window. I stopped and stared at it. It told me that it had the spirit of the American actor Broderick Crawford trapped inside it and asked for my help. I went in and rescued him. Things were getting strange. We walked on. I went into a café, sat at a table, sat Broderick on the chair opposite and ordered two strawberry milkshakes. I drank mine through a straw but it surged up into my face like molten lava and I put it down and we left. The guys wanted to go home. Come with us, they said, we'll drop the other half.

We were back in the kitchen and we'd dropped the other half. I was sitting at the table. I looked out into the garden. There was one of those round spinning clothesline things out there. It became a cartoon merry-go-round. The clothes became painted horses. There was a man there, the circus ringmaster. He held a whip in one hand. He was a cartoon too. He removed his head with his top hat when he bowed to take our applause. I saw something in the corner of my eye and turned to look. It was an LP. It was the Uriah Heep album with the cobwebbed dead face on the front. I went for a pee. I stood in the small narrow toilet and peed. I looked down at the relentless stream of sparkling urine and I felt that I was peeing away all the pain and misery and sadness that mankind had suffered since time began. All the wars, all the hatred, all the unkindness, all the grief, all the fear, the horrors of Dachau and Belsen, I pissed away disease and poverty and hunger, I pissed away my father's pointless death, I pissed away the black pantomime of my childhood. It was all going, flowing out of me. I became aware that I was involved in an act of profound expurgation. It was the Immaculate Urination. I began to cry. I cried with gratitude. I went back into the kitchen. I had an intense pain in my neck. I believed that it was the sun. The guys twigged that there was something wrong. They said they'd take me home. We went in a taxi. There was a hold-up at a bank. Men ran out firing shots behind them, leapt onto their waiting horses and galloped off. They were half cartoon and half real. There were flower baskets hanging next to people's front doors as we passed. They contained demonic heads snarling and snapping at me. We pulled up at a traffic light and the car next to us was filled with werewolves. They smiled at me. The guys dumped me off outside my house. I didn't have my key. I decided that I'd ring the doorbell and if nobody answered I'd get a big kitchen knife and cut my own throat. I was quite at ease with the idea. I rang and Mavis came. I told her what had happened. I told her that I was frightened. Vince was at work in the other psych hospital so Mavis rang him. We got in her Volkswagen and drove there. I was lost. I was gone. The werewolves had taken over. We parked in the car park and Mavis went in. I looked at the windows of the ward. There were grey-winged demons with writhing tongues straining at the leash to get out, to get to me.

Mavis came back with Vince. He handed me a medicine cup with a sweet sticky pink liquid in it and told me to drink it. I drank it and he called me a fool. Instead of going home Mavis took me to Pedro and Gerda's house. They were friends of theirs and I'd been there a few times. I went in and lay down on the carpet. I could hear them talking. They were saying that they were going to poison me. I was too tired to escape and anyway I wasn't really there. I was lying on the hard dusty ground in the middle of a herd of longhorn cattle in a corral in the old West. It took me weeks to recover. I stayed in bed as much as I could. I was trembling all the time. I wish I'd never taken acid. It opens a door which, once opened, can never be closed.

Vince and Mavis moved to a lovely flat in Gladesville. It was under the bridge, Gladesville Bridge, the longest single-span bridge in the world at that time. It was a spectacular sight. They asked if I wanted to move in with them and I did. Ted went back home to America. The back garden of the new flat was right on the harbour; the water actually lapped up to the shore. There was a boathouse where I'd sit in the evenings and watch the sharks' fins as they glided back and forth ten or fifteen yards out. Sydney harbour is the most shark-infested stretch of water in the world. There were some spectacular storms. I watched one from my window. The sky was red and black. The sea was huge. A giant battleship in dock on the far side of the harbour was being tossed up and down like a toy. I love weather. I love all types. I like rain.

I fell in with a fellow student nurse, an Englishman named Charles Kenton. His father was the boss of the London

146

School of Economics and Charles had been to public school and Cambridge University. He had in fact been sent down from Cambridge University. It was this academic setback that sent him off to Oz in search of himself. He was six-three, talked crystal upper-class English and had a physique like a professional swimmer. He was the poshest and best-looking bloke I'd ever met. He was a cross between Jeremy Irons and Jim Morrison. I had never met a man who had sex with more women. It appeared to me that he did it with every woman he ever met. They literally threw themselves at his feet, but Charles was already in love. He'd screw them, sure, but they'd never replace smack. Charles was into junk and alcohol. He was like a character from a Colin Wilson novel, larger than life, dangerous. We used to go drinking in the city. Charles drank quadruple Southern Comforts. We'd go to pubs, order round after round of lager and tip them over our own heads. We were idiots; that is the truth of the matter, but hanging around with Charles did my sex life the world of good. I'd started on twelve-hour night shifts on a residential ward where the patients were responsible for their own welfare. They could come and go as they pleased, and many held down jobs. It was easy. All I really had to do was hand out tablets once an evening and just be there. I'd bought a cheap guitar and a 'how to play' book and spent most of my work time practising chords. I had a nice little office where I could lock the door and get my head down too. I had it off with a girl in there one night. She was a nurse who turned up expecting someone else to be there, a boyfriend of hers. He'd shot through though, and she wanted sex, so I volunteered. She was a weird girl. She hardly spoke. She fucked like a rabbit, though, and introduced me to some of her friends. I shagged a girl with long red hair who wore leathers and drove a Harley. I shagged a girl with the biggest tits I'd ever seen. I shagged an English bus conductor. I was getting it right, left and centre. Life should have been good but it wasn't. I'd felt unwell since the acid trip. I felt that I was trapped like a painting in a frame. I felt afraid. I was lonely. I was sitting on a wall outside ward eight late one night when I saw a figure sitting on a chair beside the door to the charge nurse's office. It was a primitive god from deep below the earth. It had a grey face that was revolving, forever changing in its composition, and a halo of black swirling smoke. The chair had become a throne. I closed my eyes and looked away. When I looked back the subterranean god had disappeared and there was a werewolf in its place. It wore black trousers and a white, open-necked shirt.

We had a week's training course in the hospital. It was nine till five. Kenton was there, there were about twenty of us. I used to ask to go to the outside toilet early in the lesson, smoke a straight grass two-skinner, then go back. I had no idea what they were trying to teach us. There was a girl there with long, straight hair. She sat a few seats behind me and one day, me, this girl, a nice Australian hippie guy whose name I forget, Kenton and a blonde Scandinavian love goddess decided to go for lunch at a pub a short ferry ride away. We sat out in the garden and had a few drinks and chatted and found that we got along, so we decided to go back to the nice hippie's flat and carry on socialising rather than go back to the work. There was a sun shower on the way to the flat and we got drenched.

Inside we drank, listened to records and smoked ganja. The hippie was a real hippie. He believed in peace and love but not necessarily in that order. I got into an intense conversation with the girl with the long hair. She was fascinating. I told her about Leonard Cohen. I'd bought *Songs of*, *Songs from a Room* and *Songs of Love and Hate* and they spoke to me. Cohen was a poet. He had his finger on the pulse of love. He knew that we were all seeking God. I raved at the girl about specific songs, the profound and beautiful lyrics. 'And he flew you above the ribbons of rain that drove the crowds from the stands.' I began to cry with the intensity of it all. The girl said 'Do you want to come and lie down?' The girl's name was Catherine Knight and she was to become my wife.

We got into a lot of shit for getting back to school late. We got kicked off the course and put on warnings. It was back to the wards for us. Cathy came back to my place. We made love again and I kicked a hole through the wall in the throes of it. She was slender and beautiful. She smelled of the sea. We were an item from that moment on. She was in the process of moving house and I went over to the new place in Ford Street, Balmain, to meet her new housemates. I took a dozen bottles of Tooheys, for the lads I thought, but the lads weren't drinkers. I drank all twelve myself to the utter amazement of Ian, a piano teacher who couldn't believe that anyone could drink that much. He was the only resident I got to talk to that night. He was a nice gentle guy. It never dawned on me that he was gay. I didn't realise it till months after I'd moved in. Cathy and I were kindred souls. She was a brilliant woman. She had degrees in psychology and Sanskrit. She took me about in her blue Hillman Minx. We went to huge outdoor swimming pools and ate Kentucky Fried Chicken. We got drunk a lot. She loved The Beatles, especially George. We were standing outside Vince's place one evening and she asked me if I'd like her to invoke the West Wind, I said, sure I would. She closed her eyes for several minutes and a fresh breeze blew.

THE WIZARD OF OZ

The other people living in Ford Street were Cathy's friend Petah Martin and her little boy Jeshua, and John Bowden and his Finnish girlfriend Rita. There were four bedrooms and a veranda upstairs and a large communal living room, a kitchen and a shower room downstairs. There was a cat there when I moved in. It was very old and dying of cancer. It shat in the cupboards and it smelled foul. It died a week or so later and to this day I am sorry that I didn't befriend it and show it some love in that time. All the people in the house with the exception of Jeshua and Rita were recently initiated members of an occult group who called themselves The Dawn of Isis. It was based on the Kabbala, ancient Jewish teaching and ritual that had been passed down by word of mouth. The name was a nod to the Order of the Golden Dawn, which was a British occult society in the late nineteenth century. W. B. Yeats had been a prominent member, as had Aleister Crowley. It involved some of the cream of Britain's literary world and was riddled with scandal. It was an attractive template for the hippie-inclined. Most of the group members were highly intelligent, highly educated people. They had energy. They were beyond accepted truth. They were magicians. My girlfriend was a magician. I got to meet the group. There were about a dozen of them. They had been studying under a guru for several years. His name was John Strangeways. He shagged all of the women and more than one of the blokes. John was older than everyone else. He was in his early forties but he looked great. He looked like Jesus, in fact. He was a 'Master'. He was worshipped. The system wasn't slavishly Kabbalistic. It embraced such things as numerology, Egyptology, the tarot, the I Ching, healing techniques, auric manipulation and astral travel. It was a broad church. The coolest bit was ritual. They had a temple in an old warehouse in Glebe. It was paid for from the common purse. It had a circle bound in gold, four thrones, purple velvet curtains, sceptres, golden cups and sacred crowns. It was impressive. I found the entire thing immensely suspicious. I thought that John was a charlatan out for his own hedonistic ends. They weren't as clichéd a phenomenon then as they are now, but I was a cynic, I suppose. Then again, converting cynics was John's stock in trade and he had the tools to accomplish it. He was intelligent and sophisticated, really sharp, and he had formidable charisma. He was cool too, an excellent blues guitarist and singer and an admired artist. His commissions came from those who worshipped him and they were never disappointed. They paid a fair whack too. John used to shag them in the rest breaks when they were posing. His right hand man was Chris Boomp De Boomp, who played bass guitar with him in pubs and clubs around the city. Chris was a huge guy who looked almost exactly like the cowardly lion in the *Wizard of Oz*. He suffered from big mate of the guru smugness unfortunately, that was his flaw. He picked up John's crumbs at the picnic of lust. Despite his unwarranted arrogance I felt sorry for him. He didn't understand fuck all about what was going on. His sister was nice though.

Despite my profound misgivings I went to see John to ask if I could join the second tier of members for the next intake. You had to ask John personally so that he could look at your aura to see if you were predestined to join. Fortunately most people were, so I got in. I had my magic seal cut out of silver plate; I engraved the sacred name of Hermes Tresmajestus along the edge in ancient script. I had the two stars made, one five-pointed in gold, the other six-pointed in silver. I wore them on a black leather thong around my neck, the seal at my throat. I began doing Kabbalistic Crosses. 'Atoh, Malkuth, Ve Geburah, Ve Gedulah, Le Olam Amen' four times a day. I read text-books by Dion Fortune, Israel Regardie and MacGreggor Mathers, *The Art of True Healing*, *A Garden of Pomegranates*, *The Ladder of Lights*. I did relaxation and imagination exercises every night. I stared at coloured cards in a particular order to help me control my dreams. Being a neophyte meant that you couldn't smoke dope. It was the price you had to pay for enlightenment. John and the initiates had gone through that and they smoked like choo-choo trains. It was a test of one's seriousness. There were weekly meetings in the temple. John would give us lectures on various things. His gist was that there was going to be a remarkable happening in Australia in the near future. A world-famous politician was going to arrive at Sydney Airport. It would be live on television. The politician would get off the plane and collapse dead on the tarmac. Then a man would come from the crowd and bring him back from the dead. This act, witnessed by tens of millions of people all over the world, would fundamentally alter people's perceptions of the nature of existence and they would turn to magic to make sense of them. That would be our time. I got the impression that the healing stranger would be one of our own group. It could even have been me. John had regular meetings with other masters and deities on the astral plane to prepare for this event. We had to be naked at these lectures. It was so our auras wouldn't get in the way. John had the biggest cock in Australia. It was the size of a cheese baguette when flaccid. He'd stand there chalking diagrams on the blackboard and talking as we sat around on the floor listening and it would sway in front of us at eye level like a baby elephant's trunk.

Gerry came around to my place one late afternoon when I was still living with Vince and Mavis. He was tripping off his head on mushrooms. He'd run all the way to my place, across Gladesville Bridge from Balmain in the hammering rain. He had a leather bag full of money and a service revolver. He had just robbed a bank. He stayed for a few hours then left.

I met Cathy's family. I met her mother first, actually. She came to visit one evening and was sat next to Cathy on the bed chatting and drinking tea when I burst into her room. I'd been to the fireman's pub in Drummoyne playing darts after work and Kenton came in and ripped my shirt off my back. It was in shreds. On top of that I was drunk.

Margaret Knight took it in her stride fortunately. Cathy had told her good things about me. We went to her home in Speers Point near the Blue Mountains a few weeks later. It was a large country town about two hundred miles from Sydney. The house was beautiful. Cathy took me to her room, the room where she slept as a child. It reminded me of my room. The reality was that we were still just children. Cathy read voraciously, Doris Lessing, Iris Murdoch and Lawrence Durrell. I read them after her. I read *Briefing for a Descent into Hell*, I read *The Plague*, I read *The Alexandria Quartet*. We went to a trendy cinema in Glebe and watched Andy Warhol films. I liked the bad acting, the monotone of the voices, the swearing and the uninspired sex. We saw the Lindsay Kemp Mime Troupe in the same venue. They were doing *Flowers*, their inter-pretation of Jean Genet's novel *Our Lady of the Flowers*. There was only one spoken line in it: 'Would you like a cup of our fine China tea?'

I have called my sweetheart Cathy up to now because that is what I knew her as then, but later she preferred to be called Kate and that is how I think of her now, so from this point on I'll revert to that. Kate's father, Neville, was an impressive-looking man, tall and thin with a splendidly aquiline face. Some would consider him handsome. Margaret was certainly beautiful. He was short-tempered and bullying. She was gentle and understanding. Neville didn't like the cut of my jib from the off. I heard him refer to me as a ridiculous clown-like creature or words to that effect. Kate hated him and so did her two brothers. The elder, David, lived in a shed out the back. He couldn't bear to be in the house. Neville never stopped looking for a fight. He was like a dog straining at the leash. David just kept out of his way. On the rare occasions they found themselves in the same room it was like waiting for a hand grenade to go off. The younger brother, Peter, spent all of his time skateboarding up and down the hilly streets outside the house. He was about sixteen, David a year older. I got to know them well. They were both lovely guys. Kate was twenty like me. In fact, her birthday was on the fifth of March 1951, two days before mine. We worked it out once that given the time difference between Newcastle and Vancouver and the exact times of our respective births, we were in fact born on the same day. I was sitting out with David in his shed watching TV and drinking a beer one afternoon when he suddenly picked up a small wastepaper bin and a magazine and told me not to move. He said there was a spider on the wall next to me and that he was going to get rid of it. I turned my head and there three inches from my face was a spider the size of my hand. I froze. I totally froze. I couldn't move the smallest muscle. I couldn't breathe, I couldn't swallow, I couldn't blink. David knocked it off the wall and into the wastepaper bin with the magazine in one swift move and took it outside. There are more poisonous creatures in Australia than any other continent. It was best not to dwell on it. We stayed five days then went back to Sydney.

I joined the group because Kate was in it and I loved her and wanted to be a part of whatever she was a part of, but there was more to it than that. I didn't believe what they believed, but I believed that there was something somewhere that I could believe. I was a young human being confronted by a spiritual void and I sought fulfillment. I wanted to understand who I was. It sounds crazy now getting involved in a thing like that, it highlights my naivety I suppose but that's not such a bad thing in one so young. I learned a few things too. I learned that if there is a god, be it a deity or be it an unimaginable thing, there is no one, no priest, no bishop, no wise man, no guru, no saint who has ever lived, who knows more about or is closer to that god than I am. It's not a bad thing to know.

I moved into Ford Street. Kate suggested that we should get married. I was all for it. It was February 1972. We decided on March. Hugo arrived. He was almost comatose with jetlag but I insisted on taking him out to get drunk and he acquiesced. When Kate got home from work she insisted on us going out to a rowing club nearby too, so by the time night came Hugo was out on his feet. We put a mattress and sleeping bag out for him on the living room floor and he crashed. Petah's dog Marion had been unwell and she went in and shat all over him in the night, but he was too buggered to react. We found him next morning covered in shit. He was okay though, and glad to be there.

Kate and I got married in Newcastle Registry Office on the twentieth of March. Quite a few members of the group had come up from Sydney and there were Knight family guests I didn't know. Gerry and Col and his wife and kids had driven up too. Hugo was best man and he gave an excellent speech concentrating on his fear of poisonous spiders. He told the guests that he found it perplexing because he usually got on so well with spiders and indeed believed himself to have a level of psychic communication with them. The reception was in the house and garden of the Knight family. I had my riverboat gambler's jacket on and Kate a beautiful long dress. David and Peter were stoned, I think. One of the guests that Margaret introduced me to was a cousin who was a bishop. He was a big jolly man. I'd noticed some not over-subtle classism from some of the straight guests towards Col and his family. They were a bit uncouth, someone said. The kids were running around shouting etcetera. This was just shit of course. Col's wife was a sweet and refined girl and the kids were just normal, healthy, naughty children but it was the old eye of the beholder scenario. As I was talking to the bishop, Col's kids rushed past us and the bishop made some comment about 'little bastards' – he was an Australian bishop you must remember – and I saw that Col and his wife were standing just behind him. We were in the hallway of the house. There was a silence. I closed my eyes and waited for the sound of fist on jaw or worse. Col called the kids and they went and sat outside. We left for our honeymoon that evening. Kate drove us to the family's holiday home, a house known as Windy Wappa, on the shores of Lake Macquarie. It was a long drive through forests and country towns, with narrow roads snaking through ancient landscapes. The Australian bush is eerie. It has a timeless quality. It is as though it is waiting. It is as though it has always been waiting. It is in the Dreamtime. We got to Windy Wappa late and went to bed.

When we woke up early the next morning there was a ferocious storm blowing. The sky was almost black and there was torrential rain. Lake Macquarie was swirling and churning and smashing against its shores not a hundred yards away. The house was isolated and the raging storm was unnerving. Kate was in a foul mood. It had started the previous day after the wedding. She hardly talked to me. The storm raged all day and through the following night. We stayed in bed reading. The house was taking a battering, there were noises of floorboards creaking and panels buckling coming from everywhere. It kept us awake. The next morning the storm had died down a little. The rain held off in patches and we went for a walk along the shores of the lake during one of them. I'd been practising hard on my guitar and I sang some songs I'd been learning. Kate told me that I could be a folk singer. We were so tiny there together standing by that great mass of water. The rain returned and we went back in. That night as we were walking up the stairs to go to bed I noticed that the door to the attic had been moved. It was slid to one side. It was obviously the wind or some other effect of the storm but we didn't see it that way. We believed that there was some evil entity there. We believed we were in danger. We gathered our things together and fled the house in panic. We felt that we were being driven away. That something wanted us gone. Kate drove all night.

The weekend after we got home we went on a group ritual weekend to a place called Hellhole Beach, which was on the coast between Sydney and Woolongong. It was a long drive followed by a tortuous walk down a steep, thickly wooded hillside. When I got down to the beach I was covered in leaches. There were huge ants that stung like hornets. The beach itself, however, was magnificent. I love the sea, I always have. It's humbling. This was the mighty Pacific. The beach itself was an almost perfect crescent of sand about two hundred yards across. There were high cliffs to the left and hilly woodlands drifting off to the right. We pitched our tents and assembled for some food and a chat. It was twilight. A campfire was lit. The weekend had been planned for months. It was to invoke and celebrate the power of the sun by meditation and ritual. It was a necessary step on the path to initiation. The initiates had done it before of course. This was for a small group of people who'd been in the initiates' group but hadn't completed it for some reason or another, and me. Practical Kabbala is based on the idea that there is a mechanism that exists in our auras, which can be developed and ultimately controlled by a series of precisely structured exercises or rituals, and that that control is synonymous with divinity. Like Buddhists attaining Nirvana. Most esoteric systems, including religions, promise a similar result. The structure in the case of the Kabbala is an interconnected framework made up of non-physical sephirot or spheres of light, and the pathways between them. This framework corresponds to the anatomy of the body. There are eleven of these spheres and they represent archetypes. The one at the feet represents the physical world, for example, the one at the top godhead. The ones on either side represent perceived opposites, justice and mercy, intellect and emotion, and the three others in the middle column or pillar as it is known represent the world of dreams, perfect balance and transition. This mechanism is known as The Tree of Life. Each of the spheres has a host of properties, colours, tastes, deities, archangels, animals, numbers, planets, stars, you name it, associated with it, and the idea is to solidify these spheres by intoning sacred Hebrew phrases specific to and concentrated in each. The one at the dead centre is called Tipareth. It is the pure point of balance between them all, and it is balance that the Kabbala seeks. Tipareth is the sphere of art and art is perfect balance between emotion and intellect. This weekend was held on a solstice. It was a Tipareth weekend.

We did a group ritual in a huge circle on the beach at midnight. John took it. We all had cloaks. They were different colours for how advanced you were. Mine was purple. Doing a ritual like that there in that huge natural amphitheatre was a buzz. There is a mood of common identity and purpose. Maybe that's what magic is. These were good people. They were people who wanted to change the world for the better and it is a noble cause to devote one's time and effort to. In fact there is none nobler. I have affection for them, love in some cases. We shared a part of our young lives. The next morning we did a Dawn Ritual. Ra was invoked. Waves the size of three-storey houses smashed against the cliffs to our left and the sea glowed red. We went for a frolic in the sea later and I lost my wedding ring. It was silver with leaves engraved on it. The Pacific Ocean took it. I bought another.

I was working in the hospital one afternoon when two plainclothes police officers turned up on the ward. They wanted to talk to me about Gerry. I don't know how they knew I knew him but they did. They wanted to know if I knew where he was. I hadn't seen him for a while but I'd heard he'd left Sydney and was a patient in a mental hospital somewhere, and this is what I told them. When I asked them what it was about they told me he was wanted for a racist murder that took place several weeks before. He'd shot a man in the back of the head. I never heard from him again but I found out that at the time the police were asking me about his whereabouts, he was actually a patient on another ward in the very hospital we were talking in. It didn't surprise me to hear what he had done. Gerry was insane. It was clear as an azure sky in spring.

I got transferred to the admissions ward. I liked it there. It was like an A and E ward in a general hospital. The patients were in crisis when they were brought in. They needed delicate treatment. There were a few regulars, alcoholics, and as soon as they were sober enough to walk they'd doll up in their Sunday best and hit the local pubs. There was shoe-cleaning equipment on a bench in the corridor on the way out of the ward, and they'd all take a big scoop from one of the open tins of polish with their fingers as they passed and swallow it. It would put a spring in their step. They'd straighten their ties or comb their hair or adjust their hats to a cocky angle and saunter off. I hadn't known that there was alcohol in boot polish. They used to drink Brasso too. I talked to a patient, a young girl who was brought in one evening. She was seventeen and very beautiful. I was enthralled. The next day we talked again. She told me that she'd been lying in bed in the night and an African witchdoctor had appeared in a beam of moonlight in front of her. She told me his face was painted blue. She said that he shook a rattle and smiled at her with a mouthful of rotting teeth. She said that she'd been terrified. She asked me if I knew what he wanted. The dear girl was lost in madness. I wanted to hug her but I didn't.

One day I was told that I was on Special Obs for a week. This meant that it was my responsibility to keep permanent tabs on a particular patient who was deemed to be at risk for some reason or other. I was told to watch a broken-looking guy who was severely depressed. You couldn't just sit there watching him every second because you still had your other routine work to do, but you had to know where he was. A couple of days later I was working near the charge nurse's office when the phone rang. The charge nurse was outside doing something near me and he told me to answer it. I told him I was on Special Obs, but the patient was there sat near us and he told me to do as he said. The call was about some trivial matter and when I came out to tell him I noticed that the patient was gone. I mentioned this and he told me to find him. I searched for an hour and went back and told the charge nurse I'd had no luck. He phoned the main office and a search was mounted. I went off duty. When I came in the following day I heard that the patient had drowned himself in an inlet just outside the hospital grounds. I had to go straight to the main office. When I got there I was told that I was guilty of gross negligence and I had the choice of quitting or getting fired. I was very upset about the whole thing. I told them the circumstances and that I just did what I was told to do by the charge nurse. They put in a phone call and the charge nurse and another senior nurse from came over from the ward. I asked him to confirm my story and he said that I was lying. He said he hadn't told me to answer the phone. He said that the patient hadn't been sitting there and he didn't know what I was talking about. The other nurse confirmed his story and I was fucked. I never went back to the ward. I was out. It was a big thing a patient on Obs killing himself. These guys were career nurses. They were watching each other's backs. The way they just stood there and lied. It upset me a lot. It reinforced my growing sense of cynicism. I went home and cried.

I got a job as a stock control clerk with George Salter Springs in Marrickville, a rural suburb three busses away from Balmain. It was the same George Salter who made weighing scales. I worked in an office on the factory floor. The work was horrific and once again I was rubbish at it, but I managed to cover it somehow. They were an okay bunch. The factory manager and my immediate boss was a short, no nonsense Aussie named Harry Langdon, which was also the name of a legendary American comedian. Harry was okay and it was generally accepted that he was shagging his assistant, a bouncy brunette whose name I forget, but since he was also married with two kids it wasn't brought up in conversation. We used to go to the local Ex-Servicemen's Club when business was slack some lunchtimes and play billiards and get tanked. I liked the people.

I was asked to help out on the factory floor one morning. There had been a rush order and it was all hands to the pump. I had to sit at a machine, a three-ton press, put small pieces of wire into a groove, depress the press with a foot pedal and throw the resultant small brass springs into a box. I did it for a while and my concentration wandered. I got the sequence of my actions wrong and pressed the foot pedal too soon. It was on a hair trigger and the next thing I knew I'd cut the top off the index finger on my right hand. The finger was severed below the fingernail. It was just hanging on by a piece of skin. The severed part was black. I stood up, walked over to Harry with the severed top resting in the palm of my other hand and he called me an idiot and ordered one of the other guys to drop everything and shoot me down to the hospital accident and emergency ward. The guy took him at his word and drove there like a madman. The injury was such that we didn't have to wait. I was taken to a room and the doctor who came to see me said that I needed immediate surgery. I was given a shot of pethidine for the pain and it really did the trick. This was in the early days of what was then called micro-surgery, and as fate would have it there was an American specialist in the field in the hospital at the time, training Australian surgeons in the technique. They asked if I'd mind a group of these trainees watching the American operate on me, on my finger. I was high on the pethidine at the time and would have agreed to anything so I said why not. I had another hit of pethidine before the actual op and half-a-dozen injections into the finger itself to kill the feeling, so by the time the surgeon started sewing my fingertip back on I was on another planet. I remember him working away while talking to the assembled host, and though I could hear his voice what he was saying made no sense to me. There were regular spurts of blood but it was as if it was all happening to someone else. I saw a row of tiny men dancing a jig together outside the window on the sill. I didn't find it odd. It just made me laugh. I woke up several hours later with my finger heavily bandaged and my hand hoisted up above my head by a pulley device. I remember thinking that the loss of my fingertip was the first step in a series of what were going to be ever-more-serious accidents of a similar kind. My hand would be next, then my arm and so on. I was convinced of this to the degree that I had already begun to reconcile myself to it. Fortunately I was wrong. Kate was there with me. She came in every day. One time one of the doctors said that I was a lucky fella having so many good-looking women coming to see me. He was referring to a visit from the woman Harry was shagging in work the previous day but Kate got very irate. She walked out in fact, and the doctor was visibly embarrassed. He apologised to me but I couldn't see what the big fuss was about. Kate had been jealous. It seemed an inopportune time and place to display it, but there you go. She'd calmed down by the time I got home but I was disappointed. How could she possibly think something like that of me? We'd only just got married for God's sake.

I was on the sick for four or five months. The finger was very painful and the healing process was slow. It put a stop to my guitar practice too, and I'd been getting better. I'd even started writing songs. They were really bleak dirges at first, all in minor keys. 'No slender man with twined hands wringing out his dirt on a torn train seat could affect me so without those eyes that even in reflection are brown to such a strange intensity.' My writing hadn't really improved since my early adolescence I'm afraid, but I was enjoying it and the few other people who heard my efforts were not insulting, so I found it a drag that I couldn't press on.

Kate had started making scarves from strips of material and beads. She was very artistic and practical. They were cool and she hired a stall at Paddington Market on Saturdays to sell them. Paddington is the gay suburb of Sydney which, at odds with the Australian man's self-image, is the gay capital of the world, and they sold quite well. My finger was getting better and I started to go out again. I had a hassle with George Salters, which had been investigated after the accident. There had been no safety guard on the machine when I was operating it but they put one in straight after and denied that it wasn't there at the time of the accident. They had also paid me full wages while I was off and were annoyed at how long my recovery was taking. I thought fuck them in the end and I didn't go back. Never trust an employer. It's a simple bit of advice but a good one.

It strikes me in writing this how serious we all were. How serious I was. The group members had convinced themselves of the profound importance of what we were doing. They believed that we were playing an integral part in the creation of a new human order. They believed that we had all met before in other lifetimes, that we had been magicians then too and that what we were doing now was the fruition of centuries, millennia of our effort and planning. Even though I was an acknowledged cynic it's hard not to get swept up in such a wish-fulfilling delusion. I'd started doing middle pillar and full tree rituals by this time too and they had a reinforcing quality. They could be quite moving, quite powerful in a way. John told us about how he could fly and how he could see into our souls. He gave tantalizing hints that he was Pan in human form. When confronted by people who found this personal deification incongruous to the groups' aims and ethos he'd preach against it, but he didn't preach against it very hard. I was right about John of course, he was just another product of the times, but I didn't realise how destructive to others such megalomania could be till later.

THE INITIATE

We moved to a flat in another part of Balmain. It was the second floor of a beautiful old house near the jetty where the ferry stopped to take passengers to Circular Quay. There were the macabre remains of Lunar Park, an old funfair, across the water and the Harbour Bridge to our right. The most striking thing about Lunar Park was the entrance gate: an enormous gaudily painted clown's head. It was horrific: the motiveless grin, the hate-filled eyes, the disdain. The entire place was monstrous in fact. It had been a top tourist attraction throughout the fifties and sixties but got gutted by fire and left derelict in 1966. It was like the silent, ghostly fairground in *The Carnival of Souls*. Why they hadn't pulled it down is beyond me. The flat itself was a gem. It had two huge bright airy rooms with high ceilings and white walls and a balcony. I started playing guitar again and life was good. The group rented a bigger space near where we lived and moved temple. Money was spent. It was impressive, a big room, a large storeroom of some kind probably, empty but for a purple silk marquee at one end. Inside the marquee, the temple itself, the thrones, the swords, the regalia, all set in predetermined order inside a ring of gold. There was a smell of burning charcoal and incense. We did rituals on a regular basis. It was the core activity of our lives. We discussed Magic. We shared our little triumphs and failures. Someone would have been astral travelling and they'd tell us what it was like. Someone else would be researching the tarot, say, in depth and would share his discoveries with us. Someone saw the Hindu Elephant God Ganesh during a ritual. Sometimes people would be troubled. They'd wonder if they were just kidding themselves. Some went. Jacked it in. It's okay, Sport, but not for me. Most just carried on.

Hugo and me got jobs working nights at the international telephone exchange in Underwood Lane by the Quay. Our hours were ten to six thirty, five nights a week, overtime for weekends and holidays. The pay was good. Almost all the other telephonists on the night shift were transvestites and transsexuals. They performed cabaret in a nightclub called Les Girls. One of them saw my ring and asked if I was married. I said I was and he asked 'To a boy or to a girl?' They weren't a bad bunch. The received wisdom of the time told us that we were all bisexual; I don't think anyone really believed it but it gave a context to sexual experimentation for the gay at heart. I remember hearing once that one of the initiates, a guy named Jim Starling, had been found in bed with the notorious Bruce. He'd seemed quite straight to me. The notorious Bruce, incidentally, was married to the forties-style lesbian Mouse. The group was lubricated by sex. Everyone was doing it with everyone else. Not in an orgiastic sense, though that did go on, but in a 'we are all just motes of dust in a great sandstorm anyway so why not' way. John introduced tantra into the curriculum. John thought sex was good. It was just like breathing to him. He loved to be lusted after, and indeed who doesn't. There were of course people in the group who were not like that. There were young people, people with difficult pasts, people who'd had problems, emotional and in some cases mental. There were some very delicate people who were looking for some solidity in their lives. Many were desperate to be loved. Sometimes some of these people would be drawn into John's world of the meaningless fuck and they would not be equipped to handle that love had not flowed from it. There were people going back home to live with their parents. There were breakdowns. There was madness.

Kenton lived just behind us in a communal house with some other posh English blokes and a few girls. There was a child's playground between our houses. I used to push Kate on the swings. I called around to see Kenton one afternoon. He was just on his way out to score some skag. 'Won't be long. You can come with me if you like.' He was going to a house in Drummoyne. There was a bridge between Balmain and Drummoyne. There were two lanes one each way, and two other lanes behind barriers, one on either side for busses. Charles drove like a man determined to kill himself. I've driven with some nutters in my time, some real nutters, but Charles was in a class of his own. He drove an old Volkswagen. I don't know how fast these cars go but this one was flat out from the moment we pulled out from the parking space outside his house. Flat out. He rounded corners on two wheels. He looked crazy. As we approached the bridge I saw that the traffic was backed up. Charles seemed to delay an age. He just carried on belting towards the back of the last vehicle. He slammed his foot on the brakes but it was too late. We hit the other car hard. The back was crushed in and it had shunted forward and smashed into the rear of the car in front as well. There was smoke. After the initial shock the driver of the car in front got out of his car and began to inspect the damage. Kenton reversed the Volkswagen until he smashed into the front bumper of a car that had screeched to a halt a few yards behind us, then he put the VW back into forward gear and smashed into the back of the car in front once again. Harder than the first time. A crowd had gathered. Kenton reversed again and, having moved the car in front further forward, had just enough space to pull out around it and zoom flat out the wrong way down the bus lane. Fate would have it that there was no bus coming the other way at the time. There was a ninety-degree left turn twenty yards the other side of the bridge. Kenton took it barely slowing down, and pulled to a shuddering halt outside a wooden-terraced house. 'Shan't be long, mate.' He came back five minutes later with a floppy-haired grin. 'My trip is in vein, mate. Let's go!'

Kate and I were happy. The days were long and hot. We got to know the people who lived next to us and shared our veranda. I was learning songs. I'd sit out on there in the evenings and serenade the neighbours. They didn't mind. They liked it. I started to listen to Bowie. The guys at work had told me about him. He was a big hero there because of his ambiguous sexuality. I remember sitting in the flat with Kate cutting my hair in front of the window and listening to *Ziggy Stardust* for the first time. 'Didn't know what time it was. The lights were lo-o-ow.' He was a magician. His lyrics contained endless Kabbalist references. 'I'm closer to the Golden Dawn, immersed in Crowley's uniform of imagery.' 'Oh no love you're not alone!' We delighted in such confirmation. He was one of us.

I started playing at a health food restaurant called The Marble Path. It was the kind of place where people sat on the floor to eat. It was probably vegan, in fact. I sat on a small stool in an enclave lit by candles and plucked away at my mournful ballads in half-hour stretches. I couldn't really play, sometimes I forgot how to form the chords mid-song so I'd just put my fingers anywhere and pretend it was a planned improvisation. The customers were so deeply involved in the world of esoteric hippness that they bought it too, and I'd get complimented on my avant-garde approach. I got fifteen bucks a night, which was good, and a free meal, which was inedible.

The time arrived when I was ready to do my initiation ritual. It involved a night alone in the temple and a series of banishments and invocations. I went in at six o'clock, slept in the circle and did a final initiation ritual at dawn. When I came out into the sunlight I had a great feeling of accomplishment. It had been a long and often difficult haul. I went home and slept the sleep of the dead.

A few weeks later we went on another ritual weekend, this time to a piece of land in the country which one of the ever-expanding band of new members owned. There must have been eighty to a hundred people there. The group was becoming notorious. We sat around campfires in the nights drinking wine and playing music. John and the Boomp took centre stage with their slow blues and rollicking sing alongs, 'Season of the Witch', 'Coming into

Los Angeles', 'High Flying Bird', it was good stuff. Others, myself included, would grab floor spots. I was writing songs about magic. They'd catch the mood sometimes and the stars would sparkle that little bit brighter. I had a new kudos now I was an initiate. One night I was designated to actually take a huge Tree ritual. Everyone was involved. They lay side by side in a huge circle and I stood in the middle in my cloak. I took them through the relaxation stage by having them visualise a journey through the planets, then we did the ritual sphere by sphere using imagination and incantation. The sound of all of those people intoning the beautiful words of the spheres in the still night air together was very moving. Such is the power of common thought and purpose. Such is the power of human connection. It was a great success. I was a natural. Later that night a blonde woman sat next to me and fond-led my arse. She said she wanted to shag me. I declined but I had a hard on like Cleopatra's Needle. She said she'd suck my cock. I declined again. I was a married man.

I started getting ill a lot. I felt tired. I'd tremble for no reason. I'd get mysterious rashes. I started to believe that I was seriously ill. There was a hospital near where we lived and I went to the A and E ward regularly, often in the early hours of the morning in a state of panic. One night I got it into my head that I'd been bitten by a poison-ous caterpillar and was actually dying. A lump came up on my forearm and I was sure that it was cancerous. I had spasms. I became convinced that I was going to die. I was paralysed with morbid thoughts. This lasted for several months but then faded. I changed jobs. I joined the Civil Service, tax again. I caught the ferry to and from work –

a large office in a tower block. My immediate boss was a young guy with thick glasses who was a noted long-distance runner. He was very nice, good at his own job but no slave driver. The work was shit, needless to say, but I developed a system whereby I didn't do it. I just hid the files when they came to me and people assumed they'd been actioned and sent to some other department. I hid them in an old metal storage cupboard in a corridor. No one ever caught me. There were other heads working there. We formed a little group. Rodney Dobelle was a short, heavily bearded young guy with a permanent bemused smile. I first met him in the staff toilets where he'd taken an urgent file and was ripping it into pieces and flushing it down the pan. He was my kinda guy. There were two others, Peter West, a tough-looking, working-class lad, and another big guy with heavy eyebrows. There was a staff recreation room with a table-tennis table and comfortable chairs where most people spent their lunch breaks on the floor below us. We got into a routine where each of us would bring in a three skinner every day and we'd meet up and smoke them in the basement of the stairwell. Then we'd go to a local sandwich shop, get two pressed chicken, cucumber and mustard sandwiches on white bread and return to the recreation room to eat them and play table tennis for the rest of the break. The stairwell stank of ganja right up to the top floor. We'd be as ripped as rats and our games would soon degenerate into clownish mayhem. We'd fling ourselves around like madmen trying to get to impossible shots. We'd crash into people sitting around or land on the table and collapse it with a bang. How they didn't twig that we were zomboid is beyond me. Rodney came back to my place a few times and we became mates. He joined the group. There was another new member named Rodney Speed so our Rodney became known as Slow Rodney to differentiate.

We stayed with Kate's family quite often at this time. I got to know them better. Margaret was a refined and sensitive woman. She was always sad. I assumed perhaps wrongly that she was grieving for a wasted life. Neville came across as an arrogant, unkind, unthinking man. His own children despised him. I think that that is what made Margaret so very rueful. I think that she had wanted her children to have a father they could love and respect. I think that she wanted a husband she could love and respect. I also got the feeling that she had once believed him to be that man and was proven wrong. Neville used to sit up until three in the morning when everyone else had gone to bed listening to classical music. He listened to recordings of an American radio comedian named Stan Freburg too. They were very good, brilliant in fact. Neville had heard them hundreds of times. He'd sit in his special armchair in his dressing gown and slippers and drift away. He'd drink a half a bottle of whisky too. I began joining him. It was then that I discovered that he was a drug addict. He was addicted to prescription drugs, downers, Mogodon. Downers are sleeping tablets, very strong ones. People who get into them in a druggie way take them then force themselves to keep awake and then, often enhanced with the use of alcohol, they enter into a euphoric state of inert contentment. The company of downer freaks is normally unbearable. Neville was an exception to this rule. We talked. We had long involved conversations. I discovered that he held the record for the fastest motorbike ride between Sydney and Newcastle. I discovered that he thought that the natural order of things was that he should be obeyed. I discovered that he had been bankrupting the family by feeding a secondary addiction to poker machines, which is what the Aussies call one-armed bandits. I discovered that on some days he'd lose a thousand dollars. All in coins pushed into slots. He was in the business, the poker machine business. It was a bit shady. He had a handgun and a licence to use it. He told me that he'd been going to a particular pub for a while, a club, and there was a big fat guy there, another businessman, who used to bump people out of the way with his big fat stomach. He told me the guy was a prick, a bully. When he did this it was presented as a joke, a bit of fun, but he and everyone else knew it was done to belittle the other man. He knew that the time would come when this guy did it to him and sure enough it did. Neville could see the fat guy waddling toward him as he stood at the bar. As the guy neared, Neville turned to face him with his jacket open, casually revealing his pistol strapped into a shoulder holster. Neville said the guy stopped, looked at him for a moment, and thought better of it. I think the guy made a wise choice. Neville was respected. He moved in high circles at a local level. I think he was a Freemason. He too felt profoundly disappointed with how his life had turned out. He should have been an army officer in time of war. He needed the grand stage to express what was in him but he'd ended up as a scrabbling businessman in a backwater town. Worse, he'd accepted it. No wonder he hated himself. I don't know if it was anything to do with me, with our chats, but I thought that he became a nicer person in the time that I knew him. I do remember that I grew to like him.

AWED MAN OUT

We moved house again, this time to a small, whitewashed cottage just off the main shopping street in Balmain, further towards town. It stood back off the road in its own patch of land and was a sort of fairytale place, unexpected in that environment. We had two rooms, a bedroom and living room with kitchen. A slim brunette woman and her boyfriend, a quiet straight transvestite, lived in the rest of the place. She worked in some sort of office job and got dressed in a smart black suit to go to work each day. The rest of the time she was a hippie. They had a lovely little dog, a poodle. She adored it. We had hamsters. They were a sweet little bunch and we made a hutch outside for them to live in. Kate was earning money by painting people's portraits at fifty bucks a time. They were good. She started one of me on a piece of hardboard but never finished it. It just sat there in the corner, my head and face staring uselessly, my glasses reflecting untrue light. Kate's brother David had moved to Sydney to work and we saw quite a lot of him. He and Kate had a difficult relationship. I think he identified her with his father. She certainly had some of his qualities. She sought conflict. She could be cutting and hurtful. David was determined not to continue being fucked around now he had escaped from his father and Speers Point and gave as good as he got. He was a deep person, taciturn, but wary of that giving the wrong impression. We were good mates. He was tough too, and I sometimes got put in the embarrassing position of having to intervene on Kate's behalf in raging arguments. He understood my position, though, and would retreat from the conflict out of deference to my

176

dilemma. He could have knocked me out cold with little effort but he was too much of a man for that. He'd just leave and come back a few days later.

I went up the road to do some shopping one afternoon and found my neighbour's poodle dead at the side of the road – it had been hit by a car. I picked it up and carried it home. She was in work and her boyfriend was away somewhere for a few days, so after giving it some thought I dug a hole in the garden and buried it. I met her outside when she came home and told her what had happened. She broke down. It was very sad. We put up a cross with the little creature's name on it and held a short ceremony. I cuddled her and she sobbed into my shoulder. What a fragile thing life is and how fragile we are. I'd started to feel uneasy.

We'd been socialising with some people from the group who'd rented a house nearby. We'd started studying acupuncture. There was a bloke called Doctor Lock of the Hong Kong School of Acupuncture and we were studying with him to get a practitioner's certificate. The people in the house were fellow students and we'd go around to test each other and to chill. I was drinking a lot; I'd got into Southern Comfort. We used to sit around and get plastered. It was a weird scene. There was a seedy decadence. Everyone was so self-obsessed. That meant that nothing mattered because things only matter when people matter. Kate didn't come home one night. She went out to see someone and she didn't come back. It turned out that she'd spent the night with Rodney Speed, one of the blokes who lived in the other house. Rodney was a soft-spoken Jesus lookalike from Bristol who'd come to

Australia as an adult a few years before. He had brown eyes. His trip was to play the overwhelmed boy, a common ploy to get laid at the time, and it worked. He drove a powerful motorbike too, and that gave him a frisson of butchness. He just wanted to love and be loved. This was run-of-the-mill fare within the social scene of the time but I had never considered that it could happen to me. She came home eventually and I found out what had happened. I was devastated. I didn't know what to do. I had a profound fear of abandonment. Things got even harder to relate to when Kate told me that she was going to carry on shagging Rodney and I'd just have to lump it. I was disoriented. I'd thought that we were special. I thought that we had been lovers in lifetime after magical lifetime. I thought we were different from the others. A lot of people think that about their relationships. The truth is of course is that no one is different. It was simple lust that broke the spell, as it so often is. Kate wanted to have sex with other blokes and Rodney was the first. I wanted to have sex with other women. At that age I can honestly say that I never met a woman I didn't want to have sex with. I can more or less say it now but I had eschewed that path at that time in favour of our mystical bond. Kate was true to her word and spent most nights with her new beau. I hit the boozers big time. I played pool with Kenton. I went to parties. I got stoned. I was sure that everyone knew and as far as I can remember they did. Most refused to take sides. The common reaction was 'What's the big deal? Everyone fucks every-one. Why is he so uncool about it?' But there was pity too. Can you imagine being pitied in a situation like that? Not one single voice said 'To hell with her!' I watched the big cranes moving the containers down in the floodlit dockyard from our veranda all through the night. Kate would come back some nights. She'd even sleep in our bed but it was like sleeping with a murderer. To think of him, Rodney, touching her, fucking her, having his cock sucked by her, was more than I could bear. I knew that they had gone to visit friends in Ford Street one night and I walked up there and stood opposite the house in the dark. His motorbike was parked outside. I could see lights on inside and heard laughter coming from the front room. It was raining heavily. I wanted to die. If I had been mentally or physically capable I would have gone over there and kicked the bearded Bristolian bastard's teeth down his throat. I found myself at a party in a house I didn't know down by the harbour a few nights later and ended up in bed with the woman who lived there, the one who was throwing the party. She appeared to know me from somewhere. She might have been a nurse. Everyone had gone and we started kissing. She stripped off and went into the bedroom. I followed her. The following morning she got up early to go to work and I was sent packing. I felt crazy. I felt like I was the craziest man in the world. I was considering killing myself. Then it finished. I don't know why but Kate forsook Rodney and came back home to carry on as we had before. I accepted the situation. What else could I do? I loved her.

Things returned to normal with ease. We listened to *Led Zep 4* and *Transformer*. We met in town for lunch in the park. We watched *Hogan's Heroes*. I played in a concert in a converted church in Kings Cross. A guy named Reno Dahl promoted it; I'd met him some time before at a party.

He'd followed me around all night dressed as Sherlock Holmes. It wasn't a fancy dress party, he was tripping. He was in the company of half-a–dozen-cool young people of his ilk. They were theatrical. Anyway, I think he saw me play somewhere and dug it so when he organised this concert he stuck me on. Kate made me a beautiful sequined T-shirt and I had my face painted with a pastel landscape. Sounds daft now but I was deadly serious. Even now, broken and disillusioned as I was, I was still the lead actor in the film. There were about a hundred people at the gig. A Chinese guy played first, one of Reno's friends. He played slide guitar and had a voice like an angel. His name was Phillip Mar. John Strangeways and Chris Boomp De Doomp played next. They were really good. They were brilliant, in fact. John played with a full deck of fingerpicks and a permanent bottleneck in the form of a thick glass ring. His only problem was the one that dogged him in everything. I saw it, I knew it, I recognised it. Though excellent at many things, John wasn't good enough at any of them. I went on last and sang a little cycle of songs. I began it with a mantra that we used, 'All things in all times in all places are one and that thing is love,' and then went into 'East Berlin', a song I'd written about the crucifixion. I segued into 'Lily Marlene', 'And we will meet there once again, beside the lantern in the rain. As once Lily Marlene. As once Lily Marlene.' It went down very well.

Me and Kate had talked about going back to Wales to visit and the time seemed right. We didn't know how long we were going to be away so Petah and Jeshua and her brother Lyndsay took over our lease till we got back. We quit our jobs and went to Speers Point to for a few days before leaving. Neville took us out on his motorboat. He was laughing, he had the wind in his hair. He was in his element.

SHOOTING STAR

I read *The Man in the Glass Case* by Colin Wilson on the flight to London. It was about a serial killer who leaves quotes from the works of William Blake at the scenes of his murders. It quite disturbed me. Kate had never been on a long flight like this before and she loved it. We watched the movies and drank gin and tonics. Ool met us at Heathrow. He'd driven up with Sion. We drove back to Wales on a wet and misty winter's afternoon. Australia, as I have said, is a stunningly beautiful country. Its colours are sharp, its landscapes huge and savage, it is thrilling. Wales, on the other hand, is a land of forests and gentle hues. If Australia is painted in oils, Wales is painted in watercolours. I'd missed it. Kate was knocked out. Britain seemed so much classier than Australia, the newspapers were serious, the television was markedly superior, intellectual discussion wasn't frowned on. As far as I can figure it this would have been the end of 1973. We got Naine's room and she moved into my old room for the duration of our stay. Kate was an impressive and likeable person. She got along famously with everyone. Ool thought her a 'lovely girl', Naine had unspoken reservations, of course, but they remained unspoken. My mother enthused in a manic, almost hysterical, way and Audrey thought her a bit stuck up. By my family's standards this was a thumbs up. It was cold. Kate got cold in a sauna. Here she was Frosty the Snowgirl. Her nose got all red and sniffly. I kept her as warm as I could. I kissed her a lot. We had a few weeks of visiting people and sightseeing, the usual suspects, old friends, relatives, Cardiff Castle, and then it was Christmas. We found Mel. He'd got married and moved to a rough housing estate in Trebanog. Him and his brother Robert called in at the house. He played us some cassettes, Bad Company, Shooting Star. I played a few songs on my guitar. We went out and got drunk. I caught up with Steve Dudley. He was living in Mill Street. We got into some guitar playing. He was still great. It was cool seeing old friends. The Glam Rock era was in full swing. Kate loved *Top of the Pops*, Marc Bolan, Slade, Bowie, Queen. We had a welcome home drink in the rugby club. Kate found Welshmen very gentlemanly. Christmas was a success. Uncle Ike turned up sober. I think he had been severely warned. We watched a film about Jack the Ripper on TV. *Carnal Knowledge* was on too. We were enjoying ourselves. Kate hit it off with Brian and particularly Frances. We'd go up to their house and drink tea and have quizzes. Brian had been unwell for some time. He had problems with his bladder and recurring back pain. It was getting him down. He was the manager in the betting shop next to the Red Cow. Horse racing played a big part in his life. He was more or less obsessed with it; it was in the family. Frances found it hard, I think she felt alone. Blaine drove down from Scotland and took us back up to stay with him over the new year. It started snowing the moment we crossed the border. It was pitch black and the snow was spectacular. It was like some huge hand had turned the world upside down and shaken it. Kate had never seen the like before.

Blaine and Morag lived in a tenth-floor flat in a tower block in Wester Hailes, a huge estate on the outskirts of Edinburgh. It was a cold uninviting place. It was great being with Blaine. We'd sit up late drinking and chatting. Morag was being a bitch though, and kept calling out to him to go to bed. She was very possessive, almost hysterically so. Her brother Gary visited. I met him in Jersey where he was working, and he was a cool guy. He brought the new Bowie album, *Pinups*. Wester Hailes was a virtual ghost town. There was a bitter wind blowing most of the time we were there. Slates fell from the roof twenty storeys up and crashed to the paved walkways below like hurled flowerpots. Someone could easily have been killed. Someone had been killed the week before we got there. There were police posters up everywhere showing hideously scarred faces and saying that this knife attack had taken place within a hundred yards of where you were standing. There was one in the local fish and chip shop. The groups of tower blocks were linked by subterranean walkways straight out of *A Clockwork Orange* and the vibe was not good. We stayed a week or so then went home by train.

Since we had decided to stay for a while, a matter of months anyway, we had to figure out a way to earn a few bob, so Kate suggested we do some acupuncture. We'd both acquired our qualifications and had worked at a group-run place called The Healing Centre in Sydney for a few months before leaving, so it seemed a good idea.

We'd brought our needles and charts over with us so we decided to give it a go. We used the big front room downstairs as our work place. Kate hung white blinds in the windows to make it look clinical and, with our certificates displayed proudly on the wall we let it be known that we were there. Kate treated a few people we knew first, and there were some definite results. The word spread and before we knew it we were treating two or three people a day. Most were elderly and suffering from the traditional Welsh ailments of arthritis and rheumatism. Acupuncture is particularly good in treating these ailments and Kate was very good at it. Our name spread. We were contacted by a journalist from *The South Wales Echo* who wrote an article about us and published it with a photograph and contact details. Business took off. I was never a hundred per cent convinced about acupuncture. I kept it in my dubious box, but people seemed to respond and it was wonderful to see so many positive results. *The Echo* said that we were the first acupuncturists ever to set up a practice in Wales.

Winter drifted into spring. Although everything seemed okay I had started to get very down. My neck had started aching. You'd have thought I could have cured it with acupuncture, right, but it did no good, it became a constant pain. It was the same pain I had when I'd had the bad trip. LSD was often mixed with arsenic in those days to heighten its effect and I had assumed it was that, but I'd had no LSD this time, no arsenic. I spent a lot of time in bed. I felt nauseous. I went to the quack but he could do nothing. I had to stop the acupuncture work but Kate persevered. Brian was unwell too. He was in

The Lemmings,
Amsterdam, 1978

Charles Normal, The Lemmings,
Amsterdam, 1978

The Lemmings,
Amsterdam, 1978

The Lemmings,
Amsterdam, 1978

Boyd looking over the balcony at
155, Haarlemmerweg, Amsterdam

155, Haarlemmerweg,
Amsterdam

John, Schweppes, Leonie, Zonderman, Kate, and
Boyd. John and Leonie's wedding, Amsterdam, 1978

Charlie, John, Leonie, Sue, Schweppes, Kate,
Zonderman, Boyd, Hurk and Victor.
John and Leonie's wedding, Amsterdam, 1978

Boyd, Amsterdam, 1978

Kate, Amsterdam, 1978

The Lemmings, Bodies Music Inn, Amsterdam, 1978

John, Victor, Boyd, Charlie and Silas
on the roof of Fannius Schoultens Straat, 1978

Boyd in Holland, 1978

Silas, Victor, John, Boyd, Charlie: The Lemmings, 1978

The Lemmings, 1978

Boyd at the zoo, 1978

Victor, Charlie, Boyd, John, Silas

The Lemmings, Amsterdam

Schweppes, Boyd, Kate and Weenie the dog
in the garden, Vernon Road, Leytonstone, 1979

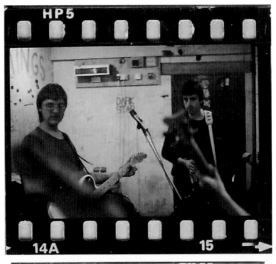

Rehearsals, London, 1979

The Lemmings, London, 1979

The Lemmings, London, 1979

Jane, Sydney, 1981

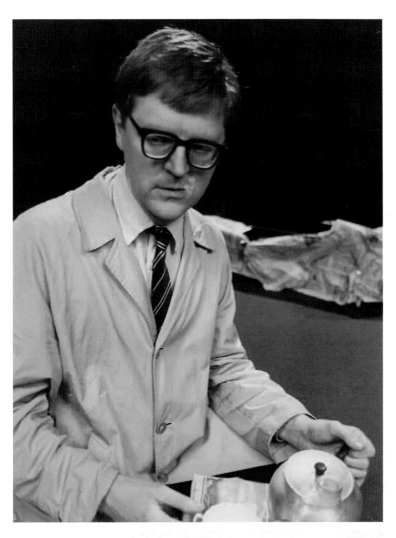

Boyd playing the title role
in 'Christie in Love',
Edinburgh, 1985

Statues of Us, Nash Point, South Wales, 1985

Boyd, Ted Dawson and Mark Lewis Jones (The Puppy),
Welsh College of Music and Drama, 1986

hospital. A neighbour took me to see him one afternoon and I began to feel ill in the car. He had to pull over and I got out and vomited uncontrollably. I was frightened. I thought that it could be something very serious. I'd lie in bed listening to the people downstairs talking and laughing as they watched TV. How could they just carry on like that when I was so ill? Getting angry only made the pain worse. Kate and I decided to go back to Sydney. Our return tickets allowed us a stop over of up to six months anywhere en route: we chose Greece. I collapsed at Heathrow airport and they put me in a wheelchair. I had to see a doctor who okayed me for the flight and we arrived at Athens on a Sunday evening. Hugo was travelling overland to join us there on his way back to Sydney, after having been back to visit his parents when we were in Wales. We met him and booked in to The Hotel Pappadopoulus in the city centre for the night. I was still feeling terrible and things came to a head. I was panicking. I thought that I was dying. At two o'clock in the morning Kate contacted reception, who gave us the number of a doctor who did emergency call outs. We rang him and he turned up an hour later. He was a short, handsome, immaculately dressed guy and he knew his stuff. I could hardly move by this time. The pain had spread down my spine. I was crying in fear. The doctor gave me a thorough examination and then began asking me questions in broken English. He wanted to know if I drank a lot of spirits. I told him I stuck to beer and he looked at my arms. He gave me an injection, which he said would help, and if it didn't I should go to a hospital the following day. The visit cost a thousand drachmas, a lot of money but fair enough in the circumstances. I slept the sleep of the dead and when I woke up I was cured. It was miraculous. The pain was gone, simply vanished.

We went to look around Athens. It was a fantastic feeling being in such an ancient and famous city. All the buildings shone in the brilliant sunlight. The colours, the noises, the traffic. We went to eat at a café. The food was tepid: spaghetti with meatballs and it was tepid. That's the way they have it. The beer was good though, German lager I think. We did a bit of shopping as I wanted sandals. I tried on a pair in a shoe shop but was undecided: they were expensive. The next day we went to the Acropolis. It glitters on a hillside within the city walls. I'd learned about the Greek Empire in history and it was strangely moving to be there in that hallowed temple in this legendary and beautiful city. I rested by a wall and looked down at the harbour. It was dominated by a huge American aircraft carrier. Two US marines stood next to me and had a fag. One was white and the other was black. They were handsome young guys and they looked almost angelic in their wing-white uniforms. We chatted and they told me they had two days shore leave from the carrier in the bay. They were incredibly polite.

I went back to the shoe shop on our way to the hotel. I'd decided to buy the sandals, but when I got there I discovered that armed police and soldiers had sealed off the shop. It had been blown up by a bomb the night before. It was just rubble. I'd had no idea, but this was a time of civil strife in Greece. A military coup was being planned to overthrow the popularly elected socialist government. This was a time of murders and bombings. It was a time of doors being knocked in the night, a time of

186

torture. When I learned this, the presence of the American aircraft carrier made sense. I felt well, really well. The doctor had thrown away the ampoule from which I got my wonder injection in a bin under the bed. It was still there. I got it out and looked at it. It was Valium.

mind games

We decided to go to stay on one of the islands which seemed a romantic idea. We got a ferry from Piraeus to Ios, a small island in the Cyclades group. The ferry ride was something else. My images of ancient Greece were more connected with the sea and islands than they were with the mainland. I think that's probably true of most everyone of my generation; we got it from films. The sea was as they depict it in those films, a greenish turquoise, and the prow of the ship cut through it leaving waves of white foam in its wake. I felt like Steve Reeves. The islands were faded greens and mauves. They watched us pass them by impassively. The sky was topaz blue, edged by rolling pink clouds, and the gulls were handkerchief white. It wasn't hard to imagine the gods up there looking down on us, moving us about like pieces on a chess board. Like I say, it was something else. We stayed in a bed and breakfast in Hora, the island's main town which was a bus ride from the harbour. White buildings, white streets, a few motor scooters, Coca-Cola and a TV set in the bar. It was pretty much inundated with Yanks. It was the same lot who came to Australia and Amsterdam. One über hippie told us that he played guitar in Jackson Browne's band and was visibly taken aback when I said I thought that Jackson Browne was shit.

We got fed up after a few days. I sat on a doorstep of one of the whitewashed buildings in the square and after a few moments I felt a presence behind me. It was a priest. He wanted to get past. I stood and let him do so. Some Greek people who were watching gave me very dirty looks. The priest himself had a formidable vibe about him. I'd been sitting on the front doorstep of his house I think. I left the square chastised. I was still afraid of God.

We decided to go to the mountains. We rented a small white house, miles from anywhere. It was more of a hut really, where the goatherd stayed in winter. There was no water, no electricity and no toilet. We were okay, though. There was bedding and an oil stove and a well nearby. There were goats too. The farmers kept them hobbled to prevent them straying, one leg trussed right up so they had to function on three. I thought it was cruel but the goats just got on with it. The local farmer or his wife would come to milk them every morning and they always left us a saucepan full outside our door. There were just two rooms. One was the living area where Hugo kipped and the other a bedroom with a raised stone bed which Kate and I commandeered. The roof was thatch. We went to Hora one day a week for supplies and lived well. Hugo had a portable cassette player and several Frank Sinatra tapes. It was there that I realised what a great singer Sinatra is. When he does 'Send in the Clowns' he leaves an almost imperceptible pause between 'Losing my' and 'timing'. There were other superb tracks on the albums too. Old Blue Eyes certainly enhanced the vibe.

I had a weird thing going on with my sleeping pattern. About an hour after going to sleep I'd wake up in a panic thinking there was something scrabbling about on my head. It felt like a bird or a bat or a large spider even. It was worrying, a sign of tension maybe. I didn't feel that wonderful despite the beautiful surroundings. I decided to stay awake one night. I just lay there next to Kate on the bed as she slept. I heard a noise in the thatch above the bed a short while later and detected movement. When it got to a point directly above my head a rat jumped down. It landed where it had been landing, on my head, and propelled itself from there off into the shadows. The scratching feeling on my face had been its little claws in the act of propulsion. Kate woke and I told her the news. It may sound daft but I like rats. Not just tame pet rats either, I like dirty rats. I like all animals. I wasn't sure at one time, I thought some were cool but others weren't. Then I found a pictorial book of snakes and there was a quote on the first page, which said 'They are not aimless wanderers, they live in little worlds of their own.' It was something I really liked about Jesus, his love of animals. He called them his children. Anyway, we decided the thing to do was to get the sort of rat trap that catches the rat in a cage and then take it somewhere away from the cottage and release it. It would no doubt have found another cottage somewhere. We went into Hora and incredibly the local shop had just the thing, so we bought it, took it home, primed it with cheese, put it under the table in Hugo's room and went to bed. We thought it best not to vary our routine or the rat might smell a rat, so to speak. We slept lightly and sure enough the rat made his customary entrance. He leapt from my head and scuttled off into Hugo's room. A few minutes later we heard the cage door snap shut. We leapt up and lit the oil lamp. The rat had a piece of cheese in its front claws and was eating away happily. He looked so cute. He was a gorgeous chap. We got dressed, though Kate was in dressing gown and slippers, and took the cage down towards the sea about a quarter of a mile by the light of the oil lamp. A strange little procession we must have looked. We opened the cage and the rat ran off into the night.

One of the really famous Greek mathematicians died on Ios. Archimedes maybe, and it was enchanting to think of him walking on these same hills all that time ago, looking at that same sea, lost in his great thoughts. I have always felt that I am living out of my time. My neck had started to hurt again. It was a pain that would not be ignored. It moved down my back. Hugo and Kate had the book *Mind Games*. It was a system of exercises that had some point to do with self-growth. I didn't really understand what it was for actually, but I did it nonetheless. It was meant to take a few weeks, with different exercises every day building up to a final breakthrough day at the end. It wasn't particularly involving and as the days went by I just got to feel more and more unwell. My neck and back were seizing up. I felt I'd been poisoned. I vomited with the pain. I began to realise that I was dying. I could feel my life draining away from me. I felt helpless and terribly sad and I talked to Kate. We came to the conclusion that I might be under attack by a succubus, an auric vampire that attaches itself to your spine, often during sex, and feeds on your Kundalini. A succubus can indeed be fatal. We decided to go straight back to Australia where I could get help from the group. John was a Master; he could handle a succubus surely. I was desperate. I'd try anything. We left Hugo behind, he was going to follow overland, and were back in Sydney three days later.

THE MESSIAH

When we got back home we went to find John straight away. He looked at my aura and said there was no succubus and so I was back to square one. I stayed in bed for weeks, a month or more, in both agonizing pain and a fatalistic torpor. Petah, Jeshua and Lindsay moved into the other part of the house when the transvestite and the beautiful poodle lover moved out. Lindsay's best mate Loci moved in shortly after. We lived together in effect. Nowhere was out of bounds, and Loci and Lindsay spent nearly all of their time in our place, drinking fresh ground coffee, watching telly and getting ripped. Petah was a strange and delicate being. She'd been taken to New York by one of her parents after they got divorced, it was her father I think, and she got pregnant and had Jeshua there by the time she was sixteen. It all sounded very exciting and romantic to me but she assured me that it wasn't. She returned to Australia and got a place of her own. She was nineteen when I met her. She and Kate were the best of friends. I liked her a lot. She seemed very brave to me, she was kind too, and funny. Lindsay was seventeen. When you first met him he appeared to be a bit thick but that was down to shyness. He was no Isaac Newton but he certainly wasn't thick either, he was a lovely lad. Loci, full name Lazlo Kosta, was eighteen and from an entire family of group members, mother, father and three sons. The father, Big Loci had fled Hungary at the time of the revolution – he'd fought and then fled when all was lost. He was a short, good-looking man with long black hair. He looked not unlike Roman Polanski. His wife Maureen was an Australian woman, short too with frizzy black hair, and somewhat birdlike features. They were a striking couple, sophisticated and modern. They wore nothing but black. Big Loci was in his early forties. They had three sons, Loci, Kerry and Marty. Their ages were close together. Little Loci was seventeen, Marty fifteen and Kerry thirteen, about that anyway. All three were short and very handsome. They all had long hair, in Marty's case very long, and had been brought up in a liberal environment. Big Loci and Maureen smoked dope with them. Sex was discussed freely. Their home had an artist's studio vibe about it. The boys all wore predominantly black too and to see them en famille was a spectacular sight. The boys were fantastic, charming and brooding. I liked them all.

Petah and Lindsay didn't have very good relationships with their parents. The mother had received a large compensation payment from a soft-drinks manufacturer after a pop bottle she was opening exploded and she was blinded in one eye by a shard of glass. I believe she lost the eye, in fact. I only ever met her once and she seemed crazy as a coot to me. The father was a tubby guy with a receding hairline and a bright red complexion. They refer-red to him as The Lighthouse because of the fiery red face and they appeared to hate him. I met him once or twice and he had an unkind, hysterical air to him. Lindsay told me that he felt physically sick in his father's presence. Anyway, these were the people I was living with at the time I took to my bed. Loci and Lindsay were permanent fixtures but I didn't mind; they were cool. Lying there in bed I'd hear the television on in the other room and it would make me cry. It was as if I'd already died and was looking back on the banality of life with profound poignancy. I was dying. Soon all of this, all the tiny physical details that make life what it is, would be lost to me forever. My neck tortured me. I could find no comfort, no position I could lie in to bring relief. Sometimes I'd get out of bed and just stand there in the curtained room. It was Hell.

One day an old boyfriend of Petah's named Allan turned up. It was a Sunday, grey and windy. I got up and sat in the living room with everyone and we had a chat. Allan was a film director. He'd been working away. He had one of those big round flat tins that they keep film in with him and he opened it up and it was packed tightly with the nicest ganja that you'd ever see. He'd brought it down from Queensland with him and was keen to get us all ripped. I hadn't smoked dope for ages, since leaving Australia to go home in fact, almost a year. I thought I'd have a toke to be sociable. Allan rolled a twelve-skinner, no mean feat, with a perfect cone. The guy knew his stuff. It got passed around and I puffed away. Ganja tastes and smells gorgeous and this particular stuff was obviously the business. It was in fact a type that was being grown in the hippie colony of Mullumbimby on the Gold Coast. It was known as Mullumbimby Madness. I got very stoned very quick, really zondered. I went back to bed and Kate came with me. We lay down in each other's arms. I could smell her lovely hair, feel it falling against my face and I relaxed. For the first time in a long time I really relaxed. Then I began to hear music, choral music, religious music. It sounded like Handel or Bach, maybe earlier. It swelled up and filled the room and it was like golden sunlight was pouring down onto me through huge stained-glass windows. We made love. Kate's skin was marble white.

My neck got better. It just got better. It's a fact that you can be ill for a long time but once you are better it fades from the memory very quickly. It figures, what's the point of dwelling on it. I regained my sparkle. By the time Hugo arrived a couple of months later we'd moved to a bigger place, a detached house on the Drummoyne to Gladesville road. It was lovely, all the houses in the road were. Kate and I had a huge bedroom at the front, Lindsay and Loci a smaller one next to us and Petah and Jeshua a medium-sized one behind them. There was a big sitting room at the back and a kitchen that opened out onto a massive garden, the left half uncultivated flowerbeds and the right lawn. There were smaller gardens to the front and sides filled with exotic plants, trees with dense hanging foliage and bushes with shining leaves and scarlet flowers the size of my fist. It was all on one storey of course, but this was a class residence. Hugo was housed in a small lean-to affair to the left of the kitchen out the back, and quite soon after we took residence Ian Bruce, the pianist, moved into the unused garage with his boyfriend, a girlish young chap with long blond hair and a beard. The household was augmented with the purchase of Sophis, a Basenji dog. He cost eighty bucks. Basenjis don't bark, they howl instead, a high-pitched, eerie howl. They climb trees too allegedly, but I never saw Sophis do it. He was the greediest son of a bitch I ever met. We were having a big meal one evening, we had guests, and I was set to peeling the spuds, fourteen pounds of them. I got it done and went to have a sit down and a spliff to recover. When I went back out ten minutes later Sophis' stomach was grossly distended. It was scraping the ground, huge and grotesque. He looked sick, really ill. The little fucker had eaten all the potato peelings, two plastic bags full of them. He would have eaten his own head if he could have reached it. Together with our cats KT, Marilyn, Mamanti and two others whose names escape me, that was our household. Oh yes, our hamsters had been killed by an Alsatian in the garden of the cottage a week before we moved. He'd ripped the front of their hutch open and torn them all to pieces. I chased him down the road with a hamster hanging from his mouth but to no avail. The hamsters were nice little chaps but I didn't really get to know them. I liked to think that they had gone to Hamster Valhalla but maybe they were in Hamster Hell. It all depended on whether they had been good hamsters or not. The Alsatian was fucked in that sense.

Kate got a job as a bus conductor, which she loved. She said that when you work on the busses the actual travelling, the moving about from place to place, ceases to have any relevance. She said it had a Zen quality. I got a job in King's Cross, working for a company called Venus Erotic Supplies. The office/warehouse was a room hidden away in the corner on the third floor of a multi-storey car park. My job was mail-order clerk. I received orders from the slips that appeared in dirty books and packed and posted them to the clients. We dealt in pornography, books and films from Germany, sex aids, vibrating vaginas and anuses, double dong dildos, wanking machines, butt plugs, S and M gear, lubricants, jellies, piss tables, dick enlargers, anything to do with fucking, you name it. It was an easy-enough job and I got to meet a lot of the prostitutes who advertised in our magazine. They thought I was very refined because I didn't want to fuck them. They offered me freebies but I declined. It wasn't easy; some of them were very tasty. The bosses were a German couple. He was an untidy, cigar-smoking bloke in his forties and she was a harsh-looking woman about the same age. They were very businesslike. What we sold was just a product. It ceased to have any shock value quite quickly. Whatever you deal in ceases to register after a while. It's the same with money when you work in a bank or as a wages clerk, it's just paper. I liked the porn though. There was one picture of a gorgeous, meaty brunette sat on a seventies-style settee with two blokes. She's sucking one of their cocks and she's got a beer bottle up her arse. She's got such a happy look on her face. They all looked so happy. You've got to admire the Germans. I was convinced that the boss and his Mrs were into all sorts of stuff but I never found out for sure. The wage was eighty dollars a week. That was a lot. The most I'd ever earned in my life.

The weather was sweltering and we put up a net between the clothes prop and the wall in the garden to create a volleyball court. We played either two or three a side for hours every day. We were all young, fit and stoned senseless and the games were whole hearted. It became a minor obsession. We sweated like we were melting and developed the routine of one of us going up the local shop between games to buy a dozen rocket-shaped iced lollies. We'd go through three or four dozen a day between us. Extreme physical exercise can be an ace buzz and this was. We'd buy half-a-dozen Sara Lee frozen apple pies too, big ones not individual. We'd bake them in the oven and have one each mashed up and drenched in cream. They were out-of-this-world gorgeous. I'd be so ripped when I was eating mine that I'd see the surface as being the surface of the moon and I'd feel as if I were walking on it. I'd actually think that I was wearing a space helmet. These were great days. I was playing guitar well too. I'd got to be friends with Phillip Mar, the Chinese friend of Reno Dahl who'd played so spectacularly at the concert in the church that time. He was an angel of a bloke, quiet, gentle and giving. He'd come over to the house and we learned some numbers together. He was infinitely better than me but he'd never give any indication that it mattered; on the contrary he was complimentary and encouraging. He wasn't from China; he was from Singapore or somewhere. His family owned a firm that made spring rolls. They were quite well off but Phillip wasn't. He lived in a flat with Reno whom he'd known since schooldays.

Don't ask me why, but I took acid again. It was a Saturday and everyone else was tripping and my memory had dimmed so I took half a tab. It wasn't as bad as the first time. When it came on I went and lay down on the grass in the back garden and stared up at the clouds. It seemed that they were weary grey creatures trudging home after a long day slaving in some hellish astral mine. Then I went indoors and sat on the floor in Petah's room with her and Kate. I was wearing Kate's gold silk dressing gown and nothing else. My pubic hair was golden red. Petah said it was beautiful. Kate and I went into our room and I started doing a slow dance in front of the dressing-table mirror. I could see stuttering silver trails left in the air by my hands and arms as they passed through it. Kate and I made love but it was uncomfortable and we abandoned it in favour of eating Kentucky Fried Chicken. That went awry too unfortunately when the pieces started to bleed. It wasn't the hell of the first time but I was glad when it was over.

Hugo was turning strange. He'd started doing primal scream therapy. It was based on the idea that we all have extremely deep unknown levels of pain from our childhood and infancy and that they disfigure our attempts to lead fulfilling lives and be happy. This was a theory expounded by Edward Janov, the writer, a psychologist with hippie leanings. Primal scream therapy involved getting back to the time these pains were initiated by relaxation and memory exercises and then releasing them through deep uncontrolled screaming. John Lennon had been extolling its virtues and Hugo threw himself into it with total commitment. He'd stay in the lean-to day and night screaming like a man being burned at the stake. It was disconcerting at first but we got used to it. Loci and Lindsay used to scream silently along with him whenever he started. Their faces would turn bright red with the effort. It was very funny, though Hugo had sacrificed his sense of humour as being distracting and he became distant and somewhat unfriendly. His state of mind was such that on top of everything else he became obsessed with *Tommy*, the rock opera by The Who. He believed it to be a profound work that spoke to him directly. It became a backdrop to the stand-off. Hugo got a girlfriend too but their relationship was such that they didn't mix with the rest of us. Hugo was crazy. He dabbled with the group from time to time but he was a loner. He had an emptiness deep inside the same as the rest of us, and this was his way of trying to fill it. He smoked ganja like it was compulsory, we all did. Loci and Lindsay made a dummy out of old newspapers stuffed into a suit. It had a head with a face and a hat and they sat it in a chair in the living room. They decided to try to see how long they could stay awake for some reason and Lindsay managed four days. He looked terrible.

We created a group newspaper. It was called *The Messiah* and we published it from home. It was very rudimentary but we sold fifty or so a time, which was cool. We had a write-in column where people would report spotting were-wolves, or lycanthropes as we called them. We regarded people who looked like lycanthropes to be lycanthropes. We'd publish a report that a lycanthrope was seen entering a supermarket in Glebe, for instance, or running for a bus in Redfern. We had a keen correspondence on the subject. There was also a whole page devoted to Victor Mature in each edition. I had become chairman of the Victor Mature Appreciation Society of Australia. I'd always been interested in him since I saw the classic *Samson and Delilah* in Ton pictures when I was about ten years old and thought that Samson, who was being played by Victor, was being played by Frankie Vaughan, a popular singer at the time. It amazed me to see Frankie like that, in a loincloth wrestling a lion. I was gripped. I learned the truth one day, of course, and since I'd always thought what a good actor Frankie was I was now forced to concede that Victor was the Boy. Not that I needed any forcing. There's a tale where Victor is doing a scene in a film and just as the cameras are about to roll the other actor stops it and asks Victor if he's all right. 'Your face, that expression, I thought...' 'That's my holy look,' Victor replied. In truth he was a good, and in some ways interesting, actor but we didn't love him for that. We loved him because when he was in frame on camera doing a scene and it called for him to exit, he always jutted his chin out in the required direction before beginning to move. It creased us up every time. I loved his performance in the Peter Sellers film *After the Fox*. He played a washed-up movie star come to Italy to make an existentialist film. He parodied himself with egoless commitment. He had the comic touch. I have the feeling that he was a nice guy. There was a gossip column, a joke page and other stuff that I forget too in *The Messiah*. It was fun. About this time I started playing at a wine bar called Ali's Oasis. It was an outdoor gig in the beer garden. They thought I was okay.

Sophis was knocked down and killed on the main road outside the house. We buried the little fellow in the garden where he used to play.

I heard that Kenton was ill. Someone said that he'd got a fungal infection of the brain from fixing up. He couldn't sleep because one of his eyes was affected and he couldn't close it. He had to go into hospital every second night for treatment and a drug-induced rest. I never saw him again. Charles was a remarkable person; I really liked him.

Reno was friends with a millionaire lighting guy named LSD Fogg. Fogg had a posh house in Surry Hills and had organised a media party to show off some new lighting equipment that he'd designed. He wanted live music so Phil Mar and I got the gig. We just sat about playing guitars and singing, basically, until everyone was ushered into a big room for the main event. The light show was very good, very trippy, but the thing that I remember it for was the music. It was the first time I ever heard *Dark Side of the Moon*. It was the continuation of my early love for Floyd. First 'See Emily Play' and now this. Floyd tap into a universal vibe. They mean a lot to me.

Phil was just the best of guys. When I went to his place to rehearse for the first time I had a look around and saw that there was only one bedroom. Who sleeps in here I asked. Me and Reno, Phil replied. But there's only one bed, I protested. I'd known Phil and Reno for years and it had never crossed my mind that Phil was gay and that he and Reno were an item. You could have knocked me down with a plectrum. This certainly wasn't Tonyrefail.

Mamanti was a black and white unneutered tomcat. His name was a Canadian Indian one, meaning Dream Walker. He was a tough little chap, all shoulders and hips. He didn't like being mollycoddled. If he deigned to sit on your lap it was a rare and commented-upon honour indeed. He was the cat that walked alone. I adored him and was concerned when he didn't turn up to eat for a few days. Toms wander quite a way, it's not uncommon for them to be gone a few days, but I fretted nonetheless. Days turned to weeks and weeks to months. I was sitting watching TV one Friday evening, just as dusk was falling. It was the film of *Quatermass and the Pit*. It was at the bit where the crane is being swung towards the huge demonic head. The room was dark. I felt a weight land on my lap. I thought it was KT or Marilyn, but no, it was the wanderer returned. He'd just walked in through the open back door. He purred. I put the light on. He had one ear badly ripped and several other facial scars. He was covered in oil too. My clothes were ruined. Still, it was worth it to have him home. He'd been away for eleven weeks: what adventures he must have had. The other cats licked him. We all loved the cats. They were a part of the family. Mamanti home, the sun shining, the angels up in heaven, things were good.

Kate became besotted with one of her fellow bus conductors. She didn't think I knew but someone in the group told me. How they knew I don't know. She told me she needed time to be herself. She asked me to move out. She was cold and brutal about it. I assumed the guy was another Rodney type. They were everywhere in Sydney, long-haired, bearded, gentle-looking guys. It was like living in Galilee. I was devastated. I went to stay at the Kostas' house in Rozelle. I spent my time moping and crying. Big Loci and Maureen were kind to me but I was inconsolable. I felt so crazy that I can't actually remember a single thing about it. I got stoned and stayed stoned. I wandered lonely as a stone. For those who are thinking, well that's why she couldn't stand him, he was stoned mindless all the time, I must point out that Kate was a devoted pot head herself, ninety per cent of the people we knew were stoners, most took acid and mushrooms too, so it wasn't that. Kate was living her own life, that's all, and often just by doing that you can inflict great pain on others. This is the danger of other people thinking that the film is about them. I was an extra. Even in my misery I still believed that the film was about me though. This was me being crushed. This was me being belittled. This was me not mattering. Something must have gone wrong with the new romance quite quickly because I was allowed back home after three or four weeks. I had no self respect left. I took up my old position in front of the TV.

I say I had no self respect left but it was more complex than that. All relationships are unequal. There is always one who loves more and one who loves less. The one who loves less is in control. The one who loves less always has the option of finding someone else they can love more. The one who loves more is a prisoner of that love. They are paralysed by it. I am by nature the one who loves more. Why this should be I don't know. It may be that I feel that to love is more profound and rewarding than to be loved. I suppose I don't expect being loved to last. I only have my love for the other to cling to. It is a love that can't be taken away, a love I can control, a love that I own. Had I not been as I am I would have left Kate and found someone else. It would not have been hard. Anyone can love anyone else. There were those who would have loved me back, there were those who were waiting for me to love them, but things were as they were and I was helpless.

The group had grown dramatically in size and we second-tier initiates were now lesser gods in our own right. We were given our own neophytes to train. Mine were a sweet girl who went on to perform burlesque under the name of

Fifi Lamour, Rita's sister Salme and a gorgeous, page-three-type girl whose name I forget. Fifi was sweet. I told her that I regarded everyone as heroic simply for being alive. She was meaty and clever. Salme was going through an acrimonious split-up with the father of her two children. We'd meet two nights a week and discuss the tarot or something and then I'd take them in a middle pillar or tree ritual. These rituals were naked and the page-three girl was enough to give Liberace a hard on. She'd lie there on her back in the candlelight and it would be heaven just looking at her. She was like a one of Dalí's nudes. She was none too bright either. She was a dish.

We went on another Magic weekend. It was in a huge field. There must have been more than a hundred vehicles. People I'd never seen before turned up, fourth and fifth generation members. There were huge ritual circles. John strutted around like a rutting stag. The new people adored him. He swung his cock as he walked through them like a policeman swinging his truncheon. On the first day a huge circle of people created a battery of energy and John, who was standing in the middle, received it and directed it towards someone who'd be sat in a little circle of their own a half a mile away in the dunes. I was one of the people in the little circle, the second of three, surrounded by long grass. I closed my eyes and concentrated on being receptive. I didn't feel anything but the desire to do so plays tricks with the senses. I opened my eyes and there were five or six little pixie-type beings looking at me from the grass with a mixture of curiosity and annoyance. I saw them as plain as day. One of them, an elderly one, looked at me for a few moments then pulled a face and pranced off. It was very weird. I am not one to believe in such things but I had the evidence of my own eyes. Who knows, there may be pixies and ghosts and hobgoblins and mermaids, who knows? I hope there are.

The following morning there was a huge sort of caterpillar-type creature wriggling along on the ground in the middle of the sleeping area. Everyone was sat around drinking coffee and waking up and the caterpillar became the centre of attention. It was a good six feet long. One end would pull towards the other and then pull away and it would move forward in steps. It was making a noise too, a spasmodic moaning grunting sound. After several minutes it seemed to have a seizure of some kind, came to a halt and keeled over onto its side. It lay there for a minute or so, then a zip opened it up from the inside and Fifi Lamour stepped out bollock naked followed a moment later by John Strangeways. Fifi walked off to do her ablutions and John strutted around the area thrusting his groin out. He actually thought that the people watching would find this behaviour admirable, and he was right. A van crashed on the way back from the weekend and two or three people were killed.

NATIONAL STREET

There was a gang-related war going on in the Sydney underworld at this time. It was in the papers and on the news every day, a beating here, a killing there, knife and gun attacks, arson. King's Cross was to Sydney as Soho was to London, the fifties Soho. It wasn't subtle. There were a lot of hard-looking bastards in suits doing the rounds. A nearby sex shop got burned to the ground. It was a very violent place. One morning going to work I got out of the lift on the third floor and began to walk across the concrete expanse to the office door hidden in the far corner. There was no one else about. It was in effect a huge echoing cavern, dark and full of shadows. I heard an immense roar approaching and a man in full leathers and a helmet with a reflecting visor screeched to a halt a foot in front of me on a Kawasaki 1250. I was frightened. He lifted the visor and shouted 'You don't want to work for those dirty bastards do you, mate?' I said I didn't, no. 'So you're going to tell them to stick their job up their arse!' Yes. Yes I am. I'll go straight in and do it now. He looked at me for a moment then smiled and said 'Well this is your lucky day then,' pulled the visor back down and belted off back down the ramp the way he'd just come. He had got his message across very well. I went into the office, told the Germans what had happened and quit on the spot. To my surprise they actually cared. They thought I was very good at my job. It hadn't even crossed my mind. I thanked them for their kind words but said that I was a coward and I was off nonetheless. They exchanged words in German. The man asked me how much they were paying me. I told him eighty dollars and he said if I stayed he'd double it. As I said earlier, eighty bucks was a very good wage, it was the most I'd ever earned in my life. It amazed me how he could double it just like that. It made me think how much they had to be getting. They told me not to worry about the threat. They said it was just a mistake and they'd see to it. There was a lot of money in porn. Still, money isn't everything. I said thanks but no thanks and went home. That guy wasn't messing. I think that if I'd been anything other than a terrified coward he would have damaged me there and then. I was grateful that he had some degree of humanity and I like to think he might have seen the funny side of it too. I wasn't from his world. He was a strong-arm man and I was a weak-arm man. It's funny, but based on that one brief meeting I quite liked the guy.

Our lease ran out in Drummoyne so we moved to a two-storey terrace in National Street, Rozelle. It was just off a main crossroads that led to Balmain, Drummoyne and the City. The house had a twenties vibe. Ian sans boyfriend had a room downstairs, the two boys had the big front bedroom with the veranda upstairs, then Petah and Jeshua's room, then Kate and me up the back. Two or three more cats joined the household; one was a ginger tom previously owned by Slow Rodney, the taxman. Slow Rodney, the cat, had his tail almost severed in an accident when a window slammed down on it. He wouldn't let anyone anywhere near it, however, and it remained permanently bent in half. He was a highly strung cat. I don't think life did him many favours. He was Slow Rodney's cat for one, he had an ossified tail, he was disliked by the other cats, people didn't like him, even cat lovers made an exception in his case. He shunned any attempt at befriending him. He seemed embittered. Marilyn was the most beautiful of cats, pure white, even her whiskers were white. She was as gracious a creature as ever walked the face of the earth and had the most gentle, lovable personality. She was a right hussy too. Toms came from miles around. I half expected them to start knocking on the door. I watched her have five kittens in a prepared cardboard box on the kitchen floor. What a thing, to give birth. There was such selfless love there, such joy. She was a queen. We'd acquired a new dog too. He looked like a bigger squatter corgi. His name was Foxy and he was a wonderful old guy. He used to play with the little kids in the street. They all knew him. I saw him walking along the street outside one evening and there was a gang of tiny tots following about ten yards behind him calling out his name, 'Foxy! Foxy!', till he'd turn around suddenly, when they'd all scream and run off. I'm sure he was aware that they were children. He had the most distinct smile I've ever seen on an animal. The smile obviously worked too. He used it to good effect on Petah's dog Marion and she had four handsome little puppies.

When you went into the kitchen late at night or early in the morning to make a cup of tea and switched the light on, the walls would be black with cockroaches. Loci and Lindsay used to kill them with rubber bands. The house was full of animals.

National Street was a golden place. Kate and I were very happy. Our bedroom had yellow lace curtains and we woke each morning in a surreal glow. Then we'd have a shower together, drink tea in bed and make love. You can't ask for much more than that. Jeshua was getting bigger. He was a cute little fellow, a typical boy, naughty and cheeky. He didn't have much time for me. One day he annoyed me so much that I tipped a saucepan full of cold water over his head. The look of shock on his face was a treat. He was too shocked to cry even. He just stood there spluttering and gasping. He told his mother what I'd done but I denied it. He and Hugo, who loved kids, became bosom pals. I thought that there was a hint of romance in the air between Hugo and Petah but nothing came of it.

Some group members felt they were being ripped off when buying ganja – the cost was high and the deals underweight – so we in the house were asked to remedy the situation by buying in bulk and selling fair deals to our fellow mystics. A bloke in Drummoyne sold us a pound for three hundred bucks. We separated it into sixteen one-ounce bags and sold them to group members at thirty dollars an ounce, which meant that selling ten would finance another pound ad infinitum. That left six ounces spare from every pound. We sold two to cover the rent and kept the other four for ourselves. We were awash with high quality ganja. I took to rolling straight grass spliffs in a rolling machine and carrying packs of twenty around with me like cigarettes. It's amazing how popular that makes a guy. 'Hey Boyd man, nice to see you, come in for a cup of tea!' As people found out about the good deals the demand rose and we ended up shifting two pounds every few weeks. Me, Loci and Lindsay would transport the stuff by bus. The bloke we bought it off and his wife were hippies. We went there to pick up a pound one day but the bloke was driving back from Queensland with it and he was running late. He'd be a few hours so we were invited to wait, which we did. The hippie wife asked us if we'd like a cup of tea and a smoke while waiting. It was a rhetorical question. She got a tin down from a shelf and rolled a two-skinner from some ancient home grown. I had two tokes and passed it on. It didn't come back to me and I was hoping she'd roll another but she didn't, she put the tin back on the shelf. A minute or so later I felt the chair I was sitting on suddenly take off vertically like a rocket ship. I've never been more ripped in my life. Her husband turned up a few hours later in the company of an American guitarist who was in the *Rocky Horror Show* band in the theatre in Glebe. It was the first production. He was a tall, thin guy, maybe six-six. We sat in the kitchen listening to him play on a twelve-string Martin. He was the business. He played 'Here Comes the Sun' and it was mesmerising. There were two women with him; he introduced them as his wives. He was a Mormon, a hippie Mormon. I ended up sitting crying and shaking like a leaf in the cwtch under their stairs at three am the next morning. That ganja was special.

I began to get paranoid. I began staying in, in fact. The only places I'd go would be group meetings, to score or to the London Café, which was on the main road at the top of National Street. The London had an air of pre-war opulence. The food was simple but good. I'd eat there sometimes. I'd dash over for a takeaway hamburger or a chocolate milkshake most days. I'd be so ripped that I couldn't speak. I'd go in and just stand there gazing at my reflection in the mirror or watching the fish in the fish tank. The owners, a Greek couple, got used to it. They'd say 'Chocolate milkshake?' as if asking a two year old, I'd give some sign of affirmation and they'd get on with it. I'd proffer my hand with payment and they'd take the correct amount. I'd be too stoned to say goodbye even.

We had a lot of visitors in National Street; it became a focal point for the more cynical group members. John was finishing his book. It was to be the New Bible. Kate was writing a chapter on the I Ching for inclusion. John called a meeting and told us initiates that in order to get to the next level of mystical advancement, to become Adepts, we would among other things have to pursue an art form. John allotted me creative writing. I said I'd pursue it but did nothing as I was too crazy to follow instructions. It was an unreal existence. When everyone you know believes in Angels and Gods and Demons the normal fare of everyday life diminishes in both significance and clarity. When people came to the house it was as if they were aware that they were entering somewhere special. A beautiful girl who I didn't know turned up to score one afternoon, and we had a smoke. She was wearing men's shorts with no knickers under them and she sat back in the wicker armchair by the door with her legs lazily apart. She was wearing a skimpy vest and her huge breasts were falling to either side. She sat there like that for a while drinking tea, just talking more or less normally, then got up and left. It was a weird scene. She obviously wanted it there and then but didn't seem offended that I wasn't responding. Looking back now I wish I had. In fact, looking back I'm really pissed off that I ever turned down any woman's sexual advances. My advice to other blokes would be to sleep with any woman you can when you can.

A Jewish guy named Jacob and his wife joined the group. He was a tall, sweet-looking man with medium-length hair and a fine moustache who owned and ran a Theatre in Education company. They toured schools with two short musical plays. One, for toddlers, was about a little boy who slips down a crack in a pavement; the other, for older kids, was about a latchkey boy named Geoffrey and his horrifying experiences at the hands of various demonic relatives. The music was composed by the director, another Jesus lookalike named John, who was a bit of a name in the Sydney music scene at the time. He wrote TV scores and had a few albums out. I auditioned for them as an actor-singer-musician. My guitar playing wasn't up to it but I knew Jacob so I got the job. It was magical nepotism. I had to play the latchkey boy Michael in one play and Freaky Freddie, a hippie weirdo who lived beneath the crack in the pavement, in the other. The plays weren't bad. There were three weeks of intense rehearsal and then we hit the road. We'd load the set and props into the van, drive to the first school, set up in the main hall and perform the play. When we'd finished we'd take the set down, return it to the van, say goodbye and set off for the next school. We often performed at four different schools a day. It was the middle of summer and the performances were very physical. We did some shows out of doors. On one occasion we performed to eight hundred kids in the playground of a school when it was a hundred and six degrees in the shade. The schools were often twenty miles apart and the sets were heavy and awkward. I can't tell you how knackering it was. We must have been so fit. The other actors were a tall, straight-looking bloke who'd been training to be a Jesuit priest and a very short, sweet-smelling bisexual girl. Both of their names elude me but they were nice people. We became quite close, a merry little band. My guitar playing got better but I was never going to be another Chet Atkins. The girl invited the priest and me back to her house for a smoke after we finished work one day. She lived on the harbour, on an island a hundred yards or so from the shore. We parked the van beneath some trees and she rowed us to her front garden in a small rowboat. It was a beautiful afternoon. The water was calm. The house was a colonial mansion. It belonged to her bloke, a rich, old guy who was away working at the time. We drank tea and had a smoke in the garden. There was something between the girl and me. I felt it strongly. She had such a beautiful face. She wasn't really a girl, she was in her early-thirties. She had to stick a moustache on for one of her roles in the play and her upper lip had become tender from using gum arabic. I wanted to kiss her. I wanted to kiss her poor, tender little upper lip. We were getting changed once behind the flats and we caught each other's eye and just stopped and looked at one another, stared at one another. The priest wasn't there. She was in her pants. She was like a porcelain doll. My advice is good, boys. Don't let those moments pass. The girl suggested that we stay there the night but the priest wasn't up for it, so she rowed us back across the harbour in the late evening and I went home.

I was going back to the office to get paid after work one Friday when I realised we were close to National Street, so I had them drop me off there. I'd pick up my wages on Monday. They were involved in a serious crash after they left me and the priest was in hospital for weeks. The back of the van behind the passenger seat where I sat was crushed flat. I would have been decapitated by the flats, which were stored behind me. Another guy took over the priest's role but I caught German measles a few weeks later and that was it. I was in bed for two weeks, deathly ill. The tiny bisexual woman visited. We sat and listened to old-fashioned songs playing on the radio. She was gorgeous.

Over the next few months a remarkable thing happened in Australian politics. Labor had won a general election and the right-wing parties hated the new Labor government with a vengeance. It was modern and trendy and determined to set Australia off on a new path. Even though Vietnam was in its end game, the Americans were determined to have military and political dominance in South East Asia, and Australia's acquiescence was a precondition of that. Up till then this had not been in question. It was a case of them saying jump and Australia saying 'How high?' But now the Labor government under Gough Whitlam was questioning this unquestioning acquiescence. They were considering the future of American missile sites in Western Australia. The opposition parties thought this verging on communism. The security services, servants of the right as ever, used the television and press to run a scandalous and illegal black propaganda campaign against their own government. It was assassination by rumour. The CIA was actively involved but in truth it didn't need to be, American interests were just as important to Australian business as they were to America. This relentless campaign of slander and false allegation reached its crescendo when a forged and highly incriminating letter allegedly sent to Gough Whitlam by a corrupt Asian businessman was published on the front page of every newspaper. Whitlam denied its authenticity, but 'he would wouldn't he?' The smears and lies against him and the Labor Party in general destroyed their credibility just as they were intended to. They were still the elected government, however, and with years left of their term in office. The Governor General of Australia was appointed by the Queen. It was a ceremonial post hung over from colonial days. The man in the post at the time was John Kerr. The Australian establishment wanted to get rid of Whitlam at all costs. It wasn't just politics, they hated Whitlam: they hated his image of what Australia could become. They didn't want pacifists and hippies and do-gooders changing the basic nature of their country. Democracy be damned. A plot was hatched whereby Kerr used an archaic and redundant piece of colonial legislation to simply sack the popularly elected government of the day and install the ultra right-wing Liberal Party in its place. It was a coup d'état. I was a socialist at the time, as were many, and we were outraged; indeed, a lot of people who weren't socialists were outraged, but it was a fait accompli. The feeling of helplessness was sobering. I was knotted up inside with frustration. Everyone was.

Ian moved out of National Street and a new group member, a girl named Sue Wright, moved in. She was tall and beautiful. Her best friend Leonie became a regular visitor. That Christmas was a buzz. I got up very early to open my presents, a habit that had stuck with me since childhood, but Sue was already up. She had baked us hash cakes. I sat in the armchair by the open window wrapped in Kate's gold silk dressing gown and ate two of them with my morning coffee. I started reading the novel *Jaws*. The hash came on heavy duty and I became more and more caught up in the story. I ended up reading the entire book from cover to cover while sitting there. It's a cracking read, better than the film even. I got right into it. I was reading a lot at the time, mostly factual stuff, stuff about Nazi Germany. I read William Shirer, *The Rise and Fall of the Third Reich, A Berlin Diary,* several biographies of Adolph Hitler and endless other books on the same topic. Everyone in the house was drawn in. John Strangeways had told us that the Hitler and the Nazi Party were tools of the Thule Society, a group of cosmic alchemists based in Iceland. Cosmic alchemists were high-level magicians with a timeless overview of the world that bypassed everyday morality in the name of an eventual greater good. It was mooted that in order to herald the dawn of the last new age, the last two thousand years in fact, it was necessary for Jesus Christ to die and that his actual physical blood was a catalyst in its creation. It was suggested that the blood of the Jewish people had the same role in the birth of the next new age, the one that we in the group were waiting for. It's rubbish of course, more than rubbish, it's shit, but we were immersed in it. We were covered in it. The group philosophies embraced both karma and reincarnation and there, stoned and paranoid, isolated and deluded, we fell into a world of madness. We began to believe that we, the people in National Street, were the reincarnations of the leading figures of the Third Reich. Kate was Heinrich Himmler, Petah was Joseph Goebbels and I was Adolph Hitler. I'd look in a mirror and see Hitler's face staring back at me. I had his sad eyes. I couldn't look at the sky without seeing the sky above Berlin, blood red as Hitler's small plane flew in on the eve of the invasion of Poland. I read about Goebbels jumping onto the train as it pulled out of Berlin Station with his lover on board, and travelling with her to Munich. I thought it breathtakingly romantic. I have heard German people saying that the entire nation fell into a dream when Hitler came to power, that they were swept along by an irresistible tide. There is no evil that cannot be embraced as good. We thought we'd been members of The Golden Dawn too. Kate and I had been burned with the other nuns at Languedoc. We'd chanted prayers in ancient Egypt. We were Jesus' disciples. We were pure energy forms looking back on the thing we now think of as reality.

There is a psychological phenomenon known as emotionalism. It is a symptom of clinical depression. It is a heightened state of empathy, which becomes morbidly poignant. I once broke down reading a shopping list. I had met the young woman who'd written it. She was a troubled person. I found the list left casually on a table. It sketched out her life. One of the items was 'A card for Nana'. I couldn't bear it; I felt like I was on fire. Well, this thing with the Third Reich induced this in me, emotionalism. I remembered the early days in Munich, the idealism, the dark beauty, the excitement. I suppose I must have been crazy but when you're crazy you don't see it that way yourself. You see it as you see it, I. That said, I did feel crazy. It wasn't specifically to do with my believing myself to be the reincarnation of Adolph Hitler though. It was a general thing.

Kate's brother, Peter, came to stay. He was a young man now, a surfer with regulation long blond hair and blue eyes. I loved him. He was such a sweet guy, my little brother-in-law. He'd had a bad experience while surfing on acid. He'd been swimming out with his board when he became aware that all the other surfers in the water were pigs, human beings with pig heads, that is. They were laughing at him, calling his name, bombarding him with insults, shouting out absurd nonsensical phrases and grunting and squealing in hellish voices. It really shook him.

There were parties at the house sometimes. I'd say hello to the guests early on, then slip away upstairs to the veranda and let them get on with it. Peter said that he could see a man with a bright red face made of clay one night when we were sitting there. He said that the man was peering around the corner of the doorway at us. The man was wearing a broad-rimmed black hat and a floor-length black cape. He said that the man was over eight feet tall.

I attacked a group of party guests with a meat cleaver in the kitchen one night. Only kidding, but you see what I mean, right. I was crazy enough to have done it, I've no doubt. I was manic and deluded. I felt like a vampire starved of blood.

We had two pounds of ganja delivered late one night. The guy from Balmain dropped it over. It was midnightish but we set to work divying it up quite happily nonetheless. Someone turned up to score. They'd heard that the eagle had landed somehow and there they were thirty bucks in hand at one in the morning. We rolled several big ones to smoke as we were working and the house was full of ganja smoke. It was like dry ice. The doorbell rang. I assumed it was another nightingale after dope so I sauntered down the hallway and opened the door. Ganja smoke poured out from all around me as if I were a demon exiting Hell. I waved the smoke from in front of my face and there were two uniformed coppers stood there, with a police Land Rover parked outside. There were small police lights blinking on the roof and the dashboard, making it sparkle like a little spaceship.

'Is this 45 National Street, Rozelle?'

'Yes.'

'Wait there a minute.'

The copper went back out to the Land Rover. I noticed what a beautiful night it was. I could hear cicadas singing. The sky was thick with stars. I told myself to calm down. I breathed deeply and strolled out onto the pavement.

'Lovely night,' I said. Then the radio in the Land Rover burst into life and a harsh metallic voice crackled out. I collapsed. I couldn't function at all. I was shaking. I could barely stand. I said 'Excuse me, I feel ill,' and ran back into the house, closing the door behind me. I dashed into the living room where the others were still apportioning the ganja and said 'Its coppers!' They were gone in a flash, out the back door, leaping over walls and fences like dogs. The ganja was left all over the floor. I ran upstairs into Sue's room. She was asleep in bed. I turned the light on and woke her. I told her that there were two coppers outside and I couldn't handle it, and that I was going to hide in her wardrobe, which I did. Sue put on her dressing gown and went downstairs to speak to them. It turned out that Sue had had her moped stolen a few weeks before and they'd found it somewhere. The incident frightened hell out of me. I felt that I was dying of radiation poisoning. I felt that my soul was being stretched between dimensions. I felt disconnected from the source.

Lindsay and Loci weren't players in the Nazi drama; they pursued their own agenda. They continued the experiments in sleep deprivation they started in Drummoyne. They'd read an article about sleep deprivation bringing on states of altered consciousness in the same way that fasting did. Group members often went on fasts. Loci and Lindsay took it on themselves to put it to the test. They stayed awake for six days and nights. They sat in the darkness till the sun came up. Their eyes burned in the harsh light of day. They weren't into conversation, not even between themselves. I found it disconcerting. Lindsay started to keep a dinner plate down the front of his shirt. He said it was to deflect bad energy. He'd begun constructing what appeared to be pieces of modern sculpture in his and Loci's room, towers of bric-a-brac, misshapen assemblages of household rubbish, boxes, bottles, pieces of metal, wire and cloth. They were sad, eerie creations. Lindsay's explanation of what he was doing was nonsensical and bizarre. They were machines that attracted energy like lightning conductors. It struck here on the top then travelled down the wires into the ground. What this energy was or what it was for was never explained. I could see that Loci was worried about Lindsay – I was too. We all were. Lindsay was such a sweet lad. We all loved him. He had been troubled for a long time. I thought he was having a schizoid breakdown. I believed that he was seriously in need of help. I thought he was dangerously ill. I voiced my fears to other group members. I talked to John Strangeways. I didn't mince words. Kate, Petah and Loci confirmed what I said. It was like talking to the air. The message was that we were being uncool. We should be respecting Lindsay's adventure into the unknown. To talk in terms of mental illness about a fellow group member was beyond the pale. Had I learned nothing? This seemed shit to me and I said so. I told them that Lindsay was ill in the same way that someone with their arm hanging off was ill, and that inaction would allow the situation to deteriorate. I was told to cool down.

It was amazing how solid this wall of denial was. They just didn't want to know.

A few days later I came home to find Lindsay in the process of making a new super machine. It started in the living room with stones and pieces of ripped-up material, then extended via the kitchen out to the back garden and down the path, ending in the small shed next to the outside toilet. It was flat to the ground. It looked like a circuit board, the termini, islands of broken crockery and ribbon, linked by the thick wire of dozens of untwisted coat hangers. There were multicoloured pieces of broken glass laid along its length so that it glittered in the sun. It led to a dense intricate pattern on the shed floor. This area was splattered with blood. The pathway had been bloodied too. Lindsay had been cutting himself with the broken glass and adding his blood to the machine. Even then the other group members refused to accept that there was anything wrong with him. It was a nightmare. Lindsay and Loci moved out into a flat a few miles away and a week or so later Lindsay took an axe to the place, the police were called and he was committed to a mental hospital. I couldn't function. I could hardly string two sentences together. I shook like a leaf on a tree.

John Strangeways turned up with Big Loci and Maureen. They were solemn. I expected an apology. I expected them to say 'Well Boyd, you were right all along. Sorry we didn't believe you.' What they did say was 'Why didn't you tell us what was going on?' They said 'This is serious. Why did you let this happen?' What they did say was 'This isn't our fault at all. It's your fault.' They sat there straight faced and lied. I was so stunned that I couldn't speak at all. My brain had been short-circuited. The play blocks of logic had been kicked away. At one point Big Loci said that I shouldn't have allowed the boys to smoke ganja. He'd given Little Loci his first spliff when he was twelve. He'd sat with us getting ripped on endless occasions, so had John. How could he say that? How could they just sit there and say this? The truth was of course that Lindsay's spectacular descent into madness had sent the bigwigs of the group scuttling. The authorities were getting involved. The real world was poking its nose into the reasons for Lindsay's condition and that would inevitably lead to the group. They would learn of rituals and drugs and sex, the words 'brainwashing' and 'cult' would be bandied. The whole caboodle could unravel. John and the others were agreeing on their story. Like the charge nurse and his mate in Gladesville when the patient on Special Obs killed himself, they were watching their backs. So much for our eternal bond. I was as paranoid as fuck. I visited Phillip Mar. He could see I was in a bad way. I slept on the couch in his living room. He was sitting on a chair by my side when I fell asleep and he was still there when I woke in the morning. He was a special person. He made me feel humble. Though I had always been a cynic I wanted to believe in the group. I wanted to believe that we were important, that magic was alive, that God was afoot, but couldn't function. I had to get away. I had to escape. Kate and I decided to go back to Wales. If it were not for her I would have died.

THE LEMMINGS

We returned to Wales with little notice and, though pleased to see us, Ool and Naine were placed on the spot. Brian wasn't well at the time. He'd been moody and irrational and Frances was finding it hard to cope with. To have us turn up and foist ourselves upon them was an extra pressure they could do without. Their disconcert was made no easier when they realised that we had no money and seemingly no plans. Though relieved to have left Australia, I felt little better. My neck had started its acid sun pain again. It got worse by the hour. I thought that I was dying. I really thought I was dying. I couldn't sit up because of the pain. I cried uncontrollably. I listened to the world passing by, aware that I was listening to it in the twilight of my own death. Then I went to sleep one night and woke up the next morning in another dimension. The pain in my neck had vanished. My brain had exploded. The acid gods had arrived. Nothing was solid. I was in a world where fear ruled. I wanted to punch people in the face. I wanted to cut my fingers off with a kitchen knife; I wanted to bite the glass I drank from and leap from upstairs windows. I could barely restrain myself from doing it. The people on TV were talking to me. The newscaster addressed me by name – he knew I was unwell. The actors in *Krakatoa, East of Java* tormented me. I was the man suspended in a wooden cage. Pirates danced in joy at my misery. I couldn't talk at all. It must have been evident that I'd cracked. Ool was devastated, Kate calm and Naine borderline hysterical. I took to staying in bed. I told Kate to leave. I was afraid I'd attack her in the night as she slept. I thought about it all the time.

She stayed. She hugged me for hours on end. She sat up next to me in bed day after day reading her books. She kissed me and ran her fingers through my hair. She was wonderful. Days became weeks and I got no better. As a matter of fact I got worse. I lay in bed and watched the rooks circling in the sky and landing on the rooftops opposite. They assembled there like an army of doomed souls. They called out to me. They'd say that I was mad and would stay mad. They told me that I'd end up killing someone I loved, that I would end my days in a back ward of a mental hospital. They said that I should kill myself. I picked up other messages too. Naine gave me a very sharp knife to eat with and it was turned so that the blade faced me. It was an invitation for me to grab it, to drive it into my face. I couldn't eat the meal. I could do nothing. I was broken.

I went to see the doctor. It was evening, pitch black and bitterly cold. There was a new doctor, one I had never met. It wasn't even him as it happened. He was on holiday so I saw a locum, an old man with wavy white hair and horn-rimmed glasses. The room was dimly lit. The desk lamp threw strange shadows on the walls. I sat opposite him and explained that my brain had gone pop and that my thoughts had been of nothing but violence and suicide. I told him that sitting there then in that room I saw him as a creature and not a human being. I said that his teeth were pronounced and I saw him grinding them in a demonic manner at me. I said that I thought that the world was full of horror and that I couldn't take it any more. I told him that I was going to kill myself that night. He let me speak without interruption, sat in thought for a moment, then wrote out a prescription and handed it to me. 'Take one of these when you get home and then one four times a day until they are used up,' he said. I took the paper from his hand and thanked him. As I rose to leave he added 'Don't take more than I've told you because these tablets can be very dangerous if you take too many.' I looked at him sitting there surrounded by pipe smoke in his tweed jacket and laughed out loud. He didn't know why. I threw the prescription away when I got out of the surgery.

Naine came home one afternoon a few days later, breathless with hysteria. I can only assume that she had phoned Kate's mother in Australia. Two more different people you would never meet. Naine had interpreted Margaret's reportage of the situation we'd fled in tabloid headline terms and started screaming that we'd been dabbling in witchcraft and someone had smashed up a house with an axe and that I'd been driven mad as punishment for heresy. I felt like I was being attacked by demons. Kate and I moved to Cardiff as soon as we could. We found a room in the attic of a private house in Kings Road, Canton. The live-in owner was a Welsh-speaking woman named Non Evans. She worked for BBC News. She hadn't wanted a couple to move in but when Kate explained our urgent need she agreed to let us the place short term while we looked for a more permanent abode. I sat cross-legged and bollock naked on a small table in front of the window thinking I was a table lamp for the first two days we were there. It was a surprisingly comforting feeling, but a compulsion to throw myself out of the window superseded it. The thing that prevented me doing so was that I realised I would probably land on the railings and that, for some reason, didn't appeal. Kate looked in estate agents' windows and scanned the local papers. She answered an ad in *The Echo* and we moved into the shared second floor of a two-storey house in Teilo Street. We got a cozy room next to the kitchen with a bay window overlooking a dainty row of back gardens. The two guys who were already there shared a room next to the communal living room at the front. Their names were John 'Benjy' Benjamin and Richard 'Longface' Carlson and they were landscape gardeners. John looked like Oddbod – the half man, half-ape creature grown from a severed finger in *Carry on Screaming* – and Richard looked like a servant in a medieval court. They met working for Norwich Union in London four years previously. Inspired by similar hippie cravings to myself, they quit and went to work landscaping on army bases in Germany, where John had grown up. His parents had been teachers there and he spoke the language fluently. They met a Welsh bloke named Phil Ferret and his wife Tarina while there and set off on the hippie trail to the Far East with them in an old bus. Richard got busted on their way back to Britain and did six months in a Belgian slammer. John came to stay in Wales with Phil and Tarina and Richard joined him on his release. Phil was a landscaper too. All three worked for a small local firm. They did commercial work in the main, maintenance of grounds and private gardens. Their basic raison d'être was getting stoned and drunk and listening to rock music.

I was like a spectre for months. I left rooms suddenly. I sat stone faced in corners. I sulked in shadows. I was as crazy as fuck. I took a walk to town through the park every day to clear my head. The path was covered in writhing snakes and the trees were chorus lines of demonic Tiller Girls. I was pursued by the wind. It mocked me and whispered about death. John and Richard had drawn the short straw. Kate must have explained the situation because they didn't hassle me for my boorish behaviour. I think they saw I was a decent-enough chap beneath it all. I kept my head down and slowly began to regain a grip on so-called reality. John and Richard were excellent fellows in fact, witty and clever. I began to spend more and more time in their company. There was a lot of high quality hash about, Zero Zero Moroccan, Green Nepalese, Red Leb, different types of Black. It was a veritable sweet shop. I didn't touch it. I was aware that my fanatical ganja smoking had contributed to my present situation. I vowed never to touch it again.

I got a job as park keeper at Plasturton Gardens, a small local park. I was supposed to pick up rubbish and tend to the flowerbeds, weeding and so forth. I soon discovered that it was backbreaking work, so I didn't do it. I just sat in the pale yellow brick hut, listened to the cricket on the wireless and drank tea. The boss came around every few days but he never really recognised the extent of my idleness. I think everyone who worked for the Parks Department was the same. It was a poorly paid job; no one was going to bust a gut. I was still crazy. I was paranoid about the trees. They were telling me to kill passers by. I got three regular gigs, the bar of the Grand Hotel, the bar of the Centre Hotel and The Frenchman, a wine bar opposite the New Theatre. I carried my guitar along the riverbank to each and I'd walk home the same way in the dark. I don't remember how I played. I think I was mediocre. There were never many people. I inspired disinterest in most. It did me good though; it was therapeutic.

I went over to Ferret's squat with John to score. It was a second-floor room in a large semi-derelict house on Newport Road. There was permanent scaffolding outside. We had to climb some very rickety stairs to get in. Tarina was lying on the bed in a reddish silk dress. She was heavily pregnant. It was the first time I met her and I was flabbergasted at how gorgeous she was. Ferret was a cool-enough looking guy but you'd never think he'd get a girl like her. She was stunningly beautiful and as sexy as a starry night. She was voluptuous. She was a lovely person too, funny and intelligent. Phil's friend Bev turned up with some heavy duty drugs and they indulged. I kept my own counsel. Who was I to tell anyone anything, right? It still took most of my energy trying to resist the temptation to tip petrol over people and set them alight when they were asleep. Ferret was a strange guy. Him and Bev, a Free-wheelin' Frank look alike, had been friends since child-hood. Both of their fathers were police sergeants up the Valleys. They left home when they were seventeen and set up residence in a cave in a nearby forest where they lived for six months before setting off into the world. They were a latter-day Ianto Clown and Billy Oof, I suppose. Bev was married too and had a little girl named Sarah, after Bob Dylan's wife and the song of the same name. He was a big guy, manic most of the time, probably due to the drugs. He was a speed freak. Essentially, they'd take anything that came to hand. I've seen Ferret snort a line of speed and fall asleep seconds later. Their metabolisms were fucked. They were both really nice guys when you caught them straight, though Phil had a nasty temper. He had had an acute anxiety state, or nervous breakdown as it was commonly called, which is what had happened to me, and I found the parallels of our symptoms fascinating. Wanting to attack people, to cut off his fingers, to bite glass, to leap from high places, he'd even been put off by the idea of landing on a spiked fence as I had, it was so specific. His unique diversion was that he'd be kept awake at night by the idea that there were huge numbers in his bedroom, actual numbers, eight, fifteen, thirty-one. He thought they reached miles into the sky. The similarities made me realise that what I was going through was far from unique. It was extremely comforting, a light in the darkness.

The urgings to violence by the trees in Plasturton Gardens got too much for me and I had to quit. The boss was very sympathetic.

I started feeling better. We went to see Doctor Feelgood, a London pub band Kate and I had got heavily into while still living in Australia, and they were fabulous. Bob Marley played Ninian Park a few months later; everyone else in the house went but I was playing in the Centre Hotel on the night and didn't go. The band didn't come on till midnight because of a power failure and there were only a few hundred people left. Bob had a huge wicker basket full of big ready-rolled spliffs and threw them into the crowd. Then he invited everyone up to the stage and played for three hours. What the hell was wrong with me? Why didn't I say fuck the Centre Hotel and just go? I regret it to this day. I learned my lesson though, and later that year I had the night off from playing at The Frenchman to see

229

the Feelgoods' second gig in Cardiff. The Feelgoods and their entourage went to the restaurant for an after-gig chill and they stayed till the early hours jamming and getting pissed. Would you believe it? I didn't go to see The Sex Pistols at the Top Rank. Everyone said they were crap except Kate, who dug them big time. I saw The Clash at the same venue but I didn't get it. The idea that you could be in a band without being a professional musician, or indeed a musician of any type, was cool though.

Sue and Leonie, our friends from Australia, arrived. They crashed with us. Things had sorted themselves out in Sydney. Lindsay was living with a girl named Wendy and had returned to his erstwhile self, more or less, but the affair had had a negative effect on the group, which had lost its sparkle and was beginning to disintegrate. John and Leonie fell in love. Richard took up with a girl named Jenny at about the same time. She treated him like shit. She bloodied his nose with a punch once because his sniffling annoyed her. The poor guy had chronic asthma but that didn't save him. John informed me that Richard had previous in abusive relationships and we assumed that he got something out of it. This didn't stop John hating Jenny though. Worse was to come. A big shambling bloke named Rhys turned up at the flat. Jenny had told him he could crash on our floor for a few nights till he got a place to stay. John and Richard knew him, he was a mate of Ferret's, so they said okay for a few nights. Rhys, however, was a downer freak and like all downer freaks he was a zombie. Lying on the floor listening to poundingly loud music twenty-four hours a day was his solitary trip. The floor being the floor of our living room where we relaxed, ate our food, chatted and watched TV. It became hellish. Rhys fell asleep one night with his boot in the fire and it melted completely off. He walked into the door and knocked himself out then got up and fell down the stairs. Once in Porthcawl he'd fallen thirty foot off the promenade wall onto rocks below and just stood up and waded off into the sea. He was still staying with us five weeks later. John asked and told him to go several times in increasingly insistent terms until he could stand it no longer and ejected him physically. Rhys continued arguing as John frog-marched him down the stairs. 'Hey man... this is uncool man. Let me get my tobacco pouch.' John threw his possessions out after him. Jenny complained. John told her she could fuck off too. She didn't come around much after that but she and Richard remained an item.

Two young blokes started turning up to my gigs. We fell into conversation. They were Danny Hoffman and Charles Normal, and they'd come to Cardiff after getting out of detention centre in Hereford. They lived in a third-floor flat in a house on Fitzhamon Embankment, a notorious theatre of alcoholism and prostitution. The flat downstairs from them was a knocking shop and Charlie and Hoffman discovered that if one of them held the other's legs as he hung upside down from the window, he could observe the girls servicing their clients.

Charlie's dad owned a business in Swansea. They didn't get on. When he was a boy his mother would drape curtains over his shoulders, put a tea cozy on his head and ride through the streets of the city on one of the open-topped tourist busses with him, waving to people as they passed by. She thought she was the Queen and that

Charlie was a prince. Hoffman was a Cockney of Greek descent. He had a profusion of curly black hair and a kind, gentle face.

I started smoking ganja again. This meant I was better. Every ganja smoker doubts the wisdom of it and determines to give up from time to time but after a while you start to realise why you smoked it in the first place. The unstoned world is such a brutal place. Ganja has done me harm, I've no doubt, but at the time the balance between that, and the joy and good times it had brought me, weighed in favour of the latter.

Charlie and Hoffman became regular visitors to Teilo Street. They were dope fiends of the first order and fitted in fine. The idea of forming a band was mooted. We'd have me on guitar and vocals, Charlie on bass and John and Ferret on guitars. We sat around stoned discussing it. We thought of names. 'Snatcher Hogger' was decided on. We put an ad in *The Echo* for a drummer. A guy named John Michael wrote a nice letter and we arranged for him to come to the flat for an audition. He was a sallow, acne-scarred youth of seventeen with a severe stutter. He didn't own any drums and had only ever had two lessons. I played him the set and he liked it and determined to get his parents to buy him some drums. We began to learn the numbers. Ferret already had an electric guitar, Charlie bought a bass, Leonie financed an electric Ovation and combo for Benjy and John Michael acquired an old, battered drum kit. Our music was a weird mixture of magic and ineptitude. We couldn't really play at all at this time but we had something huge in our favour. Something talent and hard work couldn't buy. We were us.

Charlie started shagging Sue. They were an unlikely couple. Sue was a delicate, sensitive new-age person and Charlie was a psychedelic pixie. Seeing it written down maybe they weren't such an unlikely couple at that. Charlie was in his oils. Perverted sex was his trip. He crept into strangers' back gardens late at night and stole knickers from their clotheslines. He'd hide in bushes, watching people when they didn't know they were being watched, women boiling kettles in their kitchens or sat on settees, lit by the flickering lights of TV sets, in living rooms or naked through the opaque glass of bathroom windows. It sounded great but I couldn't figure out why anyone would want to smell knickers that have just been laundered. Surely that defeats the point. Charlie said he'd far rather smell soiled ones but that they were much harder to come by, so he'd decided to settle for second best. He'd wank off in them when he got home. He had a pair of binoculars too. He'd tell us all about some half-naked girl he'd caught a glimpse of or some couple he'd seen having it off or kissing in a field. He loved it. He'd lived in Canterbury before going to DC and was sexually assaulted by a German HGV driver he hitched a lift with. The guy made Charlie suck his cock to orgasm as he drove along. Charlie wasn't the most fortunate of men. His bass playing was coming along though.

The old lady who owned our house and lived downstairs from us died suddenly. She was a sweet person. It was quite a shock. The flat became vacant and Phil and Tarina moved in. Their daughter Jamie was born at 12:01 on the morning of January the first 1977. She was the first baby of the new year. I waited at the hospital with Phil. We

233

stayed up all night and had a cooked breakfast in Asteys by the bus station the next morning. He was so happy. I got a short-term job working in a fixtures warehouse. Fixtures are screws, bolts and washers etcetera. The office was relaxed. The boss was a bloke named Lionel. I spent my time avoiding work and writing little sketches about office life to entertain my fellow workers. I stayed a month. John, Richard, Charlie and Hoffman were well into the drugs at this point. Charlie and Hoffman were lack of willpower personified. They'd taken to it like a duck takes to orange. I was into speed. Much cheaper than coke and three times as good. Coke, I have often thought, is speed for wankers. I was drinking like a fish too. It was winter, a beautiful sparkling winter. We went for a walk by the river in the snow one night and a tree uprooted itself and crashed to the ground near us.

I finished at the fixings warehouse. There'd been a young guy working there named Clive. He was a borderline punk though his favourite band was Cockney Rebel. We became friends and he came back to the flat one night and tried some hot knives with Charlie and John. He'd never smoked hash before and he loved it. His name was Clive Trevelyan but I christened him Twink one starry night while walking to the Conway pub and it stuck.

I took some methadone one night when a friend of Ferret's did a chemist's and got two big bottles of the stuff. What a buzz that was. It was oneness with the cosmos. It was Heaven on a stick. We tried to go to the pub but could get no further than the front gate. It was all too beautiful. A bloke named Brian who worked with John joined us as road manager and sound mixer. He bought a PA out of his own pocket. Another band of our acquaintance had a rich-boy keyboard player who subsidised them financially. He was Roger Brooke-Bond so Brian Davies became Dick Schweppes, Dick from his uncanny resemblance to Dick Dastardly of Wacky Races fame, Schweppes as a tipping of the hat to Brooke-Bond. He was also our mixer, of course, so the name had a double resonance. I entered the *Melody Maker* folk rock competition as a solo performer and came second in the Welsh heat. I played 'Rape in a Romantic Situation', 'Lilith' and 'East Berlin'. The review was very positive. It inspired us. We started hiring rehearsal spaces. John Michael became Victor Random. His small cymbal sounded like the lid off a Peake Frean's biscuit tin. We referred to it as such: 'Hit the Peake Frean's there, Victor.'

Victor had a thing against keeping the simple beat. It's the case with a lot of drummers. He'd always try to insert little fills. It sounded like someone kicking a tin bath down a flight of stone stairs. He got better with time. We decided that once we felt ready we'd do a few local gigs and then go to Amsterdam to make our fortune, but there was a snag. Ferret didn't want to uproot his new family. It was understandable but he took umbrage at our insistence that we were going to go and left the band. He grew ganja plants in a greenhouse in the garden. He spent less time with us. A process of alienation began. It created a bad vibe from then till we left. It was a shame. Ferret and Tarina were lovely people.

A friend from Sydney was performing with the Lindsay Kemp Mime Troupe in London and he came to see us. His name was Maurice Fame. Maurice was a dancer and mime

235

artist who'd performed some of my songs in concert in Australia. He was very camp and quite spectacularly bitchy. He was in fact the first queen I'd ever got to know. He insisted on using the women's toilet in the pub when we went out for a drink. Ferret took agin' him and Maurice talked down to Ferret. It was touch and go whether Ferret would beat the shit out of him at one point, but it passed. Maurice had released a single before leaving Australia, a cover of my song 'Massive Bringdown Fruitcake City', and was keen to discuss a project he had in mind. He invited me to London to see the Kemp show, a version of Punch and Judy, at the Roundhouse, stay the night and then meet a Portuguese film producer the following day. I went back with him. He was staying with the rest of the company in a large labyrinthine house by Battersea Power Station. We dumped our stuff off and went to the venue. The show was ace. There wasn't a huge audience but the perform-ance was cracking. There were two blokes in full-length fur coats sat in front of me. I thought it odd because it was swelteringly hot. When the show finished I saw that it was Rudolph Nureyev and another guy. I'm sure he gave me a wink but I might have been mistaken. Lindsay Kemp himself was staying in the house, and a blind guy called The Great Orlando. They were as camp as tits to a man. The Portuguese film director met us at the door of his flat in a silk dressing gown and nothing else. He didn't have a male hormone in his body. We sat on a lavish couch and discussed Maurice's idea for a film of my half-written musical *Alice Angel Starr*. It was set in a futuristic mental institution a thousand feet below the floor of the Atlantic Ocean. Alice Angel Starr is a patient there but she used to be a famous dancer, a Mata Hari figure, and her life had been full of intrigue and romance. She'd told the other patients about a place where there was still happiness and life, a magical island called Danceland. One night when the patients are asleep a wall collapses and an SS officer enters wielding a pick. He is covered in dust. His name is Karl Eikhorne and he'd escaped from Hitler's bunker as the Russians closed in by digging a tunnel. That was in 1945. He's been digging for seventy years and now he's got here. He and Alice strike it off, rescue the patients and escape with them to Danceland. That's it. I played a few of the songs on a nylon string guitar, 'Up on a Ledge', 'Summer Affair' and 'Hard Drugs'. The Portuguese producer enthused mildly over the idea but he didn't like the name Karl Eikhorne so we changed it to Rick Sabine. It was all gibberish of course, cocaine-fuelled delusion, and nothing came of it. I was glad to get back to Wales. I never saw Maurice again, but he was a cool-enough guy and I liked him. Rudolph never got in touch.

Richard moved in with Jenny and Charlie moved in with us. He drove everyone crazy with his toilet habits. He had a phobia about shit. He couldn't bear it anywhere near him. This resulted in hour to two-hour stays in the loo and the usage of entire rolls of toilet paper at one sitting. He'd polish his arsehole as far as we could tell. You could hear it from the living room. It was like someone sand-papering a wooden horse. His carryings on also resulted in spectacular blockages, which he refused to deal with himself. John had to use a coat hanger to loosen it then put his arm in a plastic bin liner and haul the wedges of shit-covered paper out. It wasn't his favourite job. Charlie took piles of porn in with him too and a good part of his time

237

was spent wanking. Indeed, it was difficult to tell by listening whether he was wanking or polishing his arsehole. Either way it kept the rest of us from doing what we needed to do and there were regular arguments through the door. Charlie would do anything he could to stay in there. He'd claim to be feeling faint. The landlord paid a surprise visit once and since Charlie wasn't staying there officially we had to hide any evidence of his presence sharpish. I grabbed his mattress from the floor and there were more than a hundred pairs of women's knickers under it.

The summer of 1976 was the hottest in fifty years. I am not normally a fan of hot weather but this was an exception. The sun entered my mind as well as the sky. We rehearsed solidly and the music was taking a recognisable shape. Kate got a job on the pumps at a nearby garage, it gave her lots of time to read and she really liked it. I'd never seen her more chilled. We watched Wimbledon on telly and Richard came up with the immortal line 'He was Bjorn Borg and he'll die Borg.' We invented a game the aim of which was to place a cup as near as possible to someone's elbow, often on the arm of the chair they were sitting on, without them knowing. The ultimate success was if they knocked it over, even more so if it was full of tea. You should try it. It's fun. Our diet was unvaried, Goblin hamburgers, tinned potatoes and tinned peas, or Mathesson's sausage and coleslaw and chips from the chip shop. We went to Southerndown beach in John's van, Ludwig, most weekends. We played cricket and had picnics on the sand. It was heavenly. Blaine visited from Scotland. He'd left his wife and children. I don't know the exact circumstances but he was already an alcoholic and I've no doubt that had a lot to do with it. He wasn't happy.

Schweppes dropped in to a rehearsal on his way back from a holiday in Cornwall and he had a mate with him, his best mate Bob Brennan. They'd grown up together in Dinas Powys. Schweppes had been involved in Bob's band Pollyanna. Bob and Schweppes were into acid and shagging. Bob looked like a Russian priest. The world was crazy. It was turning to shit in front of our eyes. We were on the brink of Apocalypse. We changed the name of the band to The Lemmings and looked for gigs. Our songs were about the coming holocaust. They were about the fucked nature of things. Elvis Presley died. There were two Teds in drapes standing outside the paper shop as I went to work one morning. They were crying. We played our first gig in the bar of Chapter Arts Centre. It was their folk night. Leonie made John a black cape with silver stars and moons on it to wear. He looked great. Victor wore his normal Tony Baretta outfit, jeans, T-shirt and a black leather jacket, Charlie wore womanly garb supplied by Sue and I wore jeans, a sequined T-shirt and my riverboat gambler's jacket. I believe I had a hat on too. The small crowd hated us. They thought we were crap. We got unplugged halfway through our third number. Our second and only other gig in Cardiff was in a pub down the docks. We played upstairs in the lounge to a tiny audience of old women. They didn't know what was going on at all. We'd finish a number, loud and discordant, I'd bark out the last word, letting it ring in the silence, then leap in the air like a gazelle and storm out of the room in hysteria, there'd be a few beats of silence and then a smattering of polite applause. I'd return to the stage in silence, unnoticed, and the cycle would be repeated. We got through the set though, every number from start to finish. These Welsh audiences weren't for us. We weren't a pub band. We were artists. We were the chosen ones. We were more convinced than ever that our decision to go to Amsterdam was correct. We quit our jobs, packed our possessions in the back of Ludwig one Friday evening and set off for Folkestone. There was John and Leonie, Victor, me and Kate. Schweppes drove behind in his car. Charlie and Sue had gone ahead a few weeks earlier to test the ground. They were living in a houseboat on the Herengracht.

AMSTERDAM

We arrived in Amsterdam late on a grey September afternoon and headed for the camping site at Vliegenbos. It was a cordoned-off field with a grey concrete toilet and shower block and a shop. John and Leonie slept in the back of Ludwig while Kate and I, and Victor and Schweppes pitched tents nearby. Once settled in, me, Schweppes and John went into the city to score. We found an art centre where we bought some ace black and sat and had a glass of beer and a spliff. Schweppes fell into conversation with a trendy, esoteric, blind Dutch guy. He asked if he could touch Schweppes' face, which Schweppes let him do but as the conversation progressed Schweppes got more and more freaked out and we had to leave. It was raining heavily by the time we got back to the camp and we spent the rest of the night in the van drinking chocolate milk and getting ripped. The next day we wandered around the city looking at the sights and trying to suss out the accommodation situation. We went to Charlie and Sue's houseboat, which was an old hulk of a place, charming but cold and wet at this time of year. They were looking for somewhere else themselves and had met some people in the squatting fraternity. Squatting was the thing in Amsterdam. It was a political movement inspired by the anarchists. We had a few quid so me, Kate, Schweppes and Victor went to a legit rental agency and decided to rent a nice flat on the top floor of a house on the Leidseplein. It was a thousand guilders a month, a fortune, but we weren't to know.

There was no furniture so we just put out our sleeping bags on the floors and settled in. The next step was to see if we could get a gig. We went to the Milky Way. They were holding a floor night for bands the next night and we got on the list. The place was packed when we went on and we played well. We did 'East Berlin', 'Hard Drugs' and 'When the Pleasure Stops'. My lead break in 'When the Pleasure Stops' was the best I ever played it. The problem of feedback from my Ovation acoustic became apparent and it remained apparent for years to come. It just wasn't suited to being hammered like I hammered it. Still they really liked us and advised us of other venues we could approach. We split our time between looking for gigs and trying to find work.

We signed up with an Uitzendbureau, an employment agency, and me, John, Victor and Schweppes got jobs on the production line at Bruynzeel's Door Factory about ten miles outside the city. We had to get up at quarter to six in order to get there to start at seven thirty. Schweppes' car was playing up and we had to push it to get it started. At that time in the morning in the pouring rain it was no fun. We'd pick John up on the way. He'd wait for us sheltered underneath a big billboard near the edge of town. We drove from there to a river, which we crossed by ferry. The ferry was packed with Bruynzeel's workers, North Africans in the main. They looked like concentration camp victims with their skeletal features and shaven heads. They had really distinctive dress sense too: garishly coloured jackets with pronounced shoulder pads, large-collared, open-necked shirts, loose trousers, pointed black leather shoes and bright yellow socks were the norm regardless of the cold and wet. They affected a macho image, constantly taunting each other and breaking into mock fights. I don't think it was heavy, just their style. I found out later that they carried knives as a matter of course. I never got close to any of them but I admired them. They refused to melt into the background. They had elan. We called them the Boneheads. We met an English bloke on the ferry one day. He was very tall and wore a floor-length battered leather greatcoat. One of his eyes was badly scarred. He'd come to Holland to start his life again after his marriage broke up. He showed us pictures of his children, two beautiful little girls with blonde ringlets. He told us he was a professional photographer. His name was Nigel but we called him Hurk, because he looked like a turkey.

The factory was enormous. It was hundreds of yards long and the section we got put to work in had one entire wall open to the elements. As you know, I am not one for hard work or for work at all, come to that, and this, the dispatch section of Bruynzeel's fire doors, was my Hell. In fact that is what we called it, Hell. Everyone called it Hell. It was Hell. The day started at seven thirty on the dot when a hooter would sound and all the lights come on as one. Until then we'd've been waiting at our stations in the dark, can you believe that? I stood by a length of track along which never-ending stacked pallets of fire doors passed. Each pallet would stop next to me and I'd take the doors off the stack and position them in a clamp, from where they were moved down the line to the delivery lorries. The stacks were above head height. The doors were as heavy as fuck and incredibly awkward to handle. By a quarter to eight I'd be sweating like a dog, it would be dripping off me. Not only that, but the manic relentlessness of the work created a sort of insanity in everyone. People would scream things out, things I couldn't understand. Men would burst into song. Some Turkish guys used to show their cocks to one another or grab their crotches and make fucking actions. One of them had been a copper back in Turkey and they shunned him. He was a slithery-looking bastard. The foreman was an ex-Nazi. We called him Rotwang after the inventor of that name in *Metropolis*. He was a bull-necked moron. There was a Dutch guy on the end of our line known as The Red Skull. He was bald headed and very tall. He looked a lot like Maine from the hospital in Jersey, in fact. He was so crazy, so indoctrinated by the work ethic, that he returned to work the day after having his thumb cut off in a machine, the very next day. The ex-thumb was just a blood-soaked bandage. There was another Dutch guy called Shark, who actually slept outside the factory gates.

243

Hell was just one section in the factory. Next to us was the Gay Section, where doors were wrapped in plastic; upstairs they had the section where only Turks worked. They were all short, extremely stocky guys. We called them The Cubes. We'd try to grab a five-minute breather in the toilets on each shift; a lot of people had the same idea so you had to dash into a vacated cubicle quick. The Cubes had the habit of eating strong salami sandwiches and smoking thick, full-strength roll ups while defecating and the smell was something wicked if you went in after one of them, but needs must. There was another section a long way away, which we'd catch a glimpse of occasionally when running an errand. It was where the young Dutch guys worked. They'd be drinking tea at their machines and had time to chat just like real people. We called it The Land of Milk and Honey and it was everyone in Hell's dream to be transferred there. It had happened. Once in a blue moon Rotwang had appeared, eyed us all up and taken some poor quivering bastard off to the Promised Land never to be seen again. When Rotwang turned up we'd all watch him like puppies in a dog pound. I was never taken. I was left to rot. We had exactly thirty minutes for lunch. The canteen was a long shed with benches and Formica tables. The Dutch diet consists of chips with mayonnaise and/or tomato sauce and/or peanut butter sauce, big lukewarm spicy sausages called Wurst and thin soup with noodles and meatballs, testicle soup as we called it. It was not haute cuisine. I've never had a more horrific job, none of us had. The question is, then, why did we stick it? Well, there were two reasons. One was the money, which we needed to live on, and the second was that we were so mindlessly stoned that we couldn't get it together to quit. We didn't smoke in work but we smoked every other second of the day and night. The street dope at the time was brown or black citrol: sticky, opiated hash from Afghanistan. It was lethal stuff. I ate a gram once and spent the next two days believing that my head was a balloon and my body a piece of string attached to it. I had to be led about.

We left the posh, unfurnished flat and cracked a squat on the third floor of an uninhabited house on Haarlemmerweg, a dilapidated street near the Red Light district. It was a murky, damp hovel of a place but it was habitable. The local squatting organiser came and attached us up to the utilities. We found some furniture in skips, cleaned the place up and settled in. We even got a telly. The place was a holiday destination for mice. We had dozens of them. If you went into the kitchen on tiptoe you'd find twenty or thirty of them of all shapes and sizes sitting on the potatoes in the potato box. They liked it there for some reason. I'd use a water spray we had for the plants on fine jet, clap my hands and watch them all skedaddle to their hole in the skirting board where I'd be waiting to squirt them as they dashed in. Sometimes their back legs would skid with the force of the water. It didn't hurt them; indeed, I had no desire to hurt them. I don't know why I did it really. The mice became confident in time, arrogant even in some cases. They'd just walk across the living-room floor while we were watching telly. They didn't even bother to run. A cat would have sorted them out but as things were they ruled the roost. Kate and I had the large bedroom and Victor and Schweppes slept on mattresses on the floor in the living room. There was another smaller room off the living room but that was kept for growing ganja plants. The straight Amsterdam people were a bizarre bunch. They had uncurtained windows at street level and packed their highly illuminated parlours with expensive furniture in an ostentatious display of their bourgoise credentials. They'd just sit there en famille reading the papers or drinking tea from bone-china cups and saucers while passers-by looked in. It was weird. The obsession with new furniture meant that a lot of perfectly good stuff was thrown out. All the squatters furnished their houses by getting to the discarded furniture before the garbage men, as indeed we had. The men had a thing about big butch dogs too. They strode around with them on thick chains. The dogs would leave enormous piles of shit wherever they felt like and the owners didn't seem to mind; in fact a lot of them seemed to encourage it. They'd look at it with pride before yanking the dog's chain and sauntering off. It was as if they'd done it themselves. They'd let them do it on people's doorsteps, anywhere. There were signs up all over saying '*Hond in de Goot*', dog shit in the gutter, not on the pavement, but they were ignored. There was a pile of German shepherd shit the size of a basketball outside our front door one morning, and it had a large undigested carrot sticking up from it like a transmission tower. I retched at the sight.

John and Leonie got a squat just up the road from us, and Charlie and Sue moved into the area too. Amsterdam was full of wasters and petty criminals. We scored dope off an Israeli named Mickey. His friend Hassan was the local kingpin. He robbed a nearby bank at gunpoint and fled the area. They were all Israeli army deserters. Mickey was a rip-off merchant but he had a certain charm. We became addicted to playing cards, contract whist and sergeant major. We'd play till the sun came up. There were some shows in English on the telly. We watched *De Familie Bellamy* and *De Man Van Atlantis* religiously. There was a good live music program in Dutch. We saw Blondie doing 'Denis' and I actually thought that Debbie Harry was a man. She just looked so remarkable I couldn't believe she was real. They had Bowie on and he sang 'Heroes' with a fag in his hand. Bowie was the soundtrack to Amsterdam. *Station to Station* with its Teutonic undertones was of the Zeitgeist. Amsterdam was a City of Lights, a City of Magic, a City of Dawns and Twilights, a Fairytale City. I loved it. The canals froze over in the winter and children skated on them. The black, black nights were polka-dotted with snowflakes. They'd swirl beneath the streetlights like eddying ghosts. On Friday evenings we'd go to Marnix Straat on the tram and have a bath in the public bathhouse. A huge, deep, old-fashioned bath filled to the brim with scalding-hot water for as long as you liked for two guilders. It was heavenly. We'd go to a nearby health food restaurant afterwards. It was painfully exotic.

I got some solo gigs in between band engagements. A French guy told me I was like Jacques Brel; I'd never heard of him but I took it as a compliment anyway. I played in the Tramway Café just around the corner from where we lived. They found a severed human hand in the pissoire across the road one night. I got chatting to two guys from the Midlands. One was six foot four with a huge Afro, a Zapata moustache and a poncho, the other was shorter and slim with a hillbilly beard. Their names were Terry

Mann and Nigel Aitkins and they'd come to Amsterdam with a guitarist singer named Oddball. They were looking for gigs. Terry, Zonderman as he became known, owned a Snap on Tools van named Gobbler and Nigel, Silas Master of the Celestial Fleets, played bass guitar and mandolin. They lived in a squat in Fannius Scholtenstraat, just around the corner from us. I called in on the way home for a toke. You had to enter through the house next door, go up to the third floor and crawl through a hole in the wall to get in. The first two floors of their own building were missing. It was a cool place all hidden away like that, not much better than ours but lighter and less claustrophobic. Silas and Zonder lived with Oddball, a bloke named Clive and a bloke named Don. Clive was a soft-spoken, bespectacled boffin type and Don was an alcoholic banjo player. Don had played with John Martyn and Hank Williams Junior. He was a cracking musician but his boozing had curtailed his career. Now he dossed in someone else's squat and busked for beer money. He'd drink a dozen bottles of Grolsch before noon. He was getting on too, late fortyish I'd say but still handsome. He had long straight hair and always wore denims. I bottled for him once but he was a moody guy. Like all alcoholics he had a nasty side which didn't take a lot of coaxing out. He was paranoid and thuggish. Oddball was really odd. He seemed straight to me, the sort of guy who'd become a bank manager. I didn't much like him. He took himself too seriously. Zonderman was a half caste West Indian; he'd been in Strangeways for a stretch and was an enforcer for the Big Daddy. He had a degree in fine arts. There were some fabulous murals on the walls of the squat. He was from Bradford, and Roland and Dave, two friends of his from back home, lived nearby. They were brothers. Both were half West Indian too. They were really big guys, six-four, and they sported similar Afros to the Man. We called them The Furry Freaks. They were hard as well as big. Both had done time. Rowland lived with his girlfriend Elaine. She was a dish, a lovely girl with the most beautiful, lip-licking breasts you'd ever seen. She wore tight-fitting jumpers, which showed them off magnificently too. They were all heavy drug users. Everyone in Amsterdam was. There was no point being in Amsterdam if you weren't.

Oddball disappeared from the scene. I think he went back home, and Zonder and The Freaks became Lemmings. I really liked them. We all did, they were fascinating people. Silas joined the band on second bass guitar and mandolin. He was a good musician, better than we were, and he slotted in perfectly. There were no personality clashes, nothing. Silas was meant to be. He was one of us from the moment we met. He smoked dope like he was in a competition. He used to pack a big chillum before going to bed and leave it by his pillow in case he had to get up in the night for a pee. He didn't want to waste the opportunity. Silas started referring to me as the Master. He'd tell everyone 'For he is the Master!' and greet me with the delighted cry of 'Master!' whenever he saw me. Others took it up and I became the Master. We played gigs far and near in pubs, community centres and disco- theques. Our mixture of Doom Rock and Space Time Romance numbers struck a chord with many. I wasn't surprised. The way I looked at it was that if I were someone else, anyone else, I would rather see us play than any other band in the world. 1978 was the year of The Lemmings.

Amsterdam was a place of social upheaval and violence. Gangs of anarchist thugs roamed the streets at sunset. We called them Big Boys because that is what they were, six-twoish, leather-jacketed, nasty, hard-looking, junky Dutch psychos. They sprayed graffiti '*Amsterdam ist Dood!*' in red paint, on walls and advertising billboards, everywhere. There was a huge arch over the road where Haarlemmerweg met the red-light district, which had been taken over and occupied by a bunch of art pseuds known as The White People. They dressed in science fiction white. They wore white face make-up and had white accoutrements. Some of them sported white face masks. I think it represented something. I met them at a party thrown by a friend of Charlie and Sue's, a Bowie clone named Squatting Jup. Jup showed us photographs of him and his girlfriend fucking in a forest. His mate had taken them. He showed them as if they were holiday snaps. Kate was a Winter Girl. She wore a long fur coat, her breath rose above her in clouds as she walked along, her face and ears were icy cold. She got a job making props for the Royal Dutch Opera. She was brilliant at it. I went to work with her on one occasion. There was a beach nearby, a huge grey beach with holidaymakers in deckchairs and children making castles in the sand. The sky was marbled. It made me more certain than ever that the human race was doomed. We went to the preview of *Tannhäuser* in The Hague. I fell asleep.

We gigged regularly. I walked into a pillar and broke my glasses walking onstage at the Brakke Grond. We got paid off in Groningen and Zonderman smashed into the wings of a line of cars in the car park as we drove off in Gobbler. We played two nights at a discotheque in Germany and had to sleep in the loft overnight with the barman who snored like a manatee. I was so stoned when we went on that I passed out during the intro to the first number. I thought I was home in bed. We played to a horde of French students in a small pub. John plucked out 'La Marseillaise' on his Ovation. They loved us. They danced madly. They told us that we were what music was all about. They said we were better than The Sex Pistols. They were right. We were the gateway to another dimension. Sometimes we'd drive home after a gig and have to go straight to work. The one time we couldn't face lugging the bass cab up three flights of narrow, virtually perpendicular stairs at three in the morning and left it in Gobbler, the sodding thing got pinched. It had belonged to Throbbing Gristle. It was a loss. I finished at Bruynzeel's. I had to. A compulsion to crush my hand in one of the machines became too insistent. I just quit and walked out. If only the real Hell were that easy to get out of.

Victor got up very early every morning to get to the Central Station by six am and wait with other lost souls on the off chance of getting a day's work picking fruit. He'd miss out most days and be back home in bed by half seven. I'd hear him going out and coming back. We tried to convince him to get a proper job but he wouldn't have it. His mother sent him parcels with replacement Baretta outfits in them about once a fortnight. His stutter had almost disappeared. He changed his name to Victor Ferrari. He preferred the image but it didn't stick and he returned to Random. He couldn't understand why he didn't score with women. It really got to him. He started believing that they found him repulsive. He thought that they thought that he looked like a pig. Some woman at a party had said 'Look at that guy. He's got a face like a pig!' and several girls and women had said 'pig face' under their breath as he passed them in the streets. He was in fact a handsome fellow but his brain was fucked.

Charlie developed the habit of hacking up phlegm into his mouth all of the time. It never stopped. You'd ask him to not do it for a minute, say, and he couldn't do it. He claimed it was poisons coming out because of his new diet. It was repulsive to say the very least. He'd lie awake all night listening to 'sounds' coming from behind his and Sue's bedroom wall. He believed that there was a huge machine there being manned by a team of scientists. Sue met a Chinese girl at a health food restaurant. Her name was Irene and she was a lesbian. She was obsessed with numerology. They became close friends. She took to hanging around Sue and Charlie's flat, stirring up mischief, so he believed. He hated her. She left Amsterdam but Charlie still kept seeing her. We'd be on a bus or tram and he'd dive down beneath the seat mid conversation saying that he'd just seen her getting on or passing in the street. He'd be shaking in horror. She got cancer and went to live with a tribe in South America I believe. She died there. Charlie had been jealous. He thought that she was trying to steal Sue away. Sue had an ethereal quality. She was worth keeping.

John and Leonie fell into a routine of domestic bliss in their fairytale attic. I rarely went there because you had to get onto the next door's roof and step across a narrow ledge to get in through their window, and I am terrified of heights. Accidents happened. There were a lot of people on the edge and a lot of drugs. A man in his forties moved into the attic of the house next to the Benjy's. He'd been in prison in North Africa for eighteen years. I never met him myself but I heard that he'd created a room inside the vaulted attic eight feet by six, the size of his cell in prison, and just stayed in there.

Schweppes, John and I got a job assembling windows in a window factory. It was horrific but not as horrific as Hell. An English bloke named Jim worked in the same section. He was in his late thirties and had come to Amsterdam, as many seemed to do, after his marriage broke down. He'd fallen in love with a young girl named Sophie and wanted to start a new life with her here. He'd worked as a runner at a record company in Manchester in the mid-sixties and was sent on an errand to score a pound of weed for The Beatles. He took it to them and they gave him a few big handfuls for his trouble. Sophie met some Amsterdam gigolo and left him, and he threw himself off the roof of the house they were living in. He looked like a young Michael Parkinson.

I got a regular solo gig, Friday lunchtimes in the coffee house at the Melkweg. It was quite prestigious. Hurk came to 'protect' me. He carried two handguns, a revolver and a Luger, in special pockets inside his greatcoat. He showed them to me surreptitiously and said 'Don't worry. I've got you covered.' I wasn't worried anyway. If they wanted to kill me, let them kill me was my attitude. It would have been an overreaction but *c'est la vie*. Hurk moved into Fannius Scholtenstraat with Zonder and Silas. Zonder had recently got himself a girlfriend, an English girl named Jane, who'd also moved in. There was an enormous home-made, wooden-framed settee in the living room. The back was six foot if it was an inch. Adults looked like five year olds sitting on it. Hurk slept on it and Hurk was a very strange sleeper. He always slept fully clothed, including his greatcoat, and with his eyes wide open. I remember going into the room one grey morning not realising he was there, and sitting on his head. He leapt up like a young water buffalo. It frightened the shit out of me. Hurk was a member of the League of Destroyed Middle-Aged Men. He was fucked.

Bob came to visit for a week. We went to see The Feelgoods in Groningen but it was just after Wilco left and it wasn't the same. Charlie and me got back stage after the gig on the pretence of being Dutch journalists. The band members were snorting sulphate and drinking brandy from bottles. I stood next to Lee Brilleaux but was too overawed to speak. We stopped the van for a pee on the way back and Bob fell down a steep grass embankment at the side of the road. When he didn't reappear we went to look for him and found him lying unconsciously drunk in a shallow stream.

We decided to make a demo tape. The studio we chose was in Oss, a small town about fifty miles from the city. We had eight hours to set up, record and mix four numbers. None of us had been in a studio before. The two Dutch guys operating the desk treated us with contempt as soon as they realised we weren't Dire Straits. Victor put the drum track down first, then Charlie and Silas stuck down the bass guitars, then my acoustic, then John's electric. There were twenty minutes to put down the vocals. We did 'Lucretia Borgia', 'Olympus Boogie', 'Matheson' and 'When the Chips Were Down'. The graceless jerks on the desk did us no favours but the tape captured something of what we were about nonetheless. It got us a new spurt of gigs and me and Clive, who still lived with Zonder, took it over to London to try to get some record companies to listen to it. A few took a copy but we never heard from them. One guy had a quick listen while we were there. He was recording a band at the time. He was Terry Melcher, Doris Day's son, and had produced 'Eight Miles High' by The Byrds. Melcher had been the previous tenant in Roman Polanski's house just prior to the Tate murders. It was Melcher who Manson really wanted to kill because he believed he'd reneged on a promise to give him a recording deal. Melcher listened to our tape but was unmoved. Our journey had been fruitless.

It was February 1978. John and Leonie got married. I made them a cooked breakfast then we travelled to the Registry Office by tram. It was a great day full of love and friendship. Furry Freak Rowland wasn't there. He'd been arrested in Bradford railway station on his way to visit his sick mother. They did him for GBH, committed years before, and he got three years.

I finished at the window factory and got a job in the kitchen at an old folks' home. Endless conveyor belts full of catering size pots and pans to scrub and dry, and claw the clinging shit food out of. It was relentlessly knackering and I never even got to see an old folk. I was downstairs, hidden away in the depths of the building with the Moroccans. There were two brothers, Hassan and Omar, who were heavy duty bone idle. They had it down to a fine art. They ghosted around unseen. They seemed ripped a lot of the time to me. I've no doubt they were ripped. I've no doubt they were as ripped as fuck. They had a breezy unpretentious flamboyance of character that was a delight to behold. Having permanent jobs in Amsterdam was a great position to be in for North Africans. They could apply for residence after three years. Our communication was limited to grunts and smiles and hand signals. The recurring message I got from them was to slow down and take it easy: *'Langsam. Langsam.'*

We went to see a man called Gina the White Horse. He was a prophet, a soothsayer, a foreteller of Doom. He was famous. His picture had been on the cover of *Time* magazine. He ran his organisation from a terraced house on the outskirts of Amsterdam. We travelled on three different trams to get there. We were shown into a waiting room, an annex to his inner sanctum, and told to wait. There were leaflets on a table telling us about Gina's prophesies. He believed that the Apocalypse was just around the corner. He claimed that the world was being ruled by a race of demonic lizards. They control everything, governments, armies, religions, all the great institutions, everything. Within the next five years or so Satan himself would come to lead them. He would crawl onto the papal throne in the shape of a lizard and the world would worship at his feet. Then there will be Great Wars, centuries of Great Wars between the Angels and the Demons. We will be offered the choice to die slowly from pus-filled open sores or to submit to the Beast and have his brand 666 burnt into our flesh, not the greatest of choices to have to make. Gina's beliefs were insane, no doubt, but they tallied with mine in all but detail. Whether the Demons were lizards or not I didn't know, but I certainly believed that they were there and I believed that Hell was ascending into our world second by second. We'd been sticking up stickers for months saying 'Dark Times Will Come'. It wasn't subtle.

One of Gina's assistants, a plump blonde girl from Blackpool, told us that he'd see us soon. She was dressed in a sheet thing like a Hari Krishna. We chatted. She had come to live in Amsterdam the previous year. When in Blackpool she'd fallen in with bad company, got into drugs and ended up pregnant. She had the child and determined to clean up her act. She took the baby to the beach one day and walked into the waves holding her. She wanted the child to feel the benevolent power of nature. It was a little new-age baptism. She went in slightly too far and got knocked off her feet by a wave; when she got up the baby had gone. She searched for it under the water but she didn't find it. It surfaced nearer the shore as dead as sand. She had a breakdown and had to get away, so she came here and met Gina. She realised now that everything that had happened was all a part of this great plan. Gina had taught her to forgive herself. He sat cross-legged on cushions in front of an uncurtained window so that the sun shone from all around him. He was a big guy, really big. Though American, he spoke English in an accent as if his first language was Arabic. He looked like a cross between Charles Manson and a bear. I don't mean that it an insulting way. Kate asked some questions, he answered

257

enigmatically. I don't remember what he said but it was shit. Gina didn't know doodley squat about Satan. He was a bread-head collector of broken hearts. It was an interesting meeting though. I was assured that he levitated after we left.

The band was getting nowhere. We'd gone as far as we could. Our last throw of the dice was a headline gig on the main stage at the Milky Way. I don't know how we got it. Maybe they heard the Oss tape.

There had been a growing discontent amongst us. The newlywed John and Leonie wanted to settle down. Kate had a desire to return to university. She wanted to study astronomy. Sue and Charlie wanted to go to London. Victor, Silas and Schweppes were easy whatever we did, but the die was cast. It made sense music wise. We'd learned our trade in Holland but everyone knew that it was London that really mattered in the music world. The gig at the Milky Way had a *fin de siècle* quality. It was an exercise in existential dissociation. My guitar was grossly out of tune and I couldn't breathe. I had to concentrate on the mechanics of breathing. The reflex to breathe had deserted me. Had I not forced myself I would have died. We played badly. It wasn't nervousness, it wasn't fear – it was technical inefficiency. I was reduced to screaming in between bouts of gasping for breath. I couldn't stand up. I was on my hands and knees grovelling like a dog. I can't comment on anyone else because I was too hysterical to have any awareness of what was going on around me. We got through the set somehow and left the stage to muted applause from the sparse audience. It didn't matter. They were there. They played their part in the story. I felt sorry for them. It was like waiting at a train station for a train to nowhere. It was Hell Central. It turned out to be our last gig in Holland.

I got the bullet from the old folks' home. It was a Friday afternoon and the pots and pans had been finished early for some reason. The conveyor belt had been turned off and I was having a rare breather. It was half past three. We finished at four. I'd got into the routine of having a shower in the men's locker room after I'd clocked off and Hassan told me that since there was no more work to do it would be okay if I had it then. I thanked him. Ten minutes later I was in the shower scrubbing away when there was a knock on the door. A voice told me that they wanted to see me in the office. I finished showering, got dressed and went to report. The female personnel officer told me I'd got the boot. It was for taking a shower on company time. I paused in thought. It dawned on me that Hassan was probably not in a position to give anyone permission to do anything and he'd done so out of friendly bravado. The job meant a lot more to him than it did to me so I took it on the chin, signed for my hours worked and left. Charlie and Sue had already gone to London and John and Leonie followed soon after. Kate, Schweppes, Victor and I hung about for a few more weeks then said goodbye to Amsterdam, and set off to join them. The channel crossing was flat and grey.

LOnDOn

Kate and I stayed with John and Leonie in their flat in Finchley for a week or so while we looked for a place of our own. We watched concerts by The Police and The Boomtown Rats in a series of televised university gigs. They repulsed me more than I can express with their stupid vacuous songs and strutting arrogance. I hated them. Sue told us that there was a room available in the squat where she was staying, so we moved in there on a longer temporary basis to get out of John and Leonie's hair. It was a huge house in Covent Garden just across the road from the Rock Garden. The entire row had been condemned for years and every house had been squatted. It was a cool-enough place. Siouxsie and the Banshees rehearsed there and Sid Vicious had a room. It was full of punks, in fact.

The unofficial main man was a tall angular Irish guy named Jerry, who was the singer in a band called MI5. He was a fascinating bloke. He'd left Belfast the previous year; he'd been dealing hash to British soldiers and was unwittingly used by the IRA to set up a murder. He met two squaddies in a car park, sold them a half a weight, and one of them was shot dead by a sniper as he walked away. Jerry was a hard bastard but no murderer. He left for London the following day. He was a smart guy, very politically and socially aware. I watched his band rehearsing. They had a lovely song called 'Paranoia'. They were very good. A bloke called in one evening with some sort of agenda and was rudely dismissive of Jerry's input. Jerry grabbed him by the collar, punched and kicked him down the stairs and threw him out onto the street. I'm glad I never got on the wrong side of him.

Kate went to see the education authorities about going to university. It was late in the day but she was a very impressive person and got a place studying astronomy at Queen Mary College in the East End to start that year. Her lecturer was to be Patrick Moore. She was very excited. There were quite a few Kiwis staying in the squat too. They were backpackers, drunks and stoners. They stole barrels of Guinness from the Rock Garden every second night and held regular orgiastic parties throughout the building. One of them staggered into our room in the early hours one night, fell onto our bed next to Kate, slept till dawn then got up and staggered out. We never saw him again. One of the punk girls was going out with the guy who played violin with the Electric Light Orchestra. He had just formed his own band. I think they were called Violinski.

I was sitting in the big second-storey front room with Jerry one afternoon when we noticed that the cars parked on the street outside were all being towed away by police tow trucks. The entire street was cleared. An hour or so later we were drawn to the window again by a strange roaring sound in the distance. It was coming from further up the street, around a bend, and it was getting closer. The first thing we saw were policemen on horses, five or six abreast and about ten deep. In their wake came a horde of Union Jack flags held high on poles. It was a National Front march. Jerry and the other lads in the squat were livid and began shouting out insults and challenges to them. They responded by taking up an anti-squatter chant, which inflamed the situation. Some of them threw things at the house and tried to break through the police cordon to get

261

at us. Jerry was all for going out and laying into them but the coppers were doing their job and they were moved along. They disappeared until all that remained was the distant beating of their drums. It was very comforting to see the revulsion they caused in our disparate group. It was good to see tough young lads like these ready and willing to mix it with them. To quote Jerry, 'There's no point trying to talk to these fuckers. A punch in the fucking mouth is the only language they understand.' Good on him.

We moved to Vernon Road in Leytonstone. It was a terrace with a small garden to the front and back. Schweppes moved into the downstairs front and we moved into the back. A living room and bedroom combined with a kitchen and an outdoor toilet. A group of African students lived upstairs. The bathroom was on their floor. There was a basement too where the gas meter lived. It was a nice place. The landlord, a Greek man, owned a café around the corner where I ate quite often. It was good food. He was a good man. I really liked him.

We acquired a dog named Tina. She was a motley black and white little thing with a rattish face. It was winter. Victor had left the band and gone back to Cardiff to live so we set about auditioning for a replacement drummer and we found a somewhat refined English bloke named Simon. His father had been big in MI6 in the Far East. The family returned to England after he retired and had a house out in the country. Simon himself lived with his girlfriend in a flat near Clapham Common. He was a nice guy, softly spoken and funny. He looked like a porn actor, perm, drooping moustache, stoned grin. We began rehearsals twice a week in studios owned by a bloke named Alan Gordon who'd been the drummer in some sixties one-hit-wonder band and now owned a music shop. The studios were under railway arches in Leyton, not far from where I lived. Iron Maiden rehearsed next door.

Kate had started her course at Queen Mary College and buried herself in studying. She'd never seemed happier. John and Leonie moved to a flat in Leyton a few miles away and Silas moved into a room in a house with some friends of friends. Charlie and Sue were living separately, Sue in a communal house on the other side of the city and Charlie in a flat he shared platonically with two girls. Charlie wasn't happy with the situation. Sue's housemates were new-age vegans. Charlie was convinced that one of them was esotericking his way into Sue's knickers. Charlie hated him. He hated all of them. He made plans to go there for dinner one evening and poison them. Charlie wasn't a rational man. Sue moved out in time to thwart the mass murder and Charlie's torment abated. Furry Freak Dave visited and crashed at Charlie's flat. He shagged the girls and invited them to become prostitutes under his management. Charlie was livid. Despite anguishing over Sue he'd been doing his level best to get in there himself and along comes Furry Freak Dave and 'Voila'! Such is the lot of the tormented.

It was a bitter winter that year. The snow fell incessantly and lay deep in the streets. Silas got a job labouring on a house conversion near where we lived and fell into the routine of coming to wake us up every morning at ten when he got a half-hour break. He started at seven. He'd call into the cake shop and get cream cakes on the way, then come and ring the bell. I'd get up and let him in. The poor bloke would be statuesque with the cold. His red fur-lined coat would be stiff, his beard and moustache white. He'd dash into our room, sit right in front of the gas fire and shudder and moan as he thawed out. 'Oh fuck... its fucking freezing. It's like the North Fucking Pole out there I'm telling you.' You could actually hear his teeth chattering, like a mouse playing tiny castanets. Once his hands were serviceable he'd skin up and smoke a J while making a pot of tea, then he'd sit back down and we'd drink tea and chat and eat the cream cakes till he had to go back. He'd crash on our kitchen floor some nights. When he got up at six am, he'd try to be quiet washing in the sink and making tea so as not to wake us then he'd have a little play on his banjo. He'd start to sing soon after and get louder and louder. In the end he'd be going at it hell for leather. He couldn't control himself.

Leytonstone was a rough, working-class area. Vernon Road was off Leytonstone High Road, the main road that passed through the suburb. We were near a huge pub called the Six Elms. It was always packed with young tarts and thugs. We'd do a few lines of sulphate and go there to play pool against the locals. There was another pub in the other direction where Adam and the Ants started out. It was an unpleasant dump. Further still in that direction was Whipps Cross and another huge pub that had strippers on Sunday afternoons. This was a skinhead pub though, and as nasty as fuck. We went there once but didn't hang about. The entire area was unwelcoming, in fact. There were monstrous grey tower blocks on the outskirts that were lit up at night by the tiny lights coming from the windows of the flats. We called them The Skin-heads' Temples. There was countryside nearby, though. I took Tina for long walks. I started calling her Weenie. She was hysterical ninety per cent of the time. I came home one day to find her under the bed with her weasel-like nose buried deep in an ounce of my grass she'd found. She'd eaten most of it. I should have been angry but she was so sweet there looking up at me with her damp snout speckled with flecks of ganja that I couldn't be. I scraped what I could off and gave her a kiss. We'd tried to convince ourselves that coming to London was the right thing to do for the band but I don't think any of us believed it. I certainly didn't. I had a feeling of failure. Things would never be the same again. I felt that the magic had gone.

We went to John's parents in Lincoln that Christmas. We drove up in Ludwig and got hit by a car at a roundabout on the way. Ludwig was okay but the front of the car was smashed in. It was full of students. No one was hurt though, and we carried on the journey. John's parents were both schoolteachers, really nice people, sociable, intelligent and kind. They made us feel very welcome. We went to a pub on Christmas Eve and walked home through the snow. Kate was sparkling with happiness. We slept on a made-up settee in the living room and had a night of intensely passionate sex. It felt a bit illicit under the noses of our hosts but we were young and in love. John's mother taught domestic science and was a great cook so Christmas dinner was memorable. John's maternal grand-mother was there too. She was in her eighties. I love old people. I love the way they can say what they like and not give a damn. When John's dad was handing out cups of tea around the fire that evening she touched him on the arm and said 'You know Geoffrey, you get uglier every time I see you.' 'Thanks very much,' he replied. It was a lovely Christmas.

We hibernated for the rest of the winter. Life passed in a haze of hot knives and television. The only forays out were rehearsals, the off licence and the Indian takeaway. Kate went back and forth to university of course, and there was the occasional speed-fuelled sojourn to the Six Elms. I had special shirts for smoking hash and eating. They saved my other shirts from destruction with dope burns and spilled food. I was no Viscount Lindley in the dining etiquette stakes. When someone was dishing up the food they'd say 'Boyd, put your eating shirt on.' I was pretty much a zombie. Schweppes and I spent a lot of time together. We'd sit in the small arc of heat thrown by the gas fire, get mindless and sing ridiculous songs with demented gusto. 'You take the high road' sung in a ludicrous high-pitched Scottish accent was a favourite as was the theme song from *Robin Hood*, the real one, the 'Riding through the glen' one. We'd sing them over and over. We'd play cards too. Well I say 'play cards', it was essentially cutting the deck to find Idi, the king of spades. Schweppes became obsessed with him. He'd close his eyes and concentrate fiercely in an attempt to forge a psychic link with him. He'd let his hand hover over the deck and sometimes chant his name before cutting. None of it helped of course, and Schweppes would become more and more agitated as the eponymous African eluded him. After a few dozen failures Schweppes would turn the deck over and search through it to find where he was 'hiding'. When he found him he'd say 'There! Look! Hiding near the bottom! I knew he was down there somewhere. I must have cut all around him!' On the rare occasions when he did cut him Schweppes' joy would be unbound. 'I've got him! There he is. Ha!' followed by a series of yipping noises.

We'd also become unnaturally preoccupied with the existence of lizard-souled men who were passing themselves off amongst normal people. They were marked out by having small beards and moustaches, receding hairlines and round, metal-rimmed glasses. They were led by the folk singer Roger Whittaker of 'Durham Town' fame. The basic lizard as described above we called a Skinless Lizard, and we made up a song about them which we added to our repertoire. If a Skinless shaved off his moustache he became a Faceless. They were devious creatures though. If a Skinless shaved off all his facial hair and wore contact lenses and a wig he could easily pass as human, for instance, and many did. They were everywhere. They were trying to take over the world. There were no female lizards though, which suggested a finite shelf life. We both feared and loathed them. No one else seemed bothered. I put Schweppes' and my behaviour down to hashish to be honest. We smoked like trains. We'd be ripped mindless for days on end. It was our normal state in fact. We were weed puppets. In between the petty manifestations as described we were both heavy duty unhappy. I don't know why. I never felt happy in London. My memories of the place are not good. Don't get me wrong, it's a great city. You can feel its history. You can taste its culture, its crime, its diversity. It has a beautiful veneer of immorality. I loved the city itself. It was me in the city I didn't like. Silly, defeated me slinking back to Britain with my tail between my legs. I was unhappy because I didn't sparkle. Kate seemed happy enough. She blossomed in academia. We didn't talk as much as we could have. I felt bad.

Charlie and Sue got back together and moved to a large, empty farmhouse out in the wilds about an hour from the city. We went to stay with them for a weekend. The house was made of stone and incredibly cold but the setting was forestland: England at its loveliest. I woke up on the first morning, just as dawn was breaking, and went downstairs to make a pot of tea. There was a light mist. Two deer were grazing about twenty yards from the kitchen window. They were plucking twigs from a bush. They looked so beautiful, the innocent little beings. We had a visitor in our back garden too for a week or so. His name was Horatio. He was a one-eyed hedgehog who, we assumed, had been hibernating there through the winter. How he got in there I'll never know. He did though, and when the time came he got out again. We fed him saucers full of bread soaked in milk and raw eggs. He loved it. There were tiny chinks of twilight through the gloom. I bought a small cassette recorder and spent hours recording gibberish sketches and weird, misshapen songs. Kate made herself a study space in the kitchen, basically a table with a dinosaur lamp, and hid herself away in books. Rehearsals were completed and we got half-a-dozen pub gigs lined up. I don't know who got them. It could have been Charlie. He had a certain businesslike persona at times. Yes, it must have been him. We played well and went down well, though even in the eclectic world of London bands we were not what people expected. We weren't the sharp, moody, angular type, or the narcissistic,

268

arty, punk variety. We weren't anything. It was both a strength and a weakness.

Winter became spring. Silas' landlords, two blokes in their thirties, owned the house they were living in. They were well-educated, middle-class civil servants with artistic leanings. Their names were Pete and Andy Plant, no relations. Andy was a tall blond guy with a beard and moustache. He was softly spoken. I thought he was gay. Pete was the dominant one. He sidelined in dealing coke and had a wicked habit himself. They'd heard about the band from Silas and decided to come and see us in a gig at Soho Polytechnic. It was the day of the general election when Margaret Thatcher got in. I railed against her from the stage but I was preaching to the converted. The gig was ace and the Plants, suitably impressed, approached us about becoming our managers. We agreed. That part of the business was always beyond us, we were too unimpressive as people.

Schweppes got put in touch with a landscaping contractor. We met him in a roadside café. He was a faceless lizard named Ham. He gave us small contracts to do on a self-employed basis. Since neither of us had a self-employment number Ham used to keep back a third of our money for tax. It was a fiddle of course, but we still earned a reasonable whack, so we accepted it. The actual work was delegated to us through David Izzard, Ham's sidekick. We referred to him as simply 'The Lizard'. The work was hard, shovelling, carrying, barrowing, digging, weeding, laying turf, clearing undergrowth. 'Heavy Weights: Long Distances.' We'd drive to the job, go to a café for a cooked breakfast, work like hell till lunch then go to a pub and have four or five pints, then back to work till tea time, knock off and stop off at a pub on the way home for half a dozen more. Then we'd go home, sit down and get stoned. Such was our daily routine that summer.

Victor visited from Cardiff for a weekend. He brought Twink, my mate from the fittings warehouse, and a girl named Carol, who lived in the same house as them. Victor had joined Twink's newly formed band The Bulbs. They played us a tape. It was crack hot. They came to one of our gigs in a huge pub south of the river. It was an unseasonably cold and rain-swept evening. We played great. That night Victor, Twink and Carol slept sat up in chairs around the gas fire. I woke up to have a pee and they were sat there, eyes shut, lit from beneath by the dull red glow of the flames. They looked like dead people arranged in a deliberate tableau. It was a macabre sight; I couldn't get out of bed.

We spent some evenings at the Plants. We'd go back after rehearsals and Pete would turn us on to a few lines of coke, then we'd sit around in his kitchen talking rubbish, babbling incoherently about our glowing futures. I was always uncomfortable. Pete Plant had a vacuum cleaner for a nose. I've seen him cut eight lines then snort them all himself one after another. He was a decently motivated guy but the Charlie had reduced him to a caricature. There was a girl named Rosie who lived with them. She was a tasty little feminist type. Silas told me that the second day he was there he was taking a bath and she walked in naked and had a shit in front of him. He didn't mind, of course, but it struck him as odd nonetheless. Silas had started working in an office by now. It was weird to see him all neatly coiffured in a three-piece suit. He seemed happy enough though.

Charlie and Sue had split up again and this time it seemed to be a permanent thing. Charlie moved into a flat with Bob, who'd come to London a few months earlier. Bob stayed with two friends of his, Glyn and Gub, who were sub editors at the *Daily Mail*, in their flat in Pimlico for a while, then got this new place on a fiddle. It was a council property with a low fixed rent. The bloke who was registered had gone abroad and Bob just took over. It was in Clapton, an area populated by orthodox Jews. We went out to a nearby pub quite often and got into Young's beer, a London-brewed real ale. It was good stuff. Charlie and Bob soon began to rub each other up the wrong way though. They were chalk and cheese. Bob was an ultra neat anal obsessive control freak and Charlie was a bone-idle, untidy pervert. It particularly bugged Bob that Charlie spent so much time contacting prostitutes and swingers on the phone. His mountains of casually scattered pornography became a problem too, but it was Charlie's toilet habits that were the greatest bone of contention, so to speak. Charlie would spend hours in there masturbating. He wouldn't do it quietly either. He'd moan and retch up phlegm continually as he did it. Bob would end up hammering on the door and threatening him. Charlie didn't pull his weight financially either. He must have used ten quid's worth of toilet paper a week. They ended up living in a state of mutual loathing. Charlie began to plan Bob's murder. He was going to cut up the corpse, put the pieces in black bin bags and leave them all around London. Charlie invariably resorted to planning murders when he felt under pressure. Bob had no fear though, and would challenge Charlie to 'bring it on'.

'Take your best shot Charlie, but you want to make sure it works first time or I'll fucking kill you. Have no doubt about it.'

Charlie thought that Bob was insane. 'He's fucking crackers Man.'

The atmosphere in the flat was what you'd imagine it to be like in a high security prison. I knew and loved them both, and indeed both had valid points, but the flat was Bob's and that gave him the moral edge. The situation was resolved in a remarkable and highly unexpected way. We played a gig in the Two Brewers pub on Clapham Common where Charlie caught the eye of a gorgeous American girl named Pam, and within three months they'd got married. I couldn't believe it, but there you go. It's no good trying to second guess other people's sexual or romantic choices. To be honest I could never understand how any female could fancy any bloke other than me. It may sound arrogant but I mean it. There you go though. Charlie got a place with Pam and moved out of Bob's. They had a baby not long after. It was a little boy and they named him Lewis. Bob lived alone in the flat. He was as crazy as a coot.

There was something going wrong with the band. The Plants wanted Andy Penn, a guitarist friend of Simon the drummer's, to join. There was mild manipulation. The vibe was bad. John decided he'd had enough of it and jacked it in. Andy Penn took his place. Penn was an accomplished player but he wasn't a Lemming. Come to that, neither was Simon. The truth is that The Lemmings had ceased to exist. The Lemmings were me, Kate, John and Leone, Victor, Schweppes, Charlie and Sue, Silas, Bob, Zonderman, Clive and the Furry Freaks. We only existed in Wales, where we came together, and in Amsterdam. We were of that precise time. It was exciting. It was romantic. It was magical. The London Lemmings were a different thing. I knew it at the time but I was too cowardly to face up to it. We changed drummers a short time later, Simon being replaced by Neil Conti, a young session player. He had a beautiful transparent-skinned Pearl drum kit with a couple of computer pad drums. He could really play too. Andy Penn made way for a guy named Alan who was nice enough. We carried on gigging. We made a demo tape. I was drinking too much. I'd keep a half bottle of whisky in my jacket pocket and swig it through the day. I didn't even like whisky. I was just crazy.

My brother Blaine had taken up with another Scottish girl and moved to London. I knew nothing about it. Her name was Sharon. They'd had a baby together, a girl called Rachel. After Rachel's birth Sharon was diagnosed as having post-natal schizoid reaction. This is like post-natal depression but it's a psychotic state, not a depressive one. It is very rare and in Sharon's case it didn't fade with time. It didn't go away. On top of this Blaine was a pretty chronic alcoholic. Sharon believed she was being observed by groups of people assembling in nearby churches. She thought that Blaine was the richest man in the world. She was profoundly ill. Blaine could barely stand up and they had a tiny baby to look after.

My brother Brian split up with his wife at around the same time. He'd been having mental problems resulting in him being hospitalised, and Frances told him she was leaving him for a mutual, also married, friend named Norman. Brian and Frances had recently been on a holiday with Norman and his wife. Brian was plunged into despair. He was a mentally fragile man and ill equipped for such trauma. He phoned me up one day. We hadn't spoken for years. He was wild with anger. He was mad for revenge. He was crying. I tried to discuss it but nothing I said mattered. I was really upset for Brian. He sounded so out of control. A while later he and Blaine fell out big time over some madness in a pub. They didn't speak for twenty years. I felt for Frances too. I couldn't believe this was a decision taken easily. Brian had been crazy for quite a time and he was getting crazier. Whatever the details, it was a horrific thing to have happened. Nightmares were sprouting up all around me.

We had a session in the flat one evening with just us. I OD'd on Nepalese hash and crawled out to the outside toilet. When I got there I curled up on the floor and started to believe that I was a resistance fighter in the Second World War and I'd been captured by the Gestapo and was lying there on the floor of a dark cell waiting for them to come to take me for interrogation. I was terrified. I could hear German voices muttering outside. I heard a bunch of keys being taken off a belt. Then I started stretching. I thought I was a cellophane love fish on the palm of an over-passionate hand. It's a bit disingenuous of me to be relating what I'm relating. It sounds as though it had sequence and context, but nothing could be further from the truth. I was seriously depressed. It was all a dream to me. I went back inside the house but was so frightened that I had to go into Schweppes' room and hide under his bed in the dark.

At a party at John's sister's posh flat a while later I drank a bottle of whisky and attacked someone in the bathroom, pulling them off the toilet so that I could be sick in it. I danced on the table. I punched a hole in a cupboard door. I was carried out to Ludwig and driven home. I fell asleep in the garden in falling snow and would have frozen to death if Silas had not come out and carried me inside. I was ill for two weeks. Listen, friends, I'm fed up of telling you I was mentally fucked all the time, but it's important for you to know. I was observing myself a lot of the time. I didn't know what was going on. It was terrifying. I won't say it any more though. I'll accept that you will keep it in mind. I wasn't an inch away from cutting my own head off with a carving knife.

Kate's father died. It was the clichéd businessman's death, a heart attack on the golf course. I imagined him smashing a ball with seething anger off into the late evening horizon and then staring challengingly at the setting sun to see where it had gone. I learned afterwards that he had been physically violent to Kate as a child and that tempered my affection for him considerably. He had bitten off more than he could chew by taking the sun on. Kate grieved terribly.

There was a young tramp living in a burned-out car beneath a bridge near us. His name was Eric and he had two dogs, Sarnie and Boot. He'd recently got out from a twelve-month stretch in prison and couldn't get things together. He was from the South West but didn't want to go home. It was getting a bit chilly at night so we'd let

275

him and the dogs sleep on the floor in our kitchen. He was a big bloke, with huge arms and a body-builder's chest, but he was very gentle and funny. He became a semi-permanent fixture. He loved the ganja and was happy to run up the shop when no one else could face it. Weenie got on well with the ultra-placid Sarnie and Boot so there was no problem there. Eric had a big boil on his neck, which turned out to be a cancerous growth that he had removed in Whipps Cross hospital. They told him such growths would return and they did. He was philosophical about it. We sat around playing guitar and shooting the breeze a lot. He'd won the first prize in the Bisley Small Bore competition when he was sixteen and seemed set for a life of rural bliss, but his head went wrong. He was almost incinerated in an accident at a turkey farm where he was trapped in an oven. His trousers had actually burst into flames when they pulled him out. Then he had another traumatic incident on his uncle's fishing boat. They went out on a sunny day and a storm blew up from nowhere. Eric said that it just got worse and worse, there were huge waves smashing over the bow and the boat was being tossed like a lollipop stick. Eric was frightened but his uncle, a hardbitten professional fisherman, was calmly getting on with what needed to be done. He told Eric not to worry, that he'd been in worse storms before and that the boat was sound. Eric clung to a bolted-down bench and tried to keep calm. At a certain point, however, his uncle broke down, fell to his knees and started wailing and screaming out that they were going to die, and crying out to God to save them. Eric completely lost it at this point and remembered nothing else till they were back on land.

He'd been banged away for some sort of petty theft, though he never really went into it. He had a girlfriend named Jackie, a not-very-bright sixteen year old, and she had a friend named Deborah who they used to have threesomes with. Eric would get his life back together a bit from time to time and we'd not see him for weeks, then he'd turn up when he was broke or down. He looked like a young Clive Dunn. The weirdest and to me totally unexpected thing about him was that he was vehemently racist. He was against interracial sex. He likened it to bestiality. I argued as much as I could but it was pointless. He never got angry at me but politely and good naturedly pointed out that I didn't know what I was talking about. He said that blacks were not human; he said that they were monkeys. It also transpired that he was as hard as nails, really hard. In fact he decided to take an active role in local racist life and went to one of the Skinhead Temples, located the then head of the Aryan Brotherhood in his garden and beat the living fuck out of him in front of his mates to establish a pecking order. He went on to become the manager of a seedy East End wine bar. I got the impression that it was a criminal organisation. In all the time I knew Eric we never had a cross word. He'd allow himself to be ordered around, make tea, go up the shops, wash the dishes, without a word of complaint. I really liked him. Despite everything, he had a sweet soul. He had to go to the hospital two or three more times to get growths removed. He told me he didn't expect to live long; the cancer would get him for sure.

The band was winding down and we played our last gig at a venue in Watford that had a huge dance floor with a glitter ball revolving above it. A short way into the set a side door opened and a young guy dressed in a military uniform and sporting a Hitler hairline and moustache came in, marched up to the front of the stage, pulled out a Luger and aimed it at the centre of my forehead. I stared into his eyes. He was from beyond the Valley of the Dolls. I thought 'Well that's it.' I didn't stop singing though, and there was a simple click when he pulled the trigger. It turned out that he was a well-known local nutter. Schweppes removed him.

I'd started work at an American bank called Manufacturers Hanover Trust a few train stops away in Stratford East. It was nights. I had to collect computer printouts, put them in piles relevant to different departments and distribute them before people came into work in the mornings. It was boring but easy and it paid a hundred and sixty quid a week, a fortune. My boss was a woman with short blonde hair and glasses and my fellow worker was an old cockney bloke. They were both nice enough in their way. The bloke used to tell me tales about his boyhood in the East End before the war. Him and his mates used to beat up Jews. 'We'd knock 'em darn then kick the shit art of 'em. They'd be holdin' their heads, covering up their faces, Please don't 'it me they'd say. Please don't 'urt me!' He'd recall it with a good-natured nostalgic chuckle that seemed to say 'Those were the days!' He felt really lucky to have landed this job. He felt he'd fallen on his feet.

The Plants wanted to put me, Schweppes and Neil the drummer together with two other guys they'd 'discovered', named Norman and Dave. We met them and had a knock. It was okay so we advertised for a bassist. We got a guy named Brian Diprose, who'd played for The Third Ear Band, an old sixties underground rock group. He looked like a caveman and owned six or seven bass guitars, one of which he kept in a coffin. We started rehearsing. I'd written some new numbers. They weren't great but they had a particular feel, a jerky bitterness. We called ourselves Watch With Mother. Me and Schweppes had started hiring out the PA too. It was quite lucrative and financed an upswing in our coke consumption. It was another bitter winter. Christmas came and went.

I was sitting with Kate one evening when she told me that she'd met someone else and wanted to leave. I can't remember what I said but a few days later Schweppes and I came home from a rehearsal and she was packing a suitcase. I stood and watched. She said she didn't want to hurt me, but if she did, there you go. She said I could kill myself if I liked. She just had to go. Then she got Schweppes to drive her to where the other bloke lived and said she'd return for the rest of her things when I wasn't there. She took Weenie and went. I sat in the armchair by the fire all night looking at my reflection in the dressing table mirror. I looked like a bundle of grey rags. Schweppes took her something a few days later and I went along for the ride. Kate came out to the van to say something and that was the last time I ever saw her. I can't describe how I felt without resorting to cliché. Suffice it to say I suffered the same agonies that every betrayed lover has ever felt. I was too hurt to feel bitter. I felt ugly. I kept bursting into tears. I cried myself dry. Schweppes would just sit there quietly or make me a cup of tea. We carried on rehearsing and renting out the PA. We'd get home late, unload the gear, then sit in Schweppes' room snorting coke and talking till dawn. We'd imagine that we had insight, we'd see diamonds sparkling where there were no diamonds.

Our landlord called. I told him my situation. He was kind and gently sympathetic. He put his hand on my shoulder and said 'There are more fish in the sea, my friend. Things seem black now but it will change.' I didn't feel so at the time but I was touched by his concern. I did do a bit of tomming and got my leg over a couple of times but my heart wasn't in it. I actually felt that I was using these women. I don't know why that should have bothered me but it did. I felt like a piece of shit.

The Plants booked us into some venues. We began to gig. Zonderman turned up from Holland to stay for a night. He had big cowboy boots on. He took them off and unscrewed the heels. There was a big sticky lump of black citrol in each. He'd brought them over from Amsterdam. We chased the dragon. There is a painting, by Millais I think, called *Les Enfants des Etoile*, *The Children of the Stars*, which shows two half-asleep little girls in their nightdresses being pulled along through a deep, star-filled sky by angels. That's what opium is like. Zonder left the next day. Sue came to see me and gave me a cuddle. She was as sweet and unaffected a person as you'd ever meet. Schweppes was still doing some work for Ham and he came home one day with two female kittens he'd found abandoned in a field. They were black and white and as pretty as could be. We named them Bert and Chester after two characters in the American sitcom *Soap*, and they took up residence in a drawer.

I was having trouble with my eyes, conjunctivitis. On top of everything else it was a drag. I was singing and performing well, though. My pain was fashionably evident. I was thin and hollow eyed. I was a walking scar.

My niece Sian was working as a chambermaid in the Intercontinental Hotel in Mayfair and she rang me. She wanted to meet up and since we had a gig that Friday we arranged to meet at the venue, The Queen's Head in Stockwell. She said she'd bring her friend, another chambermaid named Jane. We got there and set up early. Sian came in followed by the most gorgeous girl I'd seen in lifetimes. This was Jane. She was tall and willowy with short black hair and dreamy, sexy eyes. She had a touch of glittery face make-up on and smoked cigarettes with great style. I said hello then sat near her till we had to play. We were heckled by the other band on the bill but it was muted because we were evidently a step above them. We gave Sian and Jane a lift back into the city in Ludwig. There wasn't a lot of room so Jane sat on my lap. This caused a physical reaction in me which I'm sure she must have noticed. We dropped them off near the hotel and she gave me a little kiss goodbye. She was eighteen. I couldn't get her out of my mind. I dreamt about her.

A few days later I plucked up the courage to phone Sian and suggest she come to visit me in Leytonstone and possibly bring her friend Jane with her, if she wanted to come, that was. She did. We went out for a drink when they came and when we got back to the flat Sian said it was time to leave but Jane wanted to stay longer, so Sian left on her own. I kissed Jane. It was a beautiful kiss. We went to bed and made love. She was a child of the stars like me. I'd fallen in love with her the moment I saw her.

Zonder turned up again the following week on another citrol run. We got way out of it. Jane had no reticence. She loved it. We stood out in the back garden together drinking beer. It was a cold black night. We laughed and chatted beneath the infinite sky. The next morning Zonder left us a fair-sized lump as a thank you for letting him crash. It was enough to keep us smashed for weeks. Zonder was coming back to London the following week to get married to his girlfriend, Jane. The wedding was on the Saturday afternoon and the reception was at John and Leonie's new place in East Ham. My Jane had already arranged to stay with her parents in Cornwall that weekend and she couldn't break it, so I went on my own.

It was a lovely wedding. Zonder and Jane looked so cool and so in love. They were both heavily into the drugs and the reception was a Felliniesque dream. I found myself on the landing queuing up outside the toilet to vomit. The door was left open for more efficient rotation. When I got in I slumped on my knees and fell asleep as I was vomiting. It was a weird thing to do but I couldn't help it. I heard people commenting. They tried to wake me but I couldn't be reached. Someone went and got the Man, who lifted me onto my feet and started walking me around. 'He'll be all right. He's just overdone it a bit. Don't worry.' I believed that I was dying, lying there with my head down the toilet. I accepted it. I thought I was going to heaven there and then. I recovered as Zonder said I would, and then Jane, a trained hairdresser, gave me a haircut. It was a botched job. I looked like a ventriloquist's dummy from a horror film, but I didn't care. I was very tired by then and I was missing Jane terribly.

Schweppes dropped me off back home, then returned to East Ham on his own. I struggled to open the front door, then staggered down the dark corridor to my room and went in. I turned the light on and there was my beloved lying all curled up and sleepy in my bed. Jane had come back early. She'd missed me too. She laughed at my haircut and held me in her arms all night. Bert and Chester woke us by biting our noses.

I quit my job. Going out at half past nine at night to go to work proved impossible. How could I leave my sweet baby like that? How could I leave her? Jane quit her job at the hotel too, and we settled into a period of drug-induced stupor. Eric called around a few times. It was in his seedy wine bar manager phase. He and Jane hit it off right away. Eric was cheeky, he stood up for himself, and Jane appreciated that. Eric liked Jane back but he was a committed misogynist. 'You can't trust women' was his catchphrase. Given my recent experience with Kate I didn't particularly disagree with him. Jane was convinced that he was right. 'You can't trust them,' she'd repeat. 'Believe me!' All three of us agreed on this fact and we were right.

Our old friend Horatio turned up one evening. He was outside the back door looking rested and sprightly. Bert and Chester were delighted. Their hackles were up as they danced around him with suspicion and curiosity. Horatio rolled into a ball and both the cats got their noses and paws spiked painfully. They never bugged him again. Horatio stayed for a few days, fattening himself up, and then disappeared as he had the previous year. Bert and Chester were growing and they'd taken to climbing the trees between our house and the one that backed on to it.

They looked so beautiful up there, hopping and tumbling from branch to branch.

We had another 'gift' from Zonderman and we were pretty much out of it every day from dawn to dusk. We watched *The Martian Chronicles* on TV; Rock Hudson, very good. Schweppes and Jane got on fine but Schweppes wasn't happy. He had spent years drunk and stoned on a succession of heavy-duty drugs, just as I had, and it hadn't made him happy either. I think the death of the dream had pained and disappointed us both more than we realised. Schweppes was a great bloke, a great friend.

Jane didn't like Leonie. We'd gone out for a drink with her and John, and Leonie had warned me about Eric. She'd said he was a tramp and a parasite and that I should sever my friendship with him. Jane took umbrage at this and thought Leonie was a stuck-up bitch. I love Leonie and would trust her with my life, but Jane would not be moved. It was a bit awkward but not terminal.

Watch With Mother broke up. I had been too drugged up and mad to involve myself. The lads in the band were good fellows and good musicians but we weren't friends. It didn't really mean anything to me. The next time I saw Neil, our drummer, he was playing with Bowie at Live Aid on the telly.

It was summer. When you're really stoned summer seems more intense. Time goes slower. The colours are darker. Jane and I were suspended in the aspic of it. Her brother Michael had lived in Australia and always enthused about it to her. I asked her if she'd like to go. I was married to Kate, I could get in easily, and Jane could get a one-year working visa. She was right up for it. The main problem was that we had no money. We decided to get jobs and save up. Jane went back to chambermaiding and I got a job as a dispatch clerk for a firm called Brown and Polson Nautical Chart Suppliers in Canning Town. The office was straight out of Dickens, as were the two old guys who ran it. I received orders for various charts through the post, found them in the storeroom, packaged them up and posted them off. Canning Town was a long train journey from Leytonstone and I'd get home in the dark. It was okay at first, it had a quaint charm even, but then the horror started to seep in. Jane was getting to the end of her tether too. She decided to try to borrow the five hundred pounds we still needed from her uncle Godfrey, an unmarried scientist who worked at a secret government research centre. She wrote him a letter and Uncle Godfrey came up trumps! Jane's visa was delayed for some reason so we decided I'd go first to find us a place to stay and that she'd stay with her parents and follow on in a month's time.

Leonie told me that Kate was pregnant and that her mother had come over to visit. Schweppes and Bob decided to return to Wales. We quit the flat the day I left. I went for a haircut in the morning before leaving for the airport. The barber turned the radio on as I sat in the chair and it was playing 'A Day in the Life'. I hadn't heard it in years. It was a good omen! When the song finished the DJ said that they were playing Lennon songs all day in memory of John, who had been shot dead by a gunman in New York earlier that morning. Schweppes took Bert and Chester back to Wales with him.

ASHES TO ASHES

I got stopped at immigration control when I arrived at Sydney airport. The guy at the gate looked at my passport and, instead of handing it back, kept it and sent me to take a seat in a small room nearby. I freaked. Ten minutes later another guy, a bespectacled guy in shirtsleeves, came in and sat at the table opposite me. He had my passport. He opened it, stared at in silence for a minute or so then asked me where my wife was, why she wasn't with me. I explained that her mother was in the UK on holiday and that they'd decided to have a European jaunt together before coming back in a few weeks' time. The guy asked me a few other questions then stared at me for a moment, stamped my passport and told me I could go. I'd had it in my head they might not let me back in right from the start; I was paranoid about it. I thought they'd think that I was trying to sneak back into Australia before I got divorced. Whether that's a crime or not I don't know, but it worried me. I took a deep breath when I got out of the airport doors. The air was thick and tasted beautiful. It felt great to be back. I got a taxi to Lindsay's house. He was still with Wendy. It was great to see him and he seemed okay. He was functioning at least. They'd made up a double mattress on the floor in the living room for me to sleep on. I slept for days. It was a strange summer. It rained a lot.

I decided to go up to Speers Point to stay with David for a few days. 'What the Matter You?' was top of the hit parade. It was cool seeing David. We talked about Peter. David said he was a lot better. We talked about me and

286

Kate and his father's death. David was a taciturn guy but a great listener. We watched TV, played pool and got drunk. I went back to Sydney a week later. Lindsay told me that Little Loci was living with a mature and beautiful woman. He'd heard a tale about John Strangeways inserting himself into their relationship. He'd heard it was a pretty sordid scene. Whether it's true or not, I don't know.

A terrible thing had happened to the Kosta family. They went to live in a caravan out in the country and young Kerry committed suicide. He'd split up with a girl. He left the house saying he was going back to Sydney, but he didn't go. He went to a nearby glade by a stream and killed himself with a shotgun. His mother discovered him accidentally a few days later. Such tragedy is hard to contemplate.

I met up with Vince and Mavis. They were married. I went to their house for a meal. There was something wrong though, I think they had lost respect for me for some reason. I'm sure that it was a legitimate reason too, but I can't remember what it was. They seemed happy together. We watched cricket for a while and I said goodbye.

Jane arrived and we rested up for a week or so. She was very moody. She'd have teenage sulks. She was as crazy as hell, stomping around, refusing to talk, hating everyone and everything. She drove me nuts with her unreasonable behaviour. I ran out of the house naked during a thunderstorm to throw myself in the lake across the road from the house in desperation on one occasion. I was drunk. It was her nineteenth birthday a week or so after she arrived and I took her to see Steven Berkoff's touring company performing *The Tell-Tale Heart* and *The Fall of the House of Usher* in a small suburban theatre. It was magical. I bought a guitar the following week, a strong earthy Washburn, and named it Roderick after Roderick Usher.

We visited Reno in Darlinghurst. He lived in a communal house with a small Chinese guy, a beautiful woman, an effete young lad named Alistair, a German private eye named Klaus and a depressed lesbian. Reno had formed a band called MC ESCHER. He wrote the songs himself; Brechtian music-hall style numbers packed with confrontationally blunt homosexual content. One was called 'He Fucks Me on a Sunday' as I recall. Klaus, a tall pleasant-looking blond guy about my age, was the group's singer, but he wasn't gay and he didn't feel comfortable with the material. He confided in me as such. I saw his point. I told him I couldn't relate to the songs either. I told him there was no way I'd sing them; I'd feel like a prick. Jane and I moved into the house. The beautiful woman was a nymphomaniac. She was shagging the little Chinese guy, who was in turn shagging Reno. She'd drag him into other people's rooms and shag him on their beds. I caught them at it on the floor in the living room on one occasion. She smiled up at me and said 'Hi'. I walked in on the little Chinese guy and Reno too. It was like Peyton Place in that house but Jane and I carried on with our tempestuous courtship unaffected. On new year's eve we went into town and had a meal in a restaurant. Quail in cherry sauce. Then afterwards we walked through the park and splashed water from the fountain. It was a glorious night. We hugged and kissed, very excited to be in Australia and very happy in each other's company. We got home before midnight and watched the fireworks from our bedroom window. John and Leonie turned up. They were on holiday visiting Leonie's family. We met at a wine bar and then went back to Reno's place. Jane stayed in her room. We moved out a few weeks later.

Jane got a job as a chambermaid in The Hilton and I got back into the Civil Service, a department that helped ex-servicemen get their own homes. The office was in a skyscraper in King's Cross, a short walk from where we lived in Hopewell Street in Paddington, where we had a one-bed, ground-floor flat in a purpose-built, two-storey block. We were joined there by a small flea-ridden kitten whom we found abandoned in a hole in a wall. We named her Flea in honour of her parasites. The flats and their grounds were the home of The Moon Gang, a group of cats led by Moonface, a black and white tom. Other members included Ghengis, a strong, handsome young tabby, Juliette, a sexy little white thing, The Bookend Twins, two feral brothers, one of whom had had his right ear flattened out of shape (to differentiate between them we called that one Broken-Eared Bookend), and Lawrence, a very naughty, flat-faced kitten who belonged to the obnoxious gay air steward who lived in the flat next door to us. Flea became a member, and the consort of the virile and much in demand Ghengis. They were a fascinating group of characters and gave me endless delight. Lawrence became a particular friend. Jane left the door ajar one morning when she left for work and he wandered in from the corridor. I was still asleep, though I registered his presence. It was a boiling hot day. He was so tiny that he had to climb onto the bed even though it was just a

289

mattress on the floor. I could hear his breathing and he licked my ear. It was very pleasant. Then he curled up in my hair, still pleasant. Then I felt my head becoming warm. Lawrence was peeing on it. I had to get up and shower and change the bed clothes; he wasn't bothered. I'd delight in holding him as if he was a toy racing car, then releasing him and watching him shoot across the carpet towards Flea's saucer of food as if attached to it by a strong rubber band. He was a greedy little tyke. All of The Moon Gang were hale fellows in fact.

I met up with Peter West, my friend from the taxation department, again. He was down on his luck: his wife had left him for a woman. He came over to the flat quite often. We'd get ripped and listen to music. He was a delicate soul. The creep next door's antics became too much and we moved to a flat on the upper floor. It was much nicer. The windows were level with the tops of trees. Jane had become saner. Her job was tolerable and paid well. My job was typical Civil Service, boring beyond words. I adopted my usual system of simply not doing it. I hid files away and spent most of my day writing short stories. They weren't Tolstoy but they were quite interesting in a juvenile way. One was about a young guy in a country being racked by political violence who becomes a street entertainer, a clown in fact, and joins a student under-ground movement. He comes from a boring middle-class family. His father gets up every morning, puts on a suit and goes to work in a government department. The clown son gets rounded up in a swoop by the secret police and has his tongue torn out. He gets strapped into a chair in a basement room without windows. They leave him in his clown regalia and make-up. They don't expect to get any information out of him. They just want to torture him for the fun of it. The unknowing torturer is his father. I enjoyed writing them and they passed the time, but the prose was convoluted and the storylines were weak. I threw them all away.

A small group of us went to a bar in the basement of the building or to a nearby wine bar for lunch every day. We'd get plastered. There was a gorgeous Turkish girl in the group who fancied me. The other guys all urged me to take advantage of the situation but I couldn't do that. It was nice being in her company though, and the cheese platter in the wine bar was a joy. 'Love Will Tear Us Apart' was in the charts.

Kate phoned me in work. She'd finished with the bloke in London and returned home. She wanted to meet up for a talk but I couldn't. It would be betraying Jane's trust. She'd had her baby, a boy. I got a call from Phil Mar. He and Reno had split acrimoniously and Phillip was now living with a bald-headed bloke named Peter. He was bitter about Reno. He said that he'd been manipulated and fooled by him for a very long time. They'd been friends since their schooldays. Phillip came around and we played music together. He'd given up the guitar for the saxophone. He liked Jane. He could see beyond her spiky surface.

I received a very unpleasant letter from Reno shortly after. He accused me of stealing people from his band. I honestly didn't know what he was talking about, and though we met again on several occasions there was a distance between us. It might have been my friendship with Phillip. It upset me; I thought the world of Reno.

291

Jane went through a period of discontent. She wanted to leave Sydney. She wanted to go up country to a ranch and become a Jillaroo. I wasn't enthusiastic. Maybe she should have gone. Who knows? I wrote a novel called *You in Your Small Corner*. I'd get up early and write as the sun came up. The novel was about Amsterdam. It was the onset of Armageddon. Giant starfish with grotesquely human faces had risen from the sea and attacked the city in their hundreds. There were crowds of Satanists rampaging through the streets, deranged priests screaming sermons from the steps of gutted churches, books being burned and children murdered. I was wandering through the carnage trying to find Kate. It engrossed me at the time but it was objectively unreadable. It followed my short stories into the bin.

A tragedy happened. Flea and most of The Moon Gang were killed. There had been reports of funnel web spiders in the gardens of the flats and the council sent pest-control people to deal with it. They sprayed poison everywhere and the poor little felines got it into their systems and died. It was horrific. I complained to the authorities but there was no response.

Jane went to Bondi Beach one morning when I was working and almost drowned. She found herself out of her depth and then got sucked under the water by a huge wave. She rose to the surface twice but kept getting pulled back under by the current. She said that she'd given up hope. She said that it was very pleasant, that she felt calm; then she was rescued by a lifesaver. He'd spotted she was in trouble from the shore and hared off into the water. It was not an uncommon occurrence apparently.

No wonder these guys get laid so often. Good luck to them, especially the one who saved my sweetheart. Winter was becoming summer again and we missed home. The reality is that the year we spent in Sydney went by as if it were a day. Nothing actually happened. I was just happy to be with Jane. Nothing else mattered. We got to know each other. It was one day with someone you love. It was the day the earth stood still. We decided to return to England.

PLYMOUTH

We got into Heathrow late so we stayed in a hotel and caught a coach to Plymouth the next day: it was a long journey. Jane's father, Bernard, met us at the bus station and drove us home. We had a takeaway curry and went to bed. It was late autumn. England looked beautiful. Dartmoor was nearby so we drove there and walked across some fields. There was a sturdy little river rushing along and a small forest. Jane looked gorgeous in her wellingtons. It started getting dark early. Jane's parents, Bernard and Constance, were very nice to me. I'm sure it wasn't easy for them, meeting the thirty-year-old married bloke who'd taken up with their nineteen-year-old daughter. There was a meeting of people, friends and acquaintances of the family, at the house to promote Amway, an American get-rich-quick scheme. An old Richard Attenborough type talked about detergents and so forth for half an hour. They all sat around listening. They were a rum bunch, tragic figures in the main. When Attenborough finished they applauded him enthusiastically. A question and answer session followed. It was like a dream.

Jane's older sister Ivy came to stay one night and Constance cooked dinner. The dinner ended with Ivy telling Jane to fuck off and then storming off into the night. Bernard scoured the streets for her in his car till the early morning. There was a private boys' school to the rear of the house, its playing fields bordered the back wall. Their uniform was short black trousers and a bright red blazer. Bernard and Constance used to refer to them as the Little Bleeders. Bernard himself had been sent to a private school when he was very young and I got the impression it had been a nightmare for him but I never discovered any of the details. Bernard was a professional golfer nearing the end of his career, only playing the occasional tournament. You got the feeling that his heart wasn't in it. He'd met Constance when he was doing his national service in the Air Force. She'd been widowed with a child, Jane's brother Michael, and it was love at first sight. There is a wedding photograph of them in front of the church door, Bernard in his uniform and Constance looking beautiful. They are such a handsome couple and so very much in love. As well as playing golf, Bernard co-owned a chain of fish and chip shops in the Plymouth area with his brother Pat, a retired pharmacist. He said we could stay in the flat above their Devonport shop until we decided our next course of action.

Devonport was a charmless place. The locals were unfriendly, brute humans in the main, young junkie alcoholic thugs and their concentration-camp guard girlfriends. It was cold, grey and violent. The flat was quite nice, luxurious, even but the vibe of the town seeped in from the shop downstairs and through the ill-fitting sash windows. We spent a lot of time with Jane's parents. We'd drive out to the country and go for long walks, usually ending up in a pub for lunch and a half-a-dozen pints of real ale. We visited Uncle Pat and his family occasionally. It was strange for me. These people were middle-class Tories. Bernard and Pat in particular were to the right of Ayn Rand. They had a virulent hatred of the working classes, and Bernard was outspokenly racist. He hated Europeans and didn't like the Welsh either. He advocated detention camps in South Africa. Compared to Pat he was a liberal. There was a third brother, Mick, the eldest. He was a Colonel Blimp lookalike who could barely make himself understood, he was always so seething with righteous anger. He regarded his younger brothers as virtually hippies. I got along okay by adopting my famous non-confrontational persona. I knew that I wasn't going to get through to these guys and that it would be a waste of effort trying. I kept my head down. Jane, on the other hand, was keen for the fray. It was evident that she and her father were old foes. Her capriciousness was unstoppable. They couldn't exchange two words without it ending in a blazing row. Tears before bedtime was the norm.

I liked Jane's sister Ivy. She was a professional golfer like her dad. She was sophisticated and beautiful but her taste in men left a lot to be desired. She went out with a succession of really horrific blokes. She'd bring them home for us to meet. They were arrogant tosser golf-club types, the sort of blokes no normal bloke can stomach. They might as well have had 'I am a piece of shit' tattooed on their foreheads. Jane didn't try to hide her contempt.

After they'd gone Ivy would ask 'So what do you think of Barnaby then?' in as conversational a tone as she could muster. We'd all say he seemed very nice and Jane would say 'He seemed like a monster to me,' or some such damning phrase. That would get them going. I felt helpless to intervene. Jane's family was just a normal family in fact, but because they were English middle-class and spoke in RP, their behaviour seemed somewhat studied to me. It was like being in a play, a damn good play, Rattigan maybe. They were ordinary people but their ordinariness was new to me. I liked them.

A friend of Jane's ran the youth hostel on the Isle of Wight with her husband. We stayed there for a week. She was nice enough but he was an über zombie. He made a fuss because I drank a bottle of Mann's I found in a cupboard. He said he'd been 'keeping' it. We visited Osborne House, where Queen Victoria locked herself away after her husband died. There was a room where Tennyson had lived. His desk was still there, his huge hat and cloak hanging over the back of the chair. I was moved.

The Falklands War kicked off. Armoured vehicles ground by in the streets outside our window in the dead of night. Off-duty soldiers and sailors were getting extra drunk. Everybody agreed that the Argies had stepped over the line. They had to be sorted out. There was a bloodlust. Bernard and his mates were positively sparkling with delight. Jane, Constance and I went to the pictures on a grey Saturday afternoon and saw a double bill of *Gregory's Girl* and *Chariots of Fire*. Even I got caught up in the patriotic vibe.

Jane called me to her side one day and told me she had planned our future. We'd get married then go to live in Canada. I was a Canadian citizen and, as my wife, she would have automatic residence. It was a great idea, romantic and exciting. The problem was that I was still married to Kate. I phoned her in Australia and told her I wanted a divorce. She said okay and that she would see to it from there. It would take some time though. We had to wait. We read a lot, Kafka, Woodhouse and Tolkien. I'd read *The Hobbit* years before and now I got stuck into *The Lord of the Rings* trilogy. I listened to Del Shannon on the juke box of the local pub and watched black and white films on the telly on rainy weekday afternoons. Time crept by. Jane and I had long philosophical conversations. There was a wireless program on about the Holocaust. Someone asked why the Jews were so acquiescent in the process. Why they hadn't fought to the death rather than allowing themselves to be herded to their destruction so easily. I said some rubbish about how we Welsh would have at least tried to rush the guards or something. It was shit but I said it. Jane said that they did resist as much as they could in the circumstances. She'd read about them taking each other's hands and singing hymns together as they were led to the chambers. I felt ashamed. Jane was a special person. She was lovely. We were getting married for practical reasons but we wouldn't have done it if we hadn't loved each other. I was a lucky man.

The divorce came through and we got married in Plymouth Registry Office a month later. Uncle Mick had a few words with me as we were entering the building. He made it clear that he regarded me as a pathetic fool and wasn't over the moon about me becoming a fringe member of the family. He was blunt. It was okay though. I could see his point. The reception was back at Bernard and Constance's house. It was a nice do. They were generous, enthusiastic hosts. Unfortunately I was suffering with an eye infection and could barely keep my eyes open, so I just sat around holding my head in my hands most of the day. There was a fair smattering of my family and Lemmings there and the disparate groups melded well. I was introduced to Uncle Godfrey and Constance's aged mother, the notorious Gang-Gang. We'd paid Godfrey the money he'd loaned us to go to Australia back, as we said we would. He was an archetypical boffin, glasses, balding head, slightly dithering but very smart. He was some type of lizard, a rare one. Gang-Gang, who was Bernard's Nemesis, was a little old woman with a sparkling eye and a sharp tongue. I met other relatives too, but didn't feel capable of extended conversation. Jane wore a pink dress and I wore cricket whites, my Tonyrefail Grammar School tie and a green jacket. The day went well. We went back to the flat in Devonport in the evening and my family and the Lemmings went for an Indian meal in a nearby restaurant. I just kept my eyes shut. It was pointless opening them, they'd just burn and I'd have to close them again. Charlie pondered expertly over the wine list. He asked the waiter a few questions. He was quite impressive, finally ordering a bottle of Claret. When it arrived the waiter poured a taster in Charlie's glass. Charlie stared at it in disappointment. He'd expected it to be white.

It turned out that I had to apply for Jane's residency from Canada, so once again I went first. I took one suitcase and

Roderick. The Air France flight took me to Paris first and then on to Toronto. I had a shiver down my spine as we crossed the Canadian coastline. I stared down from the window at huge areas of forest land and sparkling blue lakes. This was Canada where I was born, where my father was buried. It was breathtakingly beautiful.

CANADA

When I got out at Toronto Airport I got a taxi, a limousine as they call them, and asked the driver to take me to a dirt-cheap hotel. The limousine ride was twenty quid and the hotel two hundred a night. I walked around with Roderick and my suitcase till I found the YMCA. It was twenty a night and I got my own little room. It was very modern, all white tiles and... well, young men, whether they were Christians or not I couldn't tell. I paid for a few nights, put my stuff safe, had a shower and went to a city-centre pub. It was an incredibly hot, humid evening. Toronto is on the Great Lakes and the weather is similar to New York. I'd never been so hot, not even in Australia. I sat at the bar and got plastered with a group of off-duty coppers. They told me that they drove down to Detroit one weekend a month to hang out. They said that I could go with them next time if I wanted to. I said I would, but can you imagine it, me getting pissed and going to heavy nightclubs in Detroit with these guys? I didn't even know what 'hanging out' meant. It was an interesting evening though. Off-duty coppers are very funny. I slept like a bell and the next morning went to a government office to get a social insurance number, a big deal in Canada, and from there to another government office in another building to fill out the necessary forms to apply for residency for Jane to come over. I met a Vietnamese guy there. He was a lot like Phillip Mar. He invited me to his house for some food the next day and gave me the address. I went to an agency that helped newly arrived immigrants the following morning, and they found me a cheap room in a boarding house off Bloor Street. I grabbed my things from the YMCA and went there on a bus. When you first get somewhere everything is so interesting, the bus, the other passengers, the tree-lined streets...

The boarding house was a detached, three-storey residence near a large park. The owners were the Chomkos, a Polish couple in their fifties. They lived on the ground floor and let out the rooms on the upper floors to single men. Mrs Chomko was a stern-looking woman who spent her time doing housework and listening to evangelist preachers ranting on television. Since the house was filled with little statues and paintings of Jesus and the Virgin Mary I assumed that she was a religious nutter, probably a Catholic. Mr Chomko made Polish sausages in the cellar. You'd often see him in his blood-stained vest with a meat cleaver in his hand. I think he did good business. Though they'd lived in Canada for over thirty years neither of the Chomkos spoke a word of English. I dealt with their daughter, a stunning-looking married woman who lived nearby. I paid a few weeks' rent and moved into a bright sunny room on the top floor. I went to visit the Vietnamese guy. He lived in an area of Toronto called Jane, which I took as a good omen. His wife didn't speak a word to me. The weather had become even hotter. I could hardly sleep at night for the mosquitoes. I'd be awake staring out of the window with sweat pouring down my face as dawn broke. I was happy though. I felt excited. I phoned Jane every day.

The other residents in Mrs Chomko's Mad House were three recently arrived young Polish guys, a pair of French-Canadian lumberjack brothers who spent four months a year in the city spending their accumulated wages on high living, an Ethiopian asylum seeker and a Yugoslavian physicist who'd fled the country a few months before. His name was Stanko. The vibe was not friendly. The Polish guys were obsessed with all things western. They bought tacky clothing and strutted about in it like male models. They were virtually hysterical ninety per cent of the time. The lumberjack brothers were misanthropic alcoholics. They had the air of murderers about them. The Ethiopian had been the manager of the biggest bank in the country but fell out of favour with some military bigwig who was stealing the assets, and had to flee in the dead of night to save his life. His wife and children were still there and he was desperately unhappy. He used to sob audibly in the nights. I went for walks in the park with him. He was tiny, five-three maybe, and as thin as a twig. We couldn't communicate well, just a little French in common, but he was a dear chap, I felt so sorry for him.

Stanko was a fascinating man. He too had fled his country. His wife and children were still there and he missed the children terribly. He didn't miss his wife that much though. I got the impression that he didn't love her. He'd worked in a nuclear research facility in Split. He told me that Yugoslavia was a desperate country. The military dictator had visited his workplace with his entourage the previous year. All the workers had to line his route and cheer as he entered the building. He passed within feet of Stanko and he told me that he was overwhelmed with disgust that such a twisted, dwarf-like creature as this had control over his and his family's lives. It was at that moment he knew he had to escape. It was either that or suicide. He borrowed money and fled across land till he got to Germany, and he'd applied to come to Canada from there. He was working delivering *The Globe and Mail*, the Toronto daily paper, door to door in the surrounding area. He looked a lot like Sig. His broken English was similar too. I'd accompany him on his delivery rounds sometimes. We'd get insulted and threatened by Canadian thugs occasionally. Stanko bit his tongue. He couldn't afford to get involved. We passed a high block of flats near the park one evening and noticed a balcony halfway up that was blackened and cracked. There'd been a fire there the week before and two people had jumped to their deaths trying to get away. Stanko was a very intelligent, very intense man. His English was remarkable given that he'd only been learning it for a few months. We were sat in the Chomkos' garden one afternoon and he asked me what we called 'these ones, these little yellow and black ones'. I told him we called them bees. I always think of bees as these little yellow and black ones now. It gives them a delightful individuality.

I was sitting in my room reading one evening and there was a knock on my door. It was the Polish guys and the lumberjack brothers. One of the more lucid Poles explained that they would like me to sign a letter they'd written to the Chomkos asking that they get rid of 'the black animal in the room down the corridor'. They said that they couldn't stand the smell and the sound of him crying when they wanted to sleep. I was too much of a coward to tell them to fuck off in so many words but I think they realised I was not going to sign, and after standing around the door for a few minutes they left. I took to going and having mint tea with the Ethiopian guy. The Poles and the Brothers Grimm noted it and the vibe became quite hostile towards me too. I actually felt under threat at times.

I walked in the park a lot. It was a beautiful place with trees and flower beds, baseball diamonds, chipmunks and prairie dogs, ice-cream vans, paddling pools, football pitches and picnic areas. It was usually filled with mothers and their children. I'd lie on the grass and stare up at the sky for hours. The Job Centre was nearby. The first time I went I was interviewed by a big young camp guy and a pretty young woman and they were very kind. They said they'd see what was about. It was their lunch hour so we went for a coffee. The bloke pulled out a nicely rolled little J from his jacket pocket. We smoked it as we walked. They were the first Canadians I'd actually communicated with and they were sweeties.

A few days later I was walking home from the park when a huge English sheep dog bounded towards me in a back garden. It leapt up onto the fence and barked. I patted its head. It was dribbling with hysteria. It was lovely. Its owner came out of the back door. He was a stocky guy about my age. He asked if the dog was bothering me. I said it wasn't. I said I liked the dog. He heard my accent. 'Are you British?' he asked. I explained that I was Welsh. 'Do you fancy a pint?' He opened the gate and we sat in his kitchen with the door open and drank half-a-dozen bottles of Budweiser. His name was Pat Prendergast. He was from London, Ontario, a city north west of Toronto. It had been called Berlin till 1914. He married his childhood sweetheart, Eva, and they moved to Toronto to work and live about a year earlier. Pat worked in an insurance company and Eva was a secretary. Eva arrived home from work. She was the cutest, sexiest little thing. There was some sort of vibe going down between them. I felt that it could be to do with my presence. Pat said that they'd be having a barbecue the next evening and I was invited. I took the hint and said I'd be there but I had to go now. Before I left Pat asked me to give my honest opinion of The Police, the band, not the law enforcers. He particularly wanted to know what I thought of Sting, the band's lead singer. Eva wanted to know too. I said I thought the band were tight and rocked it out a bit but that I personally couldn't stomach them. I said they made me feel physically sick. I said that Sting was a grotesque. I said I'd like to punch his pouting sensitive face into Roses Lime marmalade. Pat beamed with pleasure. Eva loved The Police and deified Sting. It could have been the other way around. In fact it probably was the other way around. I left. I returned the next evening. Pat was in the garden barbecuing sausages. We stood about for a bit and it started to rain. Pat attempted to carry on cooking but it proved a losing battle, so we adjourned to the kitchen. It dawned on me that no one else was coming. Eva turned out to be as sweet as she was beautiful. She apologised for her mood the previous evening. She said that it didn't matter what I thought of Sting. She just thought he was a dish, full stop. We agreed to differ. We sat at the kitchen table watching night fall through the open door. We were drinking at a fair pace. Pat asked me if I smoked. Not cigarettes I didn't. 'I'm talking weed,' he said. He got some Alaskan grass down from the shelf and we smoked some in a small pipe. It did the trick. In fact I started to feel unwell. I first noticed it when I slid off the chair onto the floor. Pat sat me back up but I couldn't remain there. I fell to the floor once again and this time I crawled towards the door. Pat called out but I waved him away. I crawled and staggered out of the house and back to the Mad House. It was raining gently. I crawled up the two flights of stairs to my room. I fell onto the bed but I couldn't sleep. The ceiling was spinning like a Catherine wheel. I fell onto the floor and started puking. I puked in the waste paper bin. It was one of those woven straw ones. I retched and puked until I fell asleep exhausted. I felt terrible when I woke up. I'd lacerated the walls of my stomach from retching. I had to clean up the puke and so forth and that set me off again. I made myself a cup of tea. What had happened the previous night was that I had been drinking with Pat and Pat was known as The Tank back in London, Ontario, due to his huge capacity for the grog. He was a legend in fact. I'd assumed that no one would be likely to drink too heavily for me to keep up with, not beer anyway, but I was wrong. Pat himself confirmed that he too had been as pissed as a rat and hardly remembered me being there.

Pat and Eva were really friendly people. They were very kind to me. I called in most days. I got to be friends with Carnaby, the dog. Eva loved Carnaby. Mrs Chomko's beautiful daughter told me that some other Polish people across the road were letting out their top floor. She said she'd had a word with them. It was ideal. I carried my stuff over and moved in. Pat drove me to the airport to meet Jane. It was late afternoon. We drove home and went to bed.

We spent the next few weeks exploring the city. Toronto is a metropolis, skyscrapers and fountains and statues and streets teeming with people of all nationalities. The weather was so hot and the sky so bright that it had a dreamlike quality. We went to a small arts cinema and saw *The Marriage of Maria Braun*. We ate out a few times but the food wasn't great. We phoned for a Chinese meal to be delivered. This was a science fiction concept to us at the time. It turned up but there was a huge dead wasp in Jane's meal and we didn't eat it. We went for walks in the park. We sat and watched a children's baseball match one evening. The standard was very high. The crowd was enthused. It was excellent. I'd got into baseball a bit from watching it on telly with Pat. It's a great game. The players are like gunslingers, especially the pitchers. It's a game of ego suppressing ego. I watched American football and ice hockey too, and both were okay, but it was baseball that did the trick for me. Jane got on well with Pat and Eva. I think Pat was knocked out at how pretty she was. Jane took to Carnaby too. It was great having them living so near.

The people who owned our new flat were a bit more animated than the Chomkos but still ultra-straight Christians. They had a son named Don who visited most days with his little boy. Don was an evangelist. He smiled like a shark coming in for the kill. He freaked me out. I felt sorry for the little boy. You could actually see him being smothered. Don't get me wrong, they were nice enough people, but there was no spark of life there. Their straightness was like a fortress. They were afraid of everything.

A letter arrived, delivered by hand. It said that I had an interview at the Job Centre that afternoon. It was for a job as a filing clerk in that very department. The two people I knew, the ones I'd had a toke with, weren't working there any longer but they'd recommended me. I was interviewed by three women and it seemed to go well. They loved my accent. I got another letter the next morning telling me I'd got the job on six months' probation and that I could start the following Monday. The old Clack charm had worked again. A new girl started with me. She was short with severe, tied-back auburn hair. Her boyfriend was a biker and she had a roughness about her. I got the impression she'd seen some hard times. We'd get a list of file numbers when we arrived in the mornings and it was our task to find them in the system and pass them to the clerk dealing with them. Most were filed away alphabetically but there were always those that had been misfiled or were out on someone else's desk for some reason. The work was relentless and tedious in the extreme but the people were okay. Our section head was a pretty woman in her thirties who lived with a police sergeant. There was an enormously fat woman with the voice of a little girl working nearby, and she was endlessly cheerful. I got sick of people saying 'You're welcome' all the time. It ceased to have any meaning. It just became an inarticulate shriek, like a baby dinosaur breaking out of its egg. To be honest the work was too hard to do much interacting, though there were a few guys who argued politics a lot and I enjoyed their passion. I hadn't realised how contentious the French question was. There was an election in the air and the Parti Quebecois was making a lot of noise. The guys in the office were all Anglophile Canadians and held no truck for them. I didn't hear the other side. Me and the biker girl ate in a nearby café and the section head joined us occasionally. I ate cooked breakfasts with skinny Canadian bacon and eggs 'easy over'. It sounded so cool saying it. I ordered pastrami on rye once just to say the words – I'd heard it so often in American films. I had wondered if I would feel anything for Canada. I did. The atmosphere was benevolent. The people were friendly and kind., they were funny too. They realised that they were regarded as bland by most of the world and they extracted humour from it. They lived in America's shadow but were distinctly un-American in their outlook. They came across as modest and dignified. I felt proud that my father had fought for them. I was happy to have been born there.

Jane and I walked along the shores of a sparkling lake one afternoon and watched otters swimming and frolicking in the water. Jane got work as a temp with a catering company run by a man named Klanklev. It was just serving in office canteens but it was better than nothing. We had a TV and a regular supply of hash courtesy of Pat.

Life was cool. The TV was interesting, seventy-eight channels and not a thing worth watching most of the time, but that didn't worry me. I watched things that were not worth watching. That said, there was a lot of sport and there were several channels that showed late films. I watched *Kagemusha*, *Seven Beauties* and Bertolucci's *1900* till the early hours. I watched *Magic* too; I was struck by what a great actor Anthony Hopkins was. We couldn't smoke dope in the house because of the smell, so I took to baking hash muffins. They did the trick. There was a channel that was like the BBC and it showed some good stuff. We watched the four-part adaptation of *Crime and Punishment* with John Hurt playing Raskolnikov. Pat and Eva thought it was interesting but low budget. We moved into autumn. Stanko came over for a cuppa sometimes but I'm afraid we fell out. He knew that I smoked dope and I think he tried to reconcile it with his upbringing, but he couldn't. He started shouting at me one day. 'Drugs! You know what I mean? Drugs! Standing outside schools... these creatures... selling drugs to little children... to babies... to the innocent ones. Drugs! How can you...' etcetera. It was an awkward situation which remained unresolved. Stanko left. The poor guy was fucked in the head. He was a character from an existentialist novel. I liked him and was sorry our friendship ended like that. I just remembered his second name. It was Stankovitch.

It started getting dark earlier. Stiff evening breezes began to blow. I thought about playing in bars. I advertised for another guitarist, someone who knew the local scene. A dozen or so guys came round the flat for a knock but each of them was crazier than the last. Maybe I worded the ad wrong. Nothing came of it. We were lying in bed one night when a mouse appeared on top of my guitar case. Jane decided that its name was Tampon and it became a regular visitor. I don't know what sex it was, that's why I'm calling it 'it'. It was wary but not terrified of our presence. It shat in a baking tray on one occasion and we had to throw away some fish, but other than that it was a good housemate.

I received a phone call in the early hours one morning. I said hello but there was no response, just the hum of an open line. I said my name and asked who was there. There was still no reply and yet I knew someone was listening. I sensed it strongly. After a while I didn't say anything. I waited in silence. Time passed. Then after what seemed an eternity I heard a croaking, servile voice. It uttered just one word, 'Master'. It was Silas! He was house-sitting in Amsterdam and got my number from Benjy. He was as stoned as an Israeli tank. We talked rubbish for over an hour. It was lovely to hear from him. Jane and I were pretty happy at this time. Nothing ecstatic, but life was kind of cool.

We woke up one morning to find the world covered in four feet of snow. It was as sudden as that and it was bloody freezing. We went to a department store and bought winter clothes, heavy duty coats, thick socks, lumberjack-type checked shirts and thermal underwear. Canada is geared up for such weather. The clothing was very effective. From that point on things just got snowier and snowier and colder and colder. While I was waiting for the bus one morning the weatherman on someone's transistor radio said that with the wind chill factor it was minus thirty-four degrees in Toronto. Strangely enough, it doesn't actually feel that cold. It just feels regular cold. I took to wearing a woolly hat. It was nice seeing people shovelling snow from their driveways so they could get their cars out. Pat did it with good-natured inevitability but some people looked really pissed off. Jane loved it. We went to Toronto Zoo. There was a reptile house and we talked to a bright-green tree boa. She said that she forgot the snow outside and just imagined she was lying on a moss-covered log in the Amazon basin. She was beautiful. If there had been no glass between us I'd have kissed her lovely nose. There were two white Siberian tigers in a large stone enclosure. The snow didn't bother them at all. They were stunningly attractive. We carried on frequenting the arts cinema. There was a complete season of Fassbinder films and we saw them all. We saw *ET* too in a big cinema full of screaming school kids. I don't believe in aliens but I do believe in post-war German social and sexual angst. I preferred Fassbinder. At home I ate hash muffins and watched a lot of TV.

We went to a party at Pat and Eva's where we met their friends. The males were overgrown boys and the females were thin neurotic women obsessed with sex. Some were from London. We got stoned in the garden and shared idiocies. Eva's parents were there too. Her dad was a good-looking Italian guy in an expensive suit. He was a businessman and a staunch supporter of American foreign policy. I didn't get involved in an argument though. I felt that it would have a negative effect on the partying. He thought I was naive. How can anyone who'd kiss a boa constrictor on the nose be thought of as naive? Pat's and Eva's circle of friends had a lot of history. There was a huge gentle guy named Gary who worried that he was violent because he'd raised his fist against an opponent in a basketball game. It made me smile. I'd expected him to have said he'd hospitalised the bloke or something, but no, the raising of the fist was enough to send Gary into an orgy of soul searching. From what I heard he should have at least broken the creep's nose, and I said so. I said that he'd have been kicked to death in Ton. They thought I was joking. The central figure in this group of friends was a bloke called Mike. He wasn't at the party but his name came up a lot. They were a close-knit, friendly bunch and I enjoyed their company. After everyone else had gone me and Pat stood on the veranda in the falling snow and wondered at the universe. I told him that I thought I was crazy and he said 'Aren't we all?'

Eva was far and away the prettiest Canadian woman I saw. Her and Pat were like Fred and Wilma Flintstone sprinkled with stardust. I liked them a lot. They invited us to London to celebrate Thanksgiving with Pat's family. We drove through pine forests, the sky white with snow, and arrived in the early dusk. The house was set back off the road. Pat's parents were very welcoming. His dad, a rotund but hard-looking man, liked a glass of whisky and we joined him. His younger brother was a handsome, strapping lad obsessed with playing sport, especially American football. He let me try on his shoulder pads and helmet. I commented that rugby was just as hard a game as football but our lads didn't wear protection like they did. I stopped short of calling them cissies but he got my point. We had tea then went downstairs to a basement room which had a bar in it. We slept soundly on a lovely feather mattress. The Thanksgiving dinner was scrumptious, turkey and pumpkin with endless vegetables followed by fruit pie. Pat's family was proud of their Irish heritage but like all Canadians they were aware of how fortunate they were. The standard of living for working-class folk was very high. There was a sense of unforced social cohesion. That night we went to a party at one of Pat's friends houses. The mythical Mike was there. He was a handsome devil with a winning smile and a charismatic presence. It was easy to see why he was loved by his friends. So were Pat and Eva. Someone started playing a guitar and I had a knock after them. Pat was well impressed. He'd never heard me play before. I avoid playing on social occasions for fear of coming across as 'the asshole with the guitar'. I've been horrified by him too often myself. Once in a while it's cool, though, and this was one of those onces. Pat beamed at his protégé. We got drunker and drunker as the night wore on, until my darling wife, who had been the focus of attention for ninety percent of the males present, fell over, unable to speak or move. I picked her up in my arms like a romantic hero and carried her back across the street to Pat's parents' house. They were still sat up watching late night TV but didn't seem put out. I said goodnight and carried my intoxicated princess off to bed. We said goodbye the following morning and drove back to T.O. in a blizzard.

It was just after this that I made a big mistake. I was watching ice hockey on the telly one Saturday afternoon when I was overcome with an attack of the munchies. I convinced myself that there would be no great harm done if I dashed down to the local shop to get some chocolate. I did so. It was bitterly cold and I was in shorts and a T-shirt. The flat was centrally heated and I often sat around like that. I started feeling ill that evening. My back ached and I developed a wicked cough. I woke the next morning in agony. The ribs in my back and sides stung with a sharp pain. Just breathing was agony. I went to see a doctor who told me that my dash to the shop had given me pleurisy. I began sweating profusely that night and, not being able to sleep, lay in bed till morning in a state of light delirium. By now the cough had become vicious and each bout tore at the muscles in my chest and back. I couldn't eat. Jane got me medicines from the chemists and made me endless cups of honey and lemon juice in boiling water, which I drank as though dying of thirst. I was really ill for five weeks. This meant that I couldn't go to work, which was a real drag, because my six-month probationary period ended during that time. I was worried I'd be marked down. No matter how ill a person is they can never be ill enough for an employer not to think they're swinging the lead. You'd have to be dead to escape that. Without work we'd be fucked. They phoned from the office every few days and their scepticism was apparent. I really wanted to go back but it wasn't possible. When I did go back the atmosphere had changed. The biker girl I worked with refused to speak to me and gave off disturbingly hostile vibes. I actually believed she was going to attack me on a couple of occasions. I think that she blamed me for being off work. Maybe she had to do my work as well as her own, which would have been hellish. She was crazy to begin with and I suppose this drove her over the edge. Her biker boyfriend had started giving her some sort of gyp just before I got ill and maybe that had got worse too. Whatever the reason, she had determined to treat me with aggressive contempt. It made work unbearable. I suppose I could have taken it to our section boss, but I didn't and I dreaded going in. I began to feel depressed. Jane sympathised. Her job was shitty too. Klanklev was a prick. She was sick of having to kowtow. We were both depressed.

Neither of us had ever been the tidiest of people and our depressive state made us untidier than ever. Housework was abandoned. The flat was simply an arena for mental anguish. It became a tip. We came home one day to find a letter pushed under the door. The owner, who was fanatically house-proud, had let herself in with her key and been horrified at the desolation. You could see her point. She said she wanted us out the following Friday. It was a devastating blow. Finding a new place by then would be all but impossible. We sat on the floor and cried. We decided to go back to England. We talked to the owner and she agreed to give us an extra week. We resigned our jobs and booked our flights. Pat took us to the airport and we had a drink in a bar as we waited to be called. We got quite drunk. We said goodbye and Jane and I boarded the 747. Canada disappeared beneath a cloud of night.

STATUES OF US

We returned to Jane's parents' new home, a large terraced house perched on a hillside overlooking Bath. It was early spring. We relaxed for a few weeks, then Bernard showed us a ground-floor studio flat he'd bought a few miles away. The idea was that we could move in, then after a few months if we liked it we could take over the lease, thus putting us on the first rung of the housing ladder. It was a tiny place with an even tinier garden, but it was very kind of him. We moved in and got a cat from the RSPCA. She was a mottled little thing who'd had some trauma and spent all her time hiding away. We called her Adolph. We'd returned from Canada with the same lack of planning as we had from Australia, and were weighing up our limited options when fate intervened in the shape of Twink, who drove down from Cardiff in the company of his mate Dickey the Postman to pay us a visit. Twink had put on a lot of weight and grown a thick, unkempt Zapata moustache. We went up the local pub for a drink and a game of pool. I beat him in the first game and he was visibly shocked. He was a cracking good player. It was luck that I won. He told me that his band, The Bulbs, had split up and asked if I'd be interested in moving to Cardiff and forming a new band with him and the remnants of the old band. I talked it over with Jane and she thought it was as good an idea as any other, so I went to stay in Cardiff for a few days to suss out the scene and meet the other guys.

Twink lived in a house on Fitzhamon Embankment opposite the river, near where Charlie and Hoffman had once lived. He had the ground floor and Carol, the girl who had visited us in London with him and Victor, lived on the top floor. The second floor had a kitchen, a communal living room and another large bedroom. I slept in a small box room which Twink, Victor and Carol had taken the trouble to tidy up for my arrival. There was a small vase of blue flowers next to the single bed. I was quite touched. The band's bass player was an old, straightish-looking bloke named Mike Kennedy. He called in on his way home from work a few days later and I played him half-a-dozen songs. He liked the numbers and was keen to get started. Jane and I moved to Cardiff. We had the large bedroom on the second floor. There was a double mattress on the floor and an old black and white television set in the corner. Adolph was still paranoid but a little bolder than she had been. I'd still never got close enough to touch her. I met the other guys in the band, Simon the drummer, very good, and Mark 'Nineto' the keyboard player, no Rick Wakeman but intrinsic to the sound. I didn't understand why Victor wasn't playing with us. He lived nearby and was always visiting, but he had given up any pretentions to rock fame. He was applying to do a degree in philosophy at Cardiff Uni. He didn't seem well to me. He looked more haunted than ever.

Twink had a new day job for a firm called Phoenix Supplies, a fastening wholesalers. He'd get home every night at five, we'd eat food he'd prepared the night before and left simmering in a slow cooker all day, then we'd get mindlessly ripped and prance about singing the songs from the set to familiarise ourselves with them. The band started rehearsing in a huge abandoned factory near Cardiff prison. Twink was a fantastic front man. He had a great voice and charisma to spare. Mike was a wonderful bass player and he and Simon were a shit-hot rhythm section. Twink lost weight, got rid of his ludicrous moustache and looked his old self again. It was summer by now. We were starting to sound very good. Jane went through several months of existential despair at being in Cardiff, but it passed and she began to like it.

Twink and I took to going to the pub at the end of the street, opposite where the alcoholics and prostitutes gathered for a few pints every evening. We'd have twelve hot knives each before going but then there'd be a delay for some reason, often a ridiculous reason such as getting soaking wet from pouring pint glasses of ice-cold water over our heads, or each other's heads, while doing silly dances in the kitchen, so we'd decide that we'd better have another twelve knives before actually leaving the house. I thought that the pub was a glittering palace. The bar sparkled with exotic drinks in multicoloured bottles, the juke box and one-armed bandit pinged and flashed with music and lights, the clientele were beautiful, mysterious people, artists, writers and philosophers. It was an oasis of light and sound. Then we went there straight one night due to a hash drought and I realised that it was in fact a crumbling shit hole full of the dregs of society. Such is the fantasy world of the hash smoker. A half-dozen pints of Brains SA, or Skull Attack as it is known colloquially, put things right again. It tasted like vomit that had been sieved into a glass but it did the business. I returned to being Verlaine in an absinthe house in nineteenth-century Paris. We played pool but my day of beating Twink had passed. He was one of those infuriating players who left the balls hanging over the lip of the pockets so that his opponent, me in fact, never had a shot to go for, then he'd pot the lot at one visit. He beat everyone. Twink was what they call a Rain Essence Man, though he'd given up chess at a serious level. His last tournament had been the World Junior Championship in Mexico City, where he'd finished eleventh.

We decided to call the band Statues of Us after one of our songs. Twink's vision of the world was as dark as mine. We wrote a few numbers together, which were good but not great. Fortunately we both had backlogs of crack hot songs so our final set was excellent material wise. Some evenings when we were driving home from rehearsals, we'd see groups of women standing outside the fire station opposite the prison calling up to their boyfriends and husbands inside, who'd gather at the barred windows and watch as the women lifted their tops to expose their breasts for them. The men would scream encouragement. There would be dozens there at times. There was a sad romance to it. Carol got a kitten, a ginger Tom named Kinnock. He was a precocious little fellow and, after an initial period of hostility, began to bring Adolph out of her shell. It was lovely to see his irrepressible bravado. Adolph took many a swing at him but to my knowledge never connected. She still wouldn't come near me but progress was being made.

There was a series of classic stage plays adapted for television on BBC 2 at the time. We watched *A Doll's House* with Anthony Hopkins as Torvald and Claire Bloom as Nora. It was wonderful. Then the following week we saw Priestley's *I Have Been Here Before* with Anthony Valentine and Herbert Lom. The boldness of the central concept of time travel combined with seeing Toby Mears from *Callan* and Doctor Korda from *The Human Jungle* being these radically different people in this dark fairytale world just slayed me. I'd never really watched a serious play before. I loved them.

I was walking down North Road one morning a few weeks later when I saw the Welsh College of Music and Drama. I stopped to take a look. It was a newish, red-brick building set back off the road. There was a modernist statue on the grass near the entrance. It looked like an ear made of black iron. I went into the foyer. There was a sign on the wall saying that they were holding auditions for the next year and that applications had to be in by that day. I asked the doorman how to apply and he handed me a form, which I filled out there on the spot and handed back to him. I don't know why I did it. I think that the plays I'd seen recently on TV had sparked something in me. I got a letter the next day telling me that I had to go for an audition the following Monday at 10 am. I had to prepare two audition pieces, each of about two minutes' length, one a classical piece, the other modern. I had to have a song ready too, and be prepared to stay all day if required. I didn't know any audition pieces so Jane and I went to the library to look some up. I knew there was a famous speech that began 'Friends, Romans, countrymen', so I asked the librarian which play it was from and found it on the shelves. There was a speech by Dr Gortler that had stuck in my head from *I Have Been Here Before*, so I got that down as well. I couldn't take the books out because I had no official address, so we wrote the relevant speeches out longhand and went home. I had never done any acting before except for the kids' theatre in Australia, and had never learned a speech, so I just started pounding the words into my head by repeating them over and over. I did it for hour upon hour every day until they started to stick and I began thinking about what they meant. I was standing on my own in the kitchen in the early hours of the Sunday morning saying 'Friends, Romans' etc, and when I came to the line 'He was faithful and just to me.' I began to cry. I was crying because of the power and beauty of the line. I'd read Shakespeare in my early teens. Sometimes I'd read pieces out to Ool in the big front room and he'd listen attentively. 'Yes, very good,' he'd say, and he meant it.

There were about forty other people auditioning on the same day as me, most of them from miles away, all over England and Wales. There were several courses in the drama stream. I was trying for the three-year performer's course. We sat around in the bar area on the first floor drinking coffee and waiting to be summoned for an initial interview. Most of the boys were posh and most of the girls were pretty. There was a lot of tension. I was called in and asked about my experience and why I wanted to be an actor and so forth. I can't remember what I said but they didn't seem over-impressed. I returned to the bar and listened to everyone else saying how they'd blown it. Next came the audition pieces. For these we were taken into the Bute Theatre. All of we would-be students sat in the front seats and watched each other's performances, and there were five assessors sat behind a long table immediately in front. Most everyone seemed very good to me, some were excellent. When my turn came I got up and did Doctor Gortler first, sat down on a chair. I remembered it all. Then I did the Shakespeare. I made one or two mistakes but I got through to the end. It seemed to pass in a second, yet when I was actually saying it, it seemed to last forever. They told a lot of people that was it, but I was asked to come back after lunch for the afternoon session when we had to sing our song. I sang 'English Psychopath', one of my own songs, then there were some movement and imagination exercises, pretending to be trees and walking round in circles and so forth. I was knackered by the end of the day. I shook hands with the teachers and said goodbye. It was a strange experience and I felt sad when I got home. There were a lot of other applicants who were better than me. I was a god, of course. I was Boyd Clack, but I was sure that the people assessing us wouldn't see it. They didn't even know that I was the star of the film.

I got a letter a few days later saying that I'd been accepted on the course and telling me how to apply for a grant. I went to the education offices and filled out the application form, but they turned me down by return post. I wrote again and they reversed the decision and offered me a full grant for the three years. I was told later that like insurance companies they turned everyone down at first, hoping you'd just forget about it. The course began in September, several months away. I bought all the books the letter said I needed, and tights for dancing and several other bits and pieces from a specialist shop in the Castle Arcade. It happened so quickly. One week I was a trembling neurotic with an uncertain future, the next I had my foot on the first rung of an exotic and exciting ladder to artistic fulfillment and fame. I never doubted that I could do the business. It never crossed my mind. This was where my future lay. I felt almost sane.

Twink had decided to buy a house in Emerald Street in Splott and he asked us if we wanted to move in to help pay the mortgage. We did so and Adolph got her third home. It was a big old Cardiff terrace in a rough part of town, but no rougher than where we'd been living and it was summer and we were happy. Twink took the small bedroom up the back, Carol got the large front bedroom and we got the medium-sized middle one. There was a living room, a smaller room, a kitchen and a bathroom downstairs and a tidy-sized, overgrown garden out the back. Jane decided to go to Rumney Technical College to get some A levels with the idea of going on to university afterwards. The Statues continued rehearsing and began looking for gigs. Twink and I started believing that we in the band had puppet alter egos. We spent hours tottering about and walking into the mobile that hung from the light-fitting in the kitchen, talking about taking our tools to the abandoned buildings, which is what we believed puppetfolk would do, in high-pitched robotic voices. We gave ourselves puppet names. I was Joe Rainbow.

Twink got a small, four-track recording system and started writing some very good songs. One of these was called 'Big Boy's Brigade' and we put it straight into the set. I met a friend of Twink's who lived nearby. His name was Neil White and he was an excellent musician, songwriter and producer. He played with Geraint Jarman, who was and still is a legendary name in Welsh-speaking music. Neil had a sixteen-track studio in a bedroom. He was an ace guy and we became mates. The band got a handful of gigs. The first was in a pub called The Cross Keys in Llantrisant, across the road from where Mike 'Perfecto' Kennedy lived. We played in the bar and went down really well. Other gigs followed and we began to acquire a small but highly enthusiastic following made up of broken people and would-be artists. The music scene in Cardiff was vibrant at the time and there were a lot of venues. We played them all. We played up the valleys too but our relative sophistication didn't go down so well there, the local taste at the time still being for heavy rock. Both Twink and I were pretty crazy. We wore ridiculous clothing and painted our faces. We spouted psychobabble between songs and I told dark stories about domestic madness. Audiences didn't know what to make of us. We played Chapter Arts Centre, where The Lemmings had been paid off all those years before, and went down a storm. We drank like fish and smoked like trains. Things were good.

Kinnock had grown into a big lad and had a heavy duty purr which gained him the nickname The Geiger Counter. I was lying half asleep in the early hours one morning listening to the distant explosions from the stone quarries when I felt a gentle thud on the duvet. I lay there in silence for a while then saw a dark, round, whiskery face appear in front of mine. It was Adolph! I was amazed. She sniffed my eyes for a few moments then curled up on the pillow next to my head and went to sleep. It was our first contact. We were great friends from that moment on.

Jane started in Rumney Tech on the same day I started at the Welsh College. We were split into three groups for practical purposes and the rest of the day was spent on orientation, introductions and being given timetables. I was one of only three who got through from my audition group. I considered the possibility that I was a token, broken, older working-class Valleys bloke chosen to add social credibility to the year. That said, I wasn't that old, and though battered about and a drunk, I still had a light glowing inside. All the other students had done fair amounts of serious acting before in school and youth theatre and were already stuck in learned habits to varying degrees, whereas I knew nothing about any of it and was totally open to instruction. I never thought anything to be too basic or a waste of time as the others often did. I worked hard too. When I'd been in grammar school I found learning impossible. I couldn't study, I couldn't bear being in a classroom even, but I now realised that that was because I'd had no interest in what they were trying to teach. With drama I was like a sponge. I loved it and it sank into me, all of it, speech, voice, movement, dance, improvisation, all of it fascinated me. I felt wonderful just getting up in the mornings and walking to the college. I had already achieved something. The college itself was set on the edge of Sophia Gardens, a beautiful park to the rear of Cardiff Castle. In its early days, when Anthony Hopkins was a student, it had been in the castle itself, but the new building was compact and state of the art and handsome in its own way. A small stream ran behind the building with a stone footbridge over it, leading to the park with its undulating greenery and patches of cherry trees. It was a relaxing environment which became magical with the onset of autumn when the leaves changed colour and the flower petals fell in pink blankets on the ground at the feet of the trees. As the weather grew colder I started wearing an old greatcoat and an incredibly long, brightly coloured, hooped, knitted scarf, and I carried a small suitcase painted in black and gold which contained my books and other paraphernalia. Everyone said that I was destined to play Doctor Who and they were right. There was no acting as such in the first year other than weekly audition pieces performed in front of the rest of the class. I felt victorious if I managed to remember the words. Others were excellent on a regular basis.

The tutor in charge of our group was John Wills, a tiny, almost dwarfish man with a receding hairline and glasses, a sort of artistic lizard. He was a camp little fellow who's main, and indeed only, claim to fame was that he had been one of the original Ovaltinies on radio. He taught speech and had a cut-glass accent and a distant air. John made no secret of his admiration and indeed affection for posh kids. He had little time for us oafs. Voice, which involved physical exercises to release the true sound of the voice, was taught by Sara Jennet, a stern-looking woman with close-cropped hair and a public school hockey teacher demeanour. She had bright eyes which were always on the brink of betraying unwarranted amazement. The lessons were exhausting but rewarding.

Dance and movement classes came as a real shock. They had us leaping and running and hopping about like a bunch of crickets for an hour and a half every morning. Most of the others found it easy enough, being young and that way inclined anyway, but it took an old, out-of-condition chap like me the entire first term to come to terms with. It didn't help that I'd interpreted 'tights' to mean the sort of tights that women wore and looked like a prick in front of everyone. I twigged it in the second term and wore track-suit bottoms instead. The dance teachers were Molly Kenny, a plump woman with graying hair tied back tightly behind her head, and Tim Hext, who'd been in The Black and White Minstrels. They were both nice enough but dance is like landscape gardening, essentially just hard work, so there was no great degree of personal interaction. Sometimes they'd teach us little routines, left, left, touch, swivel and down, stuff like that. I was not a natural. I have always thought that men look ridiculous trying to dance and I was living proof of it. There were a couple of other oafs in the class but they were thuggish types who made up for their lack of subtlety with intense physical effort. I was pleased to observe that despite that they still looked like pricks. There were a couple of guys who were very good. They wanted to be dancers or act in musicals and they had the feel for it. Chris Rickets was very good, and when we had to pair up I was often paired with Tony Coughlin, a lovely camp lad from West Wales who showed endless patience and kindness as I struggled to keep up. It was hard work but once again there was something very satisfying about it. There was one lad, Stuart from Bournemouth, who was even worse than me. I think he was made of wood. Not everyone could be a dancer but the classes gave one an awareness of movement, of one's body, and that filtered through into acting performance. It was a challenge. I enjoyed it.

The band was gigging a lot by then, mostly in Cardiff. Twink took up running. He'd leave the house in the hammering rain, run around Roath Park Lake, and return home dripping wet. He loved it and it kept him fit. He'd started getting moody though. He was an essentially morose guy and had the ability, as many such people do, to radiate his emotion and create a bad atmosphere. You could sense him sitting in his room in the evenings smouldering with discontent. I think that he carried a torch for Carol, who was knocking about with some other bloke. It could have been something else. I don't know. Jane and I spent Christmas with her parents in Bath. The world was covered in snow. I could hardly wait to get back to college.

I got to know some of the other students. There was a dashing RAF officer type named Terry Howe who was a part of the infamous Howe dynasty of actors from Ferndale. His elder brother Phillip and his younger brother Gary had already been to the college. Terry was a heavy-duty shagger of women. He was in his late twenties, a Valleys boy, a drinker and a dope smoker. Despite this he had an endearing naivety. We got along fine. There was another young bloke, a red-haired, square-jawed North Welshman named Mark Davies, who'd stayed with Terry for a few weeks at the beginning of the year while he sorted out accommodation. Terry's brother Gary, a rampant homosexual, thought he was gorgeous and chased him around the table when they first met. Gary said that Mark was just like a little puppy. Terry and I called Mark the Puppy after that, which mutated with time to the Red Dog and then just the Dog. He was a tough, friendly lad with oodles of charm. Neither Terry nor the Dog were in my group but we took to hanging about together. There was another bloke, Ted Dawson, who was in my group who joined our triumvirate. I got talking to him and his girlfriend Elaine in the bar one evening. Ted was from a farming family in the North of England and had been to private school and Leeds University, where he'd got a degree in English and a taste for drama. He and Elaine got together while there and she had come to Cardiff to be with him. She was a stunningly beautiful girl and as smart as a button. She wanted to work for a record company or in television. She and Ted had been entertainment secretaries at Leeds and were good friends with The Sisters of Mercy, a Goth band who were quite big at the time. Elaine, as I say, was a doll. She had beautiful pale lips and long blonde hair. Her eyes were sparkling and sleepy at the same time and she had a scrumptiously sexy body. She was stylish and nice too. The company of beautiful women is an exquisite thing for a man. You don't have to bed them, though that would be ideal of course, but just to be there talking to them, laughing, to be in their presence is a gift. There were several other girls, fellow students, who fell into the same category. Ted was a lucky guy but I'm not sure he appreciated it. There were other people I was getting to know and like too, of course, Alf, Ho, Larry, Craig Heart, Tricia and Theresa, Rhiannon, the Emmas, Helen, Cooky, Bethan and more. Most all of them were optimists. They were young, of course, but it wasn't just that. They had energy and confidence. Such company was unusual, well for me it was anyway. I suppose the magic group had it in a way but that seemed born of desperation, whereas this was born of aspiration. It was a healthy environment.

I started recording a series of songs with Neil White. I'd had some numbers I really liked but the band didn't want to do, so I asked Neil if he fancied working on them with me and he did. Neil did all the arrangements, played all the instruments and recorded and produced them in his studio. It took a long time but his work was inspired. He was a lovely guy and we communicated on an artistic level. Theresa and Helen, two of my college friends, provided perfect girlish backing vocals under the name The Clackettes, and the final product, twelve songs under the title *Personal Apocalypse*, was excellent. We produced fifty cassettes with a photograph of me, aged seven, in Santa's grotto in Howells in Cardiff on the front. I look so bemused. It was a very productive and rewarding experience and most of the songs were perfect. I gave the cassettes to friends and colleagues, and many fell in love with them. To do something good, to do something right, as it should be, is an unspeakable joy. Gigging was so-so at the time. Some nights it was good but some nights, arriving, setting up, doing a sound check, sitting around in a half empty shit hole watching the hate-filled psycho dregs seeping in, then playing to the cold emptiness as the rain beat down outside, it wasn't.

Twink's moodiness hadn't passed. Bob, who was living with a woman named Jan at the time, started visiting. I'd lie in bed in the early hours and hear him and Twink getting stoned and drunk downstairs. They both had deep resonant voices. It was like listening to two thunder gods planning a storm.

I saw *The Tempest* done by our third years in the Bute. It was very good. There were a lot of good actors in that year. I particularly liked Steve Smith, a cool-looking guy with black curly hair who just seemed to have it. He was an excellent bloke too. The students from our year drank in a pub called The Rummer Tavern in town. We spent many an evening of drunken revelry there. Mark the Red Dog took up with an ultra-posh, and rich, girl named Flip. All of the boys were sex mad, needless to say. They would have fucked a dead rat in the street if they could have figured out a way to do it. The girls were the same, no doubt, though they confided in me less on the topic. I was drinking a lot. The term wended its way to a close. I used to repeat lines I was learning for audition pieces over and over as I walked in to the college in the mornings, and I'm sure that a lot of people thought I was a schizophrenic. They began avoiding me. I'd try to explain sometimes, but they'd just rush off. Ah well, it was a small price to pay.

The Statues recorded two songs, 'Do You Still Love Me Terry?' and 'Suicide', in a studio in Newport. The production wasn't great but the tape helped us get more gigs. The miners' strike had begun in March and there was a lot of frustration and anger against the Thatcher government in working-class communities. It was a terrible time in British history. The country was more divided than I'd ever known it. Thatcher hated the miners because of their long socialist tradition, and she was determined not only to destroy the industry and its communities but to humiliate them. The police shamed themselves with their partisan delight in being at the boot end of this hubris. They identified with the right and behaved in a paramilitary fashion in enforcing its agenda. There were terrible scenes of organised punishment being meted out on the television news. Police thugs were bussed in from London and their behaviour disgusted even their own provincial colleagues in many cases. One of Thatcher's legacies was to be the redefining of the police/public relationship. It is a legacy that was to eat at the very core of our society. South Wales was in the thick of it. We held student union meetings in the common room to discuss developments but, though sympathetic, we were impotent. The coalmining valleys of my childhood and youth were gone forever. This was Thatcher's Britain. It was the politics of hatred. It was a winning strategy. The Tories won the next election with a landslide.

The band played a gig at the college and went down a storm. Simon the drummer got a full-time job drumming for a jazz band in Switzerland and bade his farewell. He was replaced by a young Goth-looking guy named Martin who had an electronic kit. He was very good and the kit added an interesting new dimension to our sound. Twink was still depressed and Jane and I moved out of Splott to a ground-floor flat in Llanbleddian Gardens, the street opposite the Sherman Theatre. We had a bedroom cum living room with a large kitchen and bathroom leading to a stone-paved yard out the back. The landlady lived upstairs. Adolph settled in well and made friends with two thuggish toms who lived nearby. We named them Shagrat and Gorbag after the two orcs who left their friend at Shelob's mercy in *The Lord of the Rings*. They were handsome lads. I was lying in bed falling off to sleep one night when I heard an unidentifiable noise. It sounded like a tiny army marching on gravel. I got up to investigate and discovered a slug munching away at a piece of torn wallpaper. I couldn't help but smile.

In the third term we were given the concept of the number three as a theme to create a piece of work. I wrote a poem called 'Three'. None of this subtext rubbish for me: they said 'Three'; they got Three! We performed our pieces for the other groups in our year. The poem was read in a deranged Pan-like baritone by Chris Isaacs. Chris was as weird a man as you'd ever meet. He looked like a were-wolf in both face and physique, with crazed blue eyes, a sardonic smile and a very cultured, lugubrious voice. He'd done quite a lot of theatre and specialised in grotesques. He was disliked by most of the other students and actively despised by some. Women found him creepy. He'd apparently mouthed off in the first few days of school, telling others that he was the bee's knees and knew then that he'd walk the acting prize in the third year. I didn't hear this and suspect that his unpopularity was really down to his lycanthropic appearance. It didn't bother me. I liked him. He was a one off. I admired his chutzpah. Anyway, he read the poem 'Three' while we, the others in the group struck up improbable poses in the background. It was good. The thing about working with actors in this way was that it was incredible fun. We were all so up for it. We were all eager to let our imaginations flourish and our talents show, and there were some very talented people among us. For someone like me, with no theatrical experience or history, it was dreamlike cool to watch another person, another human being, doing something brilliant and inspired there in the flesh in front of you. To be a part of this process was thrilling. I was grateful and well disposed to all of them. Bethan Davies, a lovely girl and the daughter of the legendary Welsh comic actor Ryan of Ryan and Ronnie fame, dropped out of the course, having decided it was not for her. Several other people had done the same. It wasn't a walk in the park.

With a few weeks of term left we all had to perform audition pieces to a panel of tutors for an end-of-year assessment. I did the 'tomorrow and tomorrow' speech from *Macbeth* and a piece from *A Doll's House*. It was similar to our entrance auditions but there were no other students watching. I did the pieces brilliantly and left the room almost overwhelmed by the experience. When the marks were put up on the notice board a few days later I was given forty-one out of a hundred. I was gutted. I just didn't understand it. No one offered any explanation and I just took it on the chin. I wasn't feeling great at this time and not just because of the audition. Things drifted in and out of vision. I was shivering inside. A final in-house performance of Thornton Wilder's *Our Town* was being rehearsed and I was sharing the role of the narrator with Maldwyn John, a Welsh speaker from North Wales. I went to the director and told her I wasn't up to it and she recast me in the smaller part of Simon Stimpson, the town drunk. I managed to pull it off okay but was glad to see the end of term, and of the first year at college, arrive. I needed a rest.

I got a holiday job labouring with Bob, who was landscaping for Richard 'Longface' Carlson's newly formed company. It was less relentlessly arduous than when Schweppes and I worked for Ham in London, the work being domestic in the main, but it was arduous enough for me nonetheless. That said, Bob, like Schweppes, was a human digging machine who allowed me to work at a far more sedate pace. We worked in the Penarth and Barry area in the main. Bob would pick me up from home every morning and we'd drive to the job to get there about 10 am. There was a piece of graffiti in black paint on the side of a red-brick shed affair on the way in which read 'Welcome to Barry'. Barry is one of the nastiest, most violent places in South Wales and the graffiti showed a black wit that never failed to amuse me. We did gardens mainly, turfing, weeding, fencing, that sort of thing. It was an unusually wet summer and we spent a fair amount of time stood in the rain doing spadework in the sodden earth. Bob's pace never faltered. He was a great guy with a fantastic dry sense of humour. He was digging in a garden one day as I sheltered against a wall when he drew my attention to a piece of broken-off baton on the ground. 'Stick in the mud,' he said. I pissed myself. The job was made pleasant by Bob's company and kindness. I felt refreshed and the money came in handy too.

Jane's first year at college had gone very well. She was intelligent and articulate, the work came easily for her, and she'd made some interesting friends there too. She got a part-time job as an usherette at the Sherman so things were better than they had been for a while financially. It's odd though, money isn't that important when you are pursuing a dream. I never felt poor. I felt rich. Twink's depression had waned and he was his old charming, lovable self again. I got over my disappointment at the audition results. Playing music for years had taught me to be savagely objective about my work. I knew I'd done the pieces exceptionally well and the opinion of the assessors didn't alter that. I wish that they had been more specific in their criticism, though. I had plenty of technical faults and had they been pointed out then I could have got stuck into putting them right earlier. Actors need a thick skin. It is a business of rejection. They tell you that it's not personal, that you just weren't 'right for the part' or 'not what they were looking for'. But it's not true. The unique quality that any actor brings to a part is that they are who they are. It's always personal. This is where self-belief comes in. I had it. By the time the second year arrived I was raring to go.

TWILIGHT OF THE GODS

The previous second year was now the final year and there was an added bounce to their collective step. There was a new first year too, of course. There was a tall, thin pallid fellow with short black hair who looked like a monkey. His name was Jo James. His father was the famous RSC actor Emrys James and his mother was the novelist Siân. I got into a conversation with a girl named Ri Richards in the bar one evening. We got along immediately. She was lovely. There was a group of students from Edinburgh too, Anthony Neilson, whose father Sandy was a big name in Scottish theatre and TV, the stunningly gorgeous Sue Vidler, Jim Cunningham and Steve Scott. Steve was good-looking young guy who soon became the college Romeo, and there was no shortage of would-be Juliets. He was a political activist and sold the *Socialist Worker* outside the canteen door every Thursday. There was another lad named Richard Tucker who sold a rival leftist rag at the same door. You'd hear them arguing minor points of doctrine in a heated manner, almost coming to blows on occasion. It was entertaining. A young bloke named Ian Rowlands joined our year. He looked like a blond James Dean. I liked him. I liked all of them.

The second year was more structured than the first. We had a series of projects, normally scenes from different plays put together as an exploration of a particular genre, which would be performed in-house for students from all years, a step up in pressure from the first year, when only students from our own year would attend. We started stage fighting lessons too. Sword fencing was beyond me. I have no physical coordination and the other lads were too rough. I skirted the classes like a mayfly keeping out of harm's way. If I was forced to fence I'd do it with one of the milder-tempered females or my dance partner Tony. I stopped drinking beer and started drinking wine. I thought it would help me not to get fat. I'd never liked wine before that but I soon acquired a taste for it. It took me a long time to appreciate that it was a different drink from beer, though, and I drank it to excess. I'd have three or four bottles a night while watching telly.

My mother was living in a block of flats near Ton rugby club. She was happy enough there, happier than I'd ever known her, in fact. She had a few friends to gossip with and the bingo hall was just up the hill. I went and stayed with her some weekends. Naine and Ool were well but

337

getting old. We got along better than we ever had. Brian had gone to live in Scotland with Elizabeth, the new woman in his life. He still wasn't well but she loved and looked after him. Margaret and Sion were divorced. I never figured out the details but it involved Sion jumping through the window of the bungalow where they had lived wielding an axe and Ool having to deck him with a poker. Our family life was one of relentless domestic drama.

The band did several gigs in the college and even more at Chapter Arts Centre, where we had built up quite a following. We'd started taking a settee, a television, a Hoover and an ironing board on stage with us. Twink wore a dress sometimes and I built walls out of cardboard boxes to hide behind. We were playing and performing well but not getting anywhere. It was frustrating, especially for Twink, who put so much into it. College had made me single minded and thoughtless to a degree. We didn't socialise as much as we had and I'm sorry for it. Twink was as good a friend as you could ask for.

I was given a personal tutor, a new woman named Joan Mills. She taught voice and was very helpful, particularly with audition pieces. She was complimentary about my ability. A first! A woman named Caroline Lamb started in the Dance and Movement department at the same time and she had an appreciation of the oaf in movement. Her encouragement and praise made me raise my game and I eventually became simply inept. We did a mime project with a chap from London, which I ended by tearing off my famous green Franz Kafka sweatshirt, ripping it to pieces and flinging the remnants into the audience. There was an audible gasp. Terry Howe kept the section where the name was written in silver and framed it. Mime was totally alien to me and I felt proud that I'd managed to do an impressive piece. Hard work was the key. Me and Mark the Red Dog used to meet up every day, find a rehearsal room and do an hour or more of voice exercises together. Voice was a strange thing. There were a lot of posh people in the new first year, James Lovell, Hugo Blick and quite a few more, and they all spoke received-pronunciation. This figured, they'd been brought up posh and gone to private schools, it made sense. I'd just have to work hard to try to learn it, but what I found more difficult to understand was why they also had perfect voices. They spoke from the diaphragm automatically. Their voices were strong and effortlessly resonant. Then one day it struck me. They were brought up unafraid. They used their voices to tell people what to do. 'Hey, you there, carry my suitcases.' 'Come on man. Get out of my way.' 'Hi. I'm James. Take a look at this for me.' Not for them a life of fear and doubt. No 'Oh... oh... no, let me go' or 'I didn't do it. It's not my fault.' Not for them the strangulated tones of engrained subservience. No, voice is directly linked to self-confidence and that is why these delicate pretty boys had manly voices and I sounded like a talking chicken. We began having acting theory lessons taught by Doctor Mike Reed, known to his friends as Doctor Mike Reed. He was famous for having fallen off stage while spear carrying at the RSC, and was interesting only in his complete inability to connect with the concept of humour.

The miners' strike was still rumbling on. There were some fierce debates in NUS meetings in the common

339

room. Geoff Williams, Gyp as he was known, was a forceful speaker, and he and the other socialist activists used to make regular strike fund collections around the college. The posh boys in the first year were all ardent Thatcherites and things turned nasty on several occasions. The end of term gave both sides a time out.

When the new term began I got a gig playing solo at The Philharmonic, a large pub on St Mary Street in the centre of town. A first year named Dave Davies helped me with the PA and transport. His mate, another first year named Rob Brydon, came with us from time to time. Rob was a Springsteen fan. The gig was typical of the type. There were arseholes who shouted out endless requests, normally 'Stairway!' or 'No Regrets!', there were the bellowing drunks showing off to giggling tarts and, worst of all, the thug who responds to you telling him that you don't do any Elvis songs by making a clumsy grab for your guitar to play one himself, normally 'Love Me Tender'. I varied the set with some solid senders like 'Where Do You Go to My Lovely?' and 'Vincent', together with some of my own less depressing numbers. I nearly came a cropper one evening when playing 'The Pope Is a Lizard', a country rag with the repeated hook line 'The Pope is a lizard', when a staggering Scottish psycho came up to me, put his hand across my strings, stared me deep in the eyes and asked without humour: 'Are you saying that the Pope is a lizard?' I was lost for a reply when fortunately Jock, another hard Scottish lad from the college first year, intervened, and sent him back to his seat. Mark the Dog saved me in a similar situation at a gig in another pub shortly after. I reluctantly dropped the song, a harmless little ditty, from my pub repertoire. I started gigging in a duo with a third year student named Will. We called ourselves Intelligence Limited. Will was a talented, likeable guy. It petered out after a while but it was fun while it lasted.

Our first project of term two was Restoration comedy. It was directed by Pete Wooldridge, a young bloke who'd started taking us in improvisation classes. These involved being given a scenario and characters and adlibbing dialogue to create a story from them. There was a pretty young girl named Andrea in the class who suffered from anorexia nervosa. We were in an improvisation class where I was a park keeper and she and several other students were children playing up on the swings. I went up to her to tell her off and she kneed me right in the balls. I crumpled up and the class was called to a halt. It hurt but I didn't hold it against her. She took some time off. I saw her wheeling a pram in Roath Park several years later and she looked fine. Our Restoration project was very good. I played two scenes from *The Lucky Chance*, a play by the adventuress Aphra Behn. The first scene was my character being dressed by his manservant, Mark the Puppy, and the second going to another house and arguing with its occupant, played by Ho, a lovely guy and a cracking good actor, about a stolen watch. Both sections were excellent, fast and funny. I got universally good feedback, so did the other lads. It was a buzz.

I saw a play written by John Smith, one of the third years, in the Bute one evening and was impressed. It involved a young man getting his first job in a supermarket. It set me off writing a piece myself. It was called *The Horse's Mouth*, a surrealist fantasy about the goings on in the mind of a young woman in a permanent coma. There was a hospital bed centre stage with the girl, connected by tubes to a machine with flashing lights, lying motionless on it. A demonic figure called 'The Voice That Is Never Listened To' appears and taunts her, taking her back to terrible scenarios from her past life and making her relive them. One was a picnic on an island where she was attacked with a broken bottle by her boyfriend. The night of the first performance showed me just how nerve racking the lot of the author is. I felt far worse than before anything I'd actually appeared in. I felt physically sick, in fact. It was a weird piece which I directed myself, but it worked. Writing it was fun. The actors were excellent.

My sister Audrey visited from her new home in Sweden. I hadn't seen her in years. I really loved her. Sometimes I think we were the same person, two halves of the one. I didn't see her often as an adult, I was abroad for long periods, and she made her home in Sweden, where she remarried and had another son. All the boys grew up there and I never really got to know them as adults. I'm sorry for that, they are my flesh and blood and I love them. I am sorry too that I never spent more time with Audrey. I'm sorry that I only ever really knew her as she was and never came to really know the older and no doubt wiser woman she became. I think about her every day, my beloved sister. It was wonderful to see her.

Our next project was on Naturalism. This encompassed work by writers such as Chekhov, Ibsen and, surprisingly

I thought, Oscar Wilde and Shaw. Naturalism was a school which came to the fore in the late nineteenth and early twentieth centuries. It eschewed the stylised acting that had been the norm till then in favour of trying to reflect life as it really is, on the stage. It regarded the audience as a fourth wall, observing but not addressed. The acting technique required was pioneered by the Russian director Stanislavski, whose book *An Actor Prepares* is the bible of the genre. It was developed at the Moscow Arts Theatre, which specialised in Chekhov's plays. A rival approach was that of Bertolt Brecht, the German playwright with his highly politicised Berliner Ensemble theatre. Stanislavski sought a performance based on the relived emotional memory of the actor, a performance that used reality and truth as its foundation. Brecht saw the actor as a messenger conveying the story. There has been a never-ending clash of opinions over these approaches, but most actors borrow from each. I performed two scenes in the project, one from *A Doll's House*, the other from *Candida* by Shaw. Both went well. Theresa and Tricia did a scene from *The Importance of Being Earnest* where the two young women are discussing diaries. The costumes were lovely and they looked so beautiful. They were both special actors and their performance filled me with delight. Theresa was living with Alf then. They had a flat in Colum Road. Theresa's parents were separated and she had a terrible shock when she saw her father's picture on the front pages of the daily newspapers one morning. They said that he'd been killed along with many others in a train crash near London. It was a terrible way to receive such news.

There was a rumour going around the college that Peter Palmer, the head of drama, a nice guy, was finishing the next year and that the powers that be were going to use the opportunity for a root and branch shake up of the teaching staff. I saw Martin Kingston, the head of acting, grab John Wills by the ear and pull him into a side room for a chastising on one occasion. I assumed it was to do with the rumour. Martin himself was a morose man without personal charm whose company and advice were rarely sought by anyone. That said, I quite liked him.

Jane and I spent the spring break with her parents. Bernard took me with him to the local golf club and I caddied for him in a game against two wealthy businessmen. They played for ten quid a hole and Bernard went around in sixty-seven. It was the only time I ever saw him play and I was mightily impressed. He'd hit the ball over some trees in the far distance, we'd walk after it and it would be a foot away from a hole I didn't even know was there. He was on fire. It was great. We played snooker in the club after, had a sauna and a swim and drove home together in the dark. Bernard and Constance did not appear to be happy. There were unspoken tensions. Constance revelled in the bitter sweet. Bernard had qualities that were not immediately apparent. He loved his children. He believed in hanging on to what was good and as far as possible ignoring the bad. He could easily have been devoured by his personal inadequacies but he hadn't been. He clung on. Despite their obvious differences, Jane was closer to her father than to her mother and he obviously adored her. Bernard and Constance were good to us and we spent a lot of happy times together. I felt sad for them. There was something wrong. It was love that was dying.

The first project in the new term was on Shakespeare. I played Romeo opposite Rhiannon Pugh's Juliet. Rhiannon was a lovely actress with an immensely expressive voice. We did the balcony scene. It was directed by Douglas Dempster, an elderly gay man with blue-rinse hair. He was no Peter Brook, but his delicate touch suited the piece and we pulled it off impressively. Douglas had been an entertainer on cruise ships for many years, and specialised in sword fencing. He had a small office on the third floor which was filled with memorabilia from his career. I went to have a debriefing with him after the performance and he broke down in tears. His long-time partner had died and he was distraught, the poor fellow. I offered him my sympathy and cried with him. I don't get male homosexuality but I get love. Llanbleddian Gardens had become a centre for socialising for my college mates. Mark, Terry, Gyp and Ted and Elaine visited regularly. We'd get stoned senseless then play ridiculous games. We'd take turns with a hammer, demonstrating how hard you would have to hit an intruder over the back of the head with it to be absolutely sure that they wouldn't get up and attack you back afterwards. It's surprisingly hard. We'd have contests to see who could keep their face under water the longest in the bathroom sink. Being insanely ripped pushed us all to unnatural extremes, but Mark was unbeatable. He used to frighten me sometimes. He had lungs like space hoppers.

I wrote another play, a two hander called *A Present for*

Ruth, which involved the unseen sister of one of the characters being admired by a man he meets in a dream. It turns out that the men are one and the same. There are a group of time travellers, The Weasel Gang, led by a man called Mike the Weasel, who warn him about a future tragedy, but he doesn't listen. I acted in it myself with Larry Franks, a handsome blond guy with an enormous jaw. We performed it in one of the small performance rooms upstairs and it went down seriously well. It went down so well, in fact, that I was given a small part, The English Ambassador, in the final third year public production of *Hamlet* by Martin Kingston, who'd been impressed by my acting. For a second year to get a part in a third year production was quite a feather in the cap. I was chuffed. Ted approached me and several others about taking two short plays, *The Ruffian on the Stairs* by Joe Orton and *Christie in Love* by Howard Brenton, to the Edinburgh Festival. I was to play John Reginald Christie of Ten Rillington Place fame. I accepted and we got stuck into rehearsals.

Ted and I had also been chosen to perform in a community project with Moving Being Theatre Company, which was based in St Steven's, a converted church down the docks. It was directed by Geoff Moore, a legendary figure in Welsh and indeed European theatre. It was an honour. The piece was called *Tiger Tiger* and, as well as a crop of top actors, there was a large group of people of all ages from the local area in the cast too. It traced the history of Tiger Bay during the latter half of the nineteenth century. It was an extravaganza with dancing and boxing and Chinese crime lords and street gangs, all centered on an illicit multiracial love story. I played an old-fashioned Welsh fundamentalist school teacher, a lovely part where I got to work with a group of children. My scene ended with them lined up on either side of me in the classroom with their hands out getting a damned good caning. It was terrific fun and the show, which ran for three weeks, was a resounding success. I met some great people doing it, not least Geoff Moore himself. Geoff gave me and Ted a hundred and fifty quid each, which he didn't have to do, towards our Edinburgh expenses, and he told me I'd done very well and that he'd help me out when I finished at college. This is a promise easily made and invariably forgotten in the acting business, but Geoff was made of more substantial stuff and I believed and trusted in him. I proved right to do so.

Hamlet was an experience. It was the first time I'd ever been in a full-length play. I held a spear in a few earlier scenes then came on right at the end to say the play's final speech over the scene of slaughter. The set was black with raked exit ramps on either side. It being a period piece I couldn't wear my glasses, and on the final blackout when the lights went off and we had to exit, the only way I could do it was to get down on my hands and knees and crawl off. I got a bit lost on the second night and was caught in flagrante when the lights went back up. There was a ripple of laughter behind me as my arse disappeared behind the flaps. All in all it was a buzz though. I felt great. The end-of-second-year audition pieces arrived and I did well, not as brilliantly as year one but still very well. When the results came out I'd got forty out of a hundred, lower than in the first year. I was nonplussed.

There was something not connecting between me and the current staff.

We drove to Edinburgh in a hire van and stayed in a second-floor flat in an old tenement near the town centre. The performance space was the basement of a church. We'd get in and set up as the previous company was de-rigging. I'd put on a grotesque mask with blood pouring from the mouth, put a length of clinical rubber tubing in my mouth and get into an open coffin centre stage. Then the coffin would be sealed with a tight membrane of fireproofed paper and covered with a tarpaulin and several wheelbarrows full of earth and rubbish. This represented Christie's garden, where several bodies were found. The play would open with two policemen, a constable played by Carlon Spencer and a sergeant played by Ted, digging for evidence. After ten minutes or so I would burst up through the membrane and stare at the audience, who were right up close to the action, making heavy breathing noises through the tube. It was an entrance that caused screaming and commotion if done right, and we normally nailed it. I'd have to get into the coffin twenty minutes or so before the audience were allowed in and lie there in silence throughout the opening exchange. This meant I was in there for half an hour, a long time for a claustro-phobe. Sometimes I'd contemplate the possibility, or probability as I imagined it, that I was the only man in the entire world at that moment who was lying in a coffin waiting to burst out. There may have been others, of course, but I couldn't figure out why. *Christie in Love* is an interesting, highly theatrical piece and could be genuinely disturbing at times. We went down really well. *Ruffian*, which had a cast of Ted, Gyp and Duncan Alexander, was a more hit and miss affair but I enjoyed watching it and both plays together made for a highly entertaining afternoon's viewing, I've no doubt. Our review was excellent.

Being in Edinburgh at Festival time is a fantastic experience. It is a beautiful city and the Scots are among my favourite people. There are fine restaurants, endless pubs and shows of all kinds going on from morn till night. We went to see a trendy company from Manchester putting on Berkoff's *Greek* in a nightclub. They were all super-fit, good-looking young people with frightening black-and-white-painted faces and ten-inch-high, brightly coloured Mohican haircuts. It was an ultra high energy performance but I was as drunk as a rat unfortunately, and disgraced myself by actually crawling across the stage to get to the toilet mid-performance. The young actors carried on regardless, as they should, but even in the state I was in I could sense the hatred beaming from their mascara-caked eyes as it bored into the back of my head. When I got to the toilet I could only manage to lie on the tiled floor and cool myself in the unidentified liquid that covered it till rescued by Ted. The *Greek* actors wanted to attack me when Ted hauled me out after the performance, but I was too far gone to make it worthwhile. I saw several other shows in the fortnight we were there but stayed in most nights with Gyp.

Carlon and Duncan were both gay and an item at the time, but this didn't prevent them going out on the circuit every night. They had what you'd call an open relationship. They were both really nice guys. Duncan's prize possession was a Head Boy badge pinned to his blazer.

349

We went to the Festival Bar a few times. It was where performers of all types gathered to mingle and exchange pleasantries. I jest. Actors are not in the business of being kind to other actors. One group from a posh school in London were doing *Christie* in another venue and, having been to see our show to suss out the opposition, accosted me about the generalised nature of my Northern accent. They had a point, accents have never been my forte, but it wasn't difficult to see their subtext. We were the business and they were just posh boys on holiday. Ted to his credit told them to fuck off, and they did. Doing the shows was great but spending time with the other guys and Elaine who'd come with us was even better. Jane got her A level results shortly after I got home and they were top drawer. I was excited but she was cool about it and chose to celebrate with her classmates instead of me.

We performed *Christie* in the Bute Theatre before the entire college on the Wednesday evening of the first week of the new term. We were very sharp and went down a storm. Paul Clements, the new Head of Drama, and Andrew Neil, Head of Acting, were present and extremely complimentary in the bar afterwards. The projects of the second year gave way to public performances in the third. Our first was *The Three Sisters* by Chekhov. I played Vershinin, the army officer with whom Masha, the eldest of the sisters, has an affair. He is a sad, troubled man, trapped in a neurotic marriage from which he is incapable or at least unwilling to extricate himself. It ends with him leaving for a posting in a distant part of the country and Masha being left bereft to grow old with her siblings. Vershinin disguises his moral cowardice with idealism. He talks endlessly of a future maybe two hundred years from then, when humankind will have overcome its inherent flaws and live in a state of civilised grace. This philosophising is no small part of his attraction to the stifled, provincial Masha. All the people in this world seek change in fact. The sisters dream of going to Moscow, their brother Andre of a happy marriage, his wife Natasha of being in charge of the family home and the various hangers on of purpose, love and happiness. It is a great play, full of humour and humanity. It reflects the great changes in Russian society that were happening at the end of the nineteenth century, the first stirrings of the communist revolution, in fact. It caused a huge stir when it was first produced. The technical challenge of playing Vershinin lay in the fact that he is such a bore, he says exactly the same thing, his vision of an idealised future, in each of the four scenes, and yet we have to see why Masha loves him so desperately. I had my hair and eyebrows dyed jet black for the part and looked horrific. I looked like a vampire, in fact. Masha would have been better off sticking to masturbation. I acted the part well, though, and the relationship worked. It was a great help that Rhiannon was playing Masha. She gave her an inherent sense of longing, which made my task easy. I had fantastic feedback in the debriefing from Paul and Andrew. At last people who appreciated that I was me. I was cock a hoop. Things at home weren't right, though. There was a distance falling between Jane and me. I tried to convince myself that it was just paranoia but I didn't succeed. I had been feeling unwell for some time. A darkness was descending. I noticed Adolph playing with Shagrat and Gorbag in the back yard one evening and I saw another creature in their midst. It was a large rat and on closer inspection I realised that it was very old and blind. The cats sniffed and pawed at it but didn't attack it. I found it fascinating. I thought for a moment that Shagrat was going to live up to his name but instead he actually licked it. How strange and delicate is the world of these tiny beasts. No different from our world in that way. No wonder I love them.

Our second public performance was a devised musical about a group of youngsters forming a band, which we performed on the small stage at the Sherman Theatre. It was directed by Pete Wooldridge but, though fun to do, it didn't set the world alight. We staged an end-of-year Christmas show in the Bute before breaking up for the holiday. It was a haphazard piece of cabaret loosely based on *The Wizard of Oz*. Mark the Red Dog broke his finger leaping over concrete bollards on our way to the show, during which we were all pretty drunk. Never drink alcohol before acting. They really don't go together. I never did it again. The show began with me on stage as the MC and Terry interrupting me with a greeting of 'Hello, haven't seen you in ages. Must be 1971? No. '72!' We spoke the ensuing duologue, a chat about our mother having died of cancer, in unison. We were as crazy as coots.

Jane and I spent the holiday at her parents'. My neck had started to hurt and my jaw felt as if it were made of brass. The first production of the second term was *The Weavers*, a play by Hauptmann generally regarded as one of the earliest examples of naturalism. It was about a rebellion against the terrible working conditions of weavers in Silesia in the mid-nineteenth century. I played an eighty-year-old man called Father Baumert and my highlight was where I got to eat dog on stage. It was directed to be performed in the round by Paul Clements. It was a fascinating process and Paul was infinitely helpful and patient. I had to adopt a guttural voice for the part and, though I didn't notice it, it was having an adverse effect on my everyday voice. The band had a gig at a pub down the docks after one performance and I felt a snapping feeling in my throat while singing. I did the final show but it didn't feel at all good. I went to see a throat specialist and he told me I'd strained my vocal chords. It was a pre-nodule condition which would only improve with time and rest. He advised me not to talk much. I took this to an extreme and spoke hardly at all. I communicated by writing what I had to say down on paper. I didn't realise just how tense I had become. I began breaking down and crying a lot. The second play of the second term was a modern piece based on *The Devils* by Dostoevsky. It was directed by Sue Dunderdale, who was the boss of the Soho Polytechnic in London. She was a great analyser of text, which I loved. We'd break each scene down into sections, the purpose of which we'd sum up in a single word, and then act the subtextual intention. I was given a cracking part but I told her that I was unable to do it because of my throat condition, so she reallocated it to Steve Scott from the second year, and I played several non-speaking roles. Steve was very good. He had to change his name for Equity purposes because they already had a Steve Scott registered, so he chose his family name instead and became Dougray Scott. I enjoyed watching him rehearse. He'd emote wildly and throw chairs around.

I would have played it differently but it was interesting and brave.

Jane said that she was leaving me and she did. She packed up and moved into a house with some girls she worked with at the Sherman. I was heartbroken. I cried waterfalls of tears. I wanted to be dead. She didn't give any reasons but I knew that she had been discontented for a long time. Her last words as she walked out the door were 'Try to forget about me.' I became a ghost.

I went to see Paul Clements. I still couldn't speak so I wrote down what had happened before I went and handed it to him. He was genuinely concerned and very kind. He told me to take as much time off as I needed. Twink drove me up to Rochdale where Blaine was living. I always flee to Blaine when things are at their lowest. He is the one person I can always rely on. Sharon was going through difficult times and was taken to a psychiatric hospital in Bolton when I was there. She was dogged with delusions. I visited her on the ward one evening. We sat together in silence listening to the rain hammering on the windows. I stayed with Blaine for a fortnight, then returned to Cardiff. Jane had taken advantage of my absence to clear out all of her possessions. She took Adolph. The flat was an empty shell. I went back to college in time for the performances of the Russian play. Being on stage, acting in a play, was just as real as, if not more real than, my everyday life at this point. I was in a state of brutal self-analysis. There was obviously something fundamentally wrong with me. I was impossible to love. I thought I was smart. I thought I was more intelligent than other people.

The truth was that I was an idiot. I had lived the life of an idiot, a genuine idiot. I had no idea why I existed. I walked, I talked, I thought. I had ideas, theories and opinions. I made judgments but I had no idea why I existed. All the things I thought, the things I believed, the things I held dear to me, all of them, every single one of them, could well have been bullshit. It wouldn't have surprised me one little bit. I didn't see why any of my thoughts should be rational. It worried me. I didn't like having senses but no context. If anything I'd rather it be the other way around. I was on a bus in Cardiff, sitting downstairs on a double decker. It was a warm summer's evening; we were going along a leafy suburban road when the driver suddenly slammed on his brakes and jumped from his cab. He approached a passer-by, a chubby man in a black suit, directed a few angry words at him and then punched him in the face. It was a solid punch. The bloke in the suit staggered back holding his nose. He almost fell to the ground. The driver returned to the bus. The man in the black suit recovered his equilibrium a little and realised that we, the people on the bus, were looking at him; that we had seen what had just happened. He adjusted his jacket, straightened his tie, stood up as straight as he could and walked on, mustering as much dignity as possible in the circumstances. His face was bright red from the punch, his eyes lit with tears. That's how I felt. I took to being a hermit. I stayed in bed. Friends were kind but I was somewhere that couldn't be reached.

There was a boy named Mathew Jenkins, an interesting, intense actor who made it his business to rub people up the wrong way. He was from a very straight, middle-class family. Mathew was seedily bisexual and hung about with a pale-faced, bespectacled English lad named Giles, whose father was a high-ranking RAF officer, and Ruth, a crazy, dark-eyed, Medusa-haired girl with acne. Mathew did badly in the end of year assessment and wasn't getting the parts he thought he deserved in the public performances. It depressed him to the point where he tried to hang himself with his leather belt from one of the delicately pink-flowered trees in the park behind the college. The branch snapped off. He had the bruises and the deep bright red mark around his neck for weeks. After Jane went, he, Giles and Ruth would visit me to cheer me up. They'd sit on the end of the bed drinking wine and smoking dope in the dim light of my bedside lamp. Mathew told me about how he'd pushed a black candle up another student's arse at a social get together to which I had not been invited. Sometime later he was visited by the Devil and had a cataclysmic schizoid breakdown. I haven't seen him since. No one really sees other people's suffering. We all expect someone to help us, someone stronger who can take control of the situation and save us, but that someone doesn't exist.

I left Llanbleddian Gardens during the spring break and moved back in with Twink. Carol had moved out by then so it was just me and him. We drank pints of gin and tonic till the early hours night after night while listening to 'Supper's Ready' from Foxtrot by the green light of a green light bulb. We smoked dope in industrial quantities. It was like living with a sleeping dragon. The band carried on gigging and we made a single. It was recorded in a studio in Monmouth. It was a double-A side, 'Doomsday Is Coming' and 'Plague in Paradise'. I couldn't sing and didn't play anything on it. I was unnecessary. I remember looking out at the fields beyond the studio and crying. Jane was still in Cardiff and I saw her in the streets from time to time, but she didn't see me. I'd be passing in the van or on a bus. She looked more beautiful than ever. The band played a gig in Chapter bar during which I climbed on top of one of the PA stacks while playing guitar and leapt down on the final chord. I landed on my heel and it hurt like hell. I saw a doctor who told me it was badly bruised and would take a long time to get better. I could barely walk. It was a physical manifestation of my mental and emotional despair. I went to a party with a girl from one of the technical courses and stayed the night. She was a sexy bit of stuff but obsessed with another bloke, her ex-boyfriend, a well-known local arsehole. It was disappointing but my heart wasn't in it anyway. The last term in college passed in a haze of self-pity and doubt. I don't remember any specifics. There must have been more public performances but I don't recall them. I was drunk a lot of the time, all of the time maybe. My confidence was at an all-time low. I bumped into Hugo in town. I hadn't seen him since I left Australia ten years earlier. He was married and lived in Camden Town in London. I couldn't speak so I communicated in writing while we drank a cup of coffee in a café opposite the castle. He'd become a scientologist. He worked for the organisation full-time in fact, him and his wife. He'd been to scientology HQ in America to study. He was right into it. We talked for a while and swapped addresses, then he went and I sat there on my own.

The end of term approached. It was the end of the course too. There was a ceremony in the college one evening where the diplomas and prizes were handed out. It was an emotional experience. I had grown close to a lot of my tutors and fellow students. Andrew Neil told me that I'd get professional work because companies would hire me as their token human. Andrew was a funny guy. I liked him a lot. I was surprised and delighted to be the co-winner of the prestigious Acting Prize with Maldwyn John. I'd only been in three plays, but I'd shone apparently. I left the ceremony early. I should have been happy but I wasn't. Nothing else matters when you've lost the person you love. I stood by the side of the road with a warm breeze blowing on my face. The orange sun was setting behind the city skyline. I closed my eyes. It was the summer of 1986. I was thirty-five years old.

POSTSCRIPT

In 1992 I had a catastrophic mental breakdown. My psychiatrist told me that this was the culmination of a long-standing clinical depression. He said that I'd probably been struggling with it since my late teens, when such things normally kick in. It would have involved extreme anxiety, profound unhappiness, delusions and quite possibly intermittent schizoid episodes. Obviously I wasn't aware of this at the time. In this, the first half of my autobiography, I have deliberately eschewed utilising this knowledge to explain and/or rationalise my behaviour. I have tried to put myself in the frames of mind

358

I had at the times I am writing about, and have recounted them as honestly as I can. My memory is not perfect and I am aware that my versions of events may not tally perfectly with those of other people involved. Indeed, I don't doubt that I may be wrong in some instances. I had times when I was not sure if I was recounting memories or memories of memories. It is possible that this could have resulted in a sort of internal Chinese whispers. There is nothing I can do about this. If any apologies or retractions are called for then they are given in advance. It is not and never has been my intention to be unkind or unfair to anyone involved. God knows, life is a difficult thing for everyone and I am in no position to throw stones. Quite a few of the people I've written about are dead now – Ool, Naine, my mother, my beloved sister Audrey, my beloved brother Brian, my dear friend Twink. I cherish their memories and am grateful that they were a part of my life.

I stopped this first part of my autobiography where I stopped, at the end of my time in drama school, because it seemed the natural place to do so. The second part will probably be more what is expected in memoirs, since it will involve the period of my life when I acquired some success as an actor and writer. My mental health is still an ongoing problem however, and as one of the main reasons for me putting pen to paper in this way is to explore and hopefully expunge some of my darker memories and thoughts, the second part won't exactly be a bundle of laughs either I shouldn't think. Thank you for reading this. Take care. Love, Boyd.